MW01039501

Twain at Sea

SEAFARING AMERICA

Richard J. King,
Williams College at Mystic Seaport,
Editor

Seafaring America is a series of original and classic works of fiction, nonfiction, poetry, and drama bearing on the history of America's engagement with our oceans and coastlines. Spanning diverse eras, populations, and geographical settings, the series strives to introduce, revive, and aggregate a wide range of exemplary and seminal stories about our American maritime heritage, including the accounts of First Peoples, explorers, slaves, immigrants, fishermen, whalers, captains, common sailors, members of the navy and coast guard, marine biologists, and the crews of vessels ranging from lifeboats, riverboats, and tugboats to recreational yachts. As a sailor's library, Seafaring America introduces new stories of maritime interest, reprints books that have fallen out of circulation and deserve reappraisal, and publishes selections from well-known works that reward reconsideration because of the lessons they offer about our relationship with the ocean.

For a complete list of books available in this series, see www.upne.com.

TWAIN AT SEA

THE MARITIME WRITINGS

OF

Samuel Langhorne Clemens

* * *

Edited by Eric Paul Roorda

University Press of New England

Hanover and London

University Press of New England
www.upne.com
© 2018 Eric Paul Roorda
All rights reserved
Manufactured in the United States of America
Designed by Eric M. Brooks
Typeset in Bulmer by Passumpsic Publishing

Images from the Roorda/Doyle Collection are in the author's possession.

Seafaring America is supported and produced in part by the Maritime Studies
Program of Williams College and Mystic Seaport. Williams-Mystic empowers global,
creative citizens while inspiring an enduring relationship with the ocean. We create an
open-minded, interdisciplinary academic community, with experiential learning
at Mystic Seaport, along the coasts of America, and at sea.

Library of Congress Cataloging-in-Publication Data
NAMES: Twain, Mark, 1835–1910, author. | Roorda, Eric Paul, editor.
TITLE: Twain at sea: the maritime writings of Samuel Langhorne Clemens /
edited by Eric Paul Roorda.
DESCRIPTION: Hanover: University Press of New England, 2018. |
SERIES: Seafaring America | Includes bibliographical references. |
IDENTIFIERS: LCCN 2017048949 (print) | LCCN 2017050297 (ebook) |
ISBN 9781512602739 (epub, mobi, & pdf) | ISBN 9781512602722 (cloth: alk. paper) |
ISBN 9781512601510 (pbk.: alk. paper)
SUBJECTS: LCSH: Twain, Mark, 1835–1910 — Knowledge — Sea. | Twain, Mark,
1835–1910 — Travel. | Sea in literature. | Seafaring life in literature. | Authors,
American — 19th century — Biography.
CLASSIFICATION: LCC PS1302 (ebook) | LCC PS1302.R66 2018 (print) |
DDC 818/.409 [B] — dc23
LC record available at https://lccn.loc.gov/2017048949

5 4 3 2 1

TO MY GRANDPARENTS BEP AND HENDRIK,
who gave their son an illustrated edition of
The Adventures of Huckleberry Finn
on his fifteenth birthday,
December 19, 1938.

TO MY FATHER, WILLIAM,
who gave me that book—
reading it launched my love of
Mark Twain.

MOST OF ALL, TO MY ANGELS—
A. E. DEE, ALIDA, AND FRANCES.

CONTENTS

Seafaring America

The Inupiat of far northern Alaska have for centuries said that the bow-head whale lives two human lifetimes. In *Moby-Dick*, the primary entrepôt of all American literature of the sea, Ishmael yarns about a stone lance in an old whale: "It might have been darted by some Nor'-West Indian long before America was discovered." By studying amino acids in the eyes of legally killed bowhead whales and dating the old lances of stone, ivory, and steel found buried in the blubber, twenty-first century researchers have confirmed that some individuals of this species might indeed live over two hundred years. A bowhead swimming around the thinning ice of the Arctic in 2015, when the Cuban-American poet Richard Blanco wrote, "we all belong to the sea between us," likely also swam in 1859 when Emily Dickinson penciled the lines: "Exultation is the going/Of an inland soul to sea" — and then put them in her drawer.

Since the first human settlement of our coasts, the voices expressing the American relationship with the sea have been diverse in gender, race, ethnicity, geography, and experience. And the study of maritime literature and history continues to converge and circulate with marine science and contemporary policy.

Seafaring America seeks to inspire and explore ocean study in this twenty-first century. The Taino chief Hatuey, James Fenimore Cooper, Harriet Beecher Stowe, Frederick Douglass, John Greenleaf Whittier, Winslow Homer, Alexander Agassiz, Joshua Slocum, Kate Chopin, Samuel Eliot Morison, Langston Hughes, Marianne Moore, Rachel Carson, Ursula K. Le Guin, Mark Twain, and generations of other American mariners, artists, writers, scientists, and historians have all known that the ocean is the dominant ecological, meteorological, political, and metaphorical force on Earth.

"The sea is History," wrote Derek Walcott in 1979, mourning the horrors of the Middle Passage and the drowned African American cultural memory. By the 1970s the sea was history in a new way. Americans began to perceive the global ocean as vulnerable to our destructive reach. The

realization rolled in with the discovery of the dead zone off the Mississippi River delta, industrial overfishing off New England, and the massive oil spill that spoiled the same Santa Barbara sands on which Richard
Henry Dana Jr. first landed his bare Boston Brahmin feet in 1835 after a
passage of 150 days. Yet even today, the rising seas, floods, shipwrecks,
and immutable tempests along the Great Lakes, the Gulf of Mexico, and
America's Atlantic, Pacific, and Arctic coasts continue to remind us of an
immortal and indifferent sea—a savage ocean that crashes and seeps over
the transience of *Homo sapiens.*

Seafaring America is a series of new and classic works of fiction, nonfiction, history, poetry, and drama that engages with the country's enduring relationship with the oceans and coastlines. Seafaring America strives
to introduce, revive, and aggregate a wide range of exemplary and seminal stories and verse about the American maritime heritage: to trace the
footprints on the beach, the stone lances in the blubber, and the pearls
in the drawer.

Richard J. King,
Williams College-Mystic Seaport

A NOTE ON THE TEXT

The maritime writings of Samuel Langhorne Clemens collected here are of two types: those published during his lifetime as Mark Twain, including his most famous novels and travelogues as well as stories and essays; and those published posthumously, mainly drawn from his notebooks, private letters, and the autobiography he dictated, which he intended to remain unpublished for a century. Works excerpted from the former category come from the first editions of books and from the original reports he wrote to newspapers. Those from the latter group of texts come from volumes published by the University of California Press, which make available the treasures of the Mark Twain Project at that university's Bancroft Library, where the Mark Twain Papers are housed. Variations in spelling and oddities in the original texts have been preserved. The bibliography contains a complete listing of all the sources employed in this anthology, including both those that provided Mark Twain's own words and those that offered information and insight about the author. Finally, I appreciate the support of Bellarmine University, and of Mystic Seaport —in particular, the Munson Institute of American Maritime Studies.

ACKNOWLEDGMENTS

I would like to thank editors Richard J. King, Stephen P. Hull, and Susan Abel for their help and encouragement; the anonymous outside reader for commenting graciously on the first draft of this book; and especially Rachel Shields for her hawkeyed copyediting of the manuscript, catching and correcting innumerable errors. (Any mistakes that remain are my fault alone.) I greatly appreciate the dedicated assistance that Emma McCauley and Rachel Earnhardt, student researchers from the Williams-Mystic program, contributed to this project. Thanks to Erin Grieb for designing the perfect map for this book. My gratitude also goes to Steve Telsey, a Mystic Seaport volunteer and parent of a Williams-Mystic alumna, who located images and did research on the many ships in Mark Twain's life at sea.

Twain at Sea

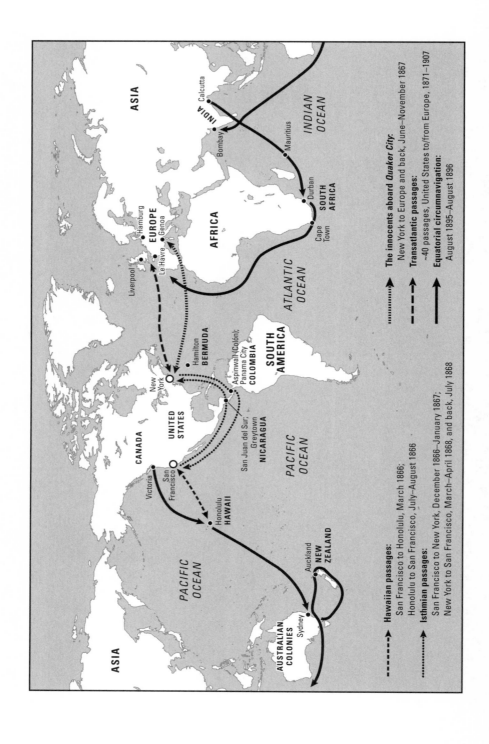

The innocents aboard *Quaker City*:
New York to Europe and back, June–November 1867

Transatlantic passages:
~40 passages, United States to/from Europe, 1871–1907

Equatorial circumnavigation:
August 1895–August 1896

Hawaiian passages:
San Francisco to Honolulu, March 1866;
Honolulu to San Francisco, July–August 1866

Isthmian passages:
San Francisco to New York, December 1866–January 1867;
New York to San Francisco, March–April 1868, and back, July 1868

The Salty Samuel C.

*S*amuel Langhorne Clemens (November 30, 1835–April 21, 1910) was a keen observer of the ocean, which he traversed repeatedly during his globe-trotting life, and of seafaring, which fascinated him. This book comprises selections from his writings about his extensive time at sea, from his first voyage — San Francisco to Hawaii in 1866 — through his 1895–1896 circumnavigation of the world by steamship, to his final ocean trips, which took him to the island of Bermuda.

As an idiom, to be "at sea" means to be completely confused, out of one's element, so to speak. Landlubbers taking their first voyage find themselves literally and figuratively at sea. They are confined within the complicated machine that is the ship, confused by the complexities of seafaring, intimidated by the limitless water surrounding them, often nauseated by the unpredictable motion of the waves, and sometimes terrified by violent storms.

Clemens was not exactly a landlubber; he was no stranger to water and navigation. He grew up on the Mississippi River and spent a formative four-year period of his young adulthood as a riverboat pilot. All told, he went on 120 Mississippi River passages, mainly between Saint Louis and New Orleans, in a professional capacity, either as an apprentice — or "cub" — pilot or as a licensed pilot.

"Mark Twain" chose his pseudonym from the lexicon of freshwater mariners, who faced many dangers. They especially had to beware of shallow water, lest they run aground and wreck the steamship. To avoid such a disaster, they sounded the depth of the muddy river by repeatedly "heaving the lead," a large lead sinker attached to a long rope. This rope, the "lead line," was marked into fathoms (six-foot intervals), which a man standing near the bow threw into the water to use as a long wet tape measure. The leadsman called out to the pilot each time he sounded the river's depth with the lead line and drew it back in, reporting the result. These repetitive "sounding calls" developed into a kind of musical form, like a sea chanty, as the leadsman, almost always an enslaved African American crewman, sang out the sounding in a loud, drawn-out, mellifluous but mournful bellow. Sounding calls were the soundtrack of a riverboat trip. "Mark twain" was the call for the second mark on the lead line, indicating two fathoms, or twelve feet, of the Mississippi beneath the steamer's keel. This was a welcome sounding call for the steamboat pilot to hear from the leadsman, because it translated to worry-free travel, at least until the next stretch of low water came along. Samuel Clemens said this about the virtues of two fathoms of water when he took the wheel of a steamboat named for him and heard that sounding call from the leadsman: "'Mark twain'—good enough water for anyone; you couldn't improve it without a little whisky."

But some literary scholars have pointed out that the words "mark twain" connote a doubling, a twoness, which carries its own significance. As with so much about the man and his work, Clemens's nom de plume reflected his fascination with duality and ambivalence. That may have been the source of his interest in the ocean, which has the capacity to be both calming and terrifying, as young Samuel Clemens discovered when he left the river and went to sea.

Despite his background as a "brown water" mariner, the writer who recast himself as Mark Twain was out of his element on the ocean. His writings about being at sea, as well as feeling at sea, reflect both his growing familiarity with voyaging and his enduring sense of amazement at the whole experience of being on the ocean. His shipboard observations also capture how the "blue water" mariners he encountered, with their salty subculture, constantly amused him, as did many of his fellow passengers, with their individual quirks. Being at sea provided the great author with abundant material for his writings.

Beginning with that first ocean voyage in 1866, maritime language infused Clemens's work, which he peppered with references to ships, frequently incorporating salty characters. When his personal life turned stormy, as it so often did, he thought about being at sea, and frequently took refuge there. He relished the experience of being aboard a ship for days or weeks at a time, which rejuvenated him, piqued his recurring intense curiosity about seafaring culture, and renewed his soulful appreciation for the sublime ocean in all its colors, textures, and moods.

Little Sammy Clemens—*very* little, after a premature birth—was a sickly child. His mother, Jane, an intense native of Kentucky who seems to have carried an extensive repertoire of supernatural and morbid beliefs and practices with her from the hollers of the Bluegrass State, despaired about her infant's health and future prospects. But she devoted herself to his survival, applying her strong will and her experience from bearing and rearing two older children, and he gradually gained strength. Clemens's father, John, who went by his middle name, Marshall, involved himself at a more superficial level in the well-being of his offspring. He was an intelligent but impractical father who failed in land speculation and legal practice and died young, only forty-nine, after undertaking an ill-advised wintertime journey and contracting pneumonia, when Sammy was eleven.

Marshall and Jane's son Benjamin had predeceased his father by five years, which was a horrifying moment for six-year-old Sam, not just because he blamed himself for the death, for reasons that remain obscure, but because his mother subjected him to an eerie encounter with his dead brother, during which she made the little boy touch the body's cold neck, which was the sort of thing her kin had done, it seems, during her Kentucky childhood. She believed Sammy had "the second sight," a kind of clairvoyance; she may well have been correct. Sam himself agreed with her.

Sammy gradually emerged from the maladies of his early childhood, although he continued to have difficulty sleeping, which was one lingering symptom of his premature birth. Nightmares plagued him (as they always would) and he somnambulated in a state of seeming wakefulness, frightening other people in the house, as sleepwalkers always do. As his general health improved, the boy's new spunk found expression in misbehavior. He developed into an accomplished prankster. He hated school. When his otherworldly mom brought him into the presence of his father's corpse to extort from him a promise of better behavior in the future, he tearfully acceded, on the condition that he would not have to go back to school. Going back to school was just what Jane had in mind. But she settled for her son's promise to toe the line—no drinking, no swearing, no mischief. Sam kept that promise to the spectral Mr. Clemens. For a while.

Up to the point of his sudden death, the dogged Marshall had dragged the Clemens clan along with him on his futile search for wealth, from Kentucky to the woods of Tennessee, on to the prairie settlement of Florida, Missouri, then to riverside Hannibal, barely able to make ends meet anywhere, as his debtors beggared him and his creditors squeezed him dry. After his death, circumstances for his surviving dependents grew even more desperate, which compelled the family's middle male child, Samuel — his little brother, Henry, came on the scene in 1838 — to go to work full-time. Samuel's choice of employment was really no choice at all. His ill-starred older brother, Orion (pronounced "oh-ree-on," not "oh-rye-un" like the constellation of the Hunter), had launched a newspaper, and he needed cheap labor. He got it from his younger sibling Sam, who apprenticed himself to the press, only to have his big brother renege on their deal and fail to pay his wages throughout the full three and a half years Sam worked for him. Orion was too much like their father. Although Sam felt fraternal affection for him, he had difficulty tolerating him.

Clemens's bond with his sister Pamela ("Pa-mee-lee-uh") was tighter. She was a brick. She married well, finding a man of un-Clemenslike stability and common sense, and she stayed close to Sam, saving his newspaper clippings for him when he had no use for such things. The saved clippings assisted the writer a great deal later on when he composed his most popular travel books, *The Innocents Abroad* (1867) and *Roughing It* (1872). The episodes recounted in those books, nerve-racking for his poor mother, included a feint at running away — or to put it more accurately, stowing away — aboard one of the massive paddle-wheel steamboats that always inspired his awe. He didn't get far when he stowed away as a small boy, but when he was a cocky eighteen years old, he "lit out" for real, not for "the territories," as Huck did to escape domestic abuse, and Jim did to escape enslavement, but rather for points east.

First Clemens went to Saint Louis and stayed with his respectable sister, now Pamela Moffett, while briefly plying his typesetting trade. From there, he booked passage up the Ohio River to Cincinnati for a spell, then headed for Lake Erie, a vast expanse of freshwater that is one of the five major basins of the inland freshwater sea called the Great Lakes. Reaching Monroe, Michigan, on the western end of the lake, he bought his fare aboard the lake steamer *Southern Michigan* for a trip to the easternmost port, Buffalo, a voyage that lasted the better part of two days. It was the first time Samuel Clemens was out of sight of land. He recorded nothing about the moment. But there is little doubt that he remembered it. How many can forget the first time they lost sight of land, and found themselves in the center of an immeasurable hemisphere of water and sky? Whether salt water or freshwater, the effect is the same: the 360-degree horizon; the outlandish scale of the scene; the immersion in the colors of that instant—blue, gray, green, purple—all instantly changeable; the prominence of the celestial orb, especially while rising and setting, in the absence of terrestrial distractions; and perhaps most indelibly, a feeling that cannot be corralled into words with satisfaction, a *je ne sais quoi* . . . Sam Clemens was headed for New York City, which he reached on Monday, August 22, 1853, and where he remained only long enough to have recollections to contrast with his many later visits, before continuing on to Washington, DC, where, again, his residency was brief but left vivid impressions that were still distinct when he returned to the nation's capital as a rising literary star in 1867.

But this picaresque interlude proved to be short-lived, and before long, Sam Clemens was back on his old Mississippi River stomping grounds. He joined his hapless brother Orion, whose Hannibal newspaper had failed, and his sister-in-law Mollie, a sweet woman who deserved a more felicitous conjugal match, in the riparian metropolis of Keokuk, Iowa, where Orion had inexplicably opted to initiate another doomed journalistic enterprise. Again, he took Sam down with him, and the younger man resolved to try something completely different. He hatched a plan to move to Brazil, where he proposed to pioneer commercial coca farming, using fifty dollars he had fortuitously found during one of the dark moments that punctuated his moody existence, a literal windfall, in the form of a currency note of that denomination that plastered itself to the exterior wall of a house, where the young man found it while walking past in a storm. He spent some of it for fare on the steamboat *Paul Jones* to New Orleans, but when he got there, instead of proceeding to South America, Sam Clemens, who had rediscovered his love of steamboats on the extended southbound trip, altered course yet again. He essentially bribed the palace steamer's pilot, Horace Bixby, to take him on as an apprentice, or "cub-pilot." Mr. Bixby accepted the offer Clemens made of $500, with a down payment of $100 that he borrowed from his brother-in-law, the balance to be garnished from his negligible salary. (Bixby settled for $350 in the end). Then the future "Mark Twain" began the most formative four years of his tumultuous, globe-trotting life.

Life on Brown Water

ammy Clemens was a difficult child. He turned his boyhood
misadventures into the published adventures of characters who
have become household names: Tom Sawyer and Huck Finn.

Mark Twain captured the way he felt about steamboats in chapters 4
and 5, "The Boys' Ambition" and "I Want to Be a Cub-Pilot," of his book
Life on the Mississippi (1883), which is part memoir, part travelogue:

* * *

From *Life on the Mississippi*

Chapter 4: The Boys' Ambition

When I was a boy, there was but one permanent ambition among my
comrades in our village on the west bank of the Mississippi River. That
was, to be a steamboatman. We had transient ambitions of other sorts,
but they were only transient. When a circus came and went, it left us all
burning to become clowns; the first negro minstrel show that ever came
to our section left us all suffering to try that kind of life; now and then we
had a hope that, if we lived and were good, God would permit us to be
pirates. These ambitions faded out, each in its turn; but the ambition to
be a steamboatman always remained.

Once a day a cheap, gaudy packet arrived upward from St. Louis, and
another downward from Keokuk. Before these events, the day was glorious with expectancy; after them, the day was a dead and empty thing.
Not only the boys, but the whole village, felt this. After all these years
I can picture that old time to myself now, just as it was then: the white
town drowsing in the sunshine of a summer's morning; the streets empty,
or pretty nearly so; one or two clerks sitting in front of the Water Street
stores, with their splint-bottomed chairs tilted back against the wall, chins
on breasts, hats slouched over their faces, asleep—with shingle-shavings

enough around to show what broke them down; a sow and a litter of pigs loafing along the sidewalk, doing a good business in watermelon rinds and seeds; two or three lonely little freight piles scattered about the "levee"; a pile of "skids" on the slope of the stone-paved wharf, and the fragrant town drunkard asleep in the shadow of them; two or three wood flats at the head of the wharf, but nobody to listen to the peaceful lapping of the wavelets against them; the great Mississippi, the majestic, the magnificent Mississippi, rolling its mile-wide tide along, shining in the sun; the dense forest away on the other side; the "point" above the town, and the "point" below, bounding the river-glimpse and turning it into a sort of sea, and withal a very still and brilliant and lonely one. Presently a film of dark smoke appears above one of those remote "points"; instantly a negro drayman, famous for his quick eye and prodigious voice, lifts up the cry, "S-t-e-a-m-boat a-comin'!" and the scene changes! The town drunkard stirs, the clerks wake up, a furious clatter of drays follows, every house and store pours out a human contribution, and all in a twinkling the dead town is alive and moving. Drays, carts, men, boys, all go hurrying from many quarters to a common centre, the wharf. Assembled there, the people fasten their eyes upon the coming boat as upon a wonder they are seeing for the first time. And the boat *is* rather a handsome sight, too. She is long and sharp and trim and pretty; she has two tall, fancy-topped chimneys, with a gilded device of some kind swung between them: a fanciful pilot-house, all glass and "gingerbread," perched on top of the "texas" deck behind them; the paddle-boxes are gorgeous with a picture or with gilded rays above the boat's name: the boiler deck, the hurricane deck, and the texas deck are fenced and ornamented with clean white railings; there is a flag gallantly flying from the jack-staff; the furnace doors are open and the fires glaring bravely; the upper decks are black with passengers; the captain stands by the big bell, calm, imposing, the envy of all: great volumes of the blackest smoke are rolling and tumbling out of the chimneys—a husbanded grandeur created with a bit of pitch pine just before arriving at a town; the crew are grouped on the forecastle; the broad stage is run far out over the port bow, and an envied deck-hand stands picturesquely on the end of it with a coil of rope in his hand; the pent steam is screaming through the gauge-cocks; the captain lifts his hand, a bell rings, the wheels stop; then they turn back, churning the water to foam, and the steamer is at rest. Then such a scramble as there is to get aboard, and to get ashore, and to take in freight and to discharge freight, all at one and the same time; and such a yelling and cursing as the mates facilitate it all with! Ten minutes later the steamer is under way again, with no flag on the jack-staff and no black smoke issuing from the chimneys. After ten more minutes the town is dead again, and the town drunkard asleep by the skids once more.

My father was a justice of the peace, and I supposed he possessed the power of life and death over all men, and could hang any body that offended him. This was distinction enough for me as a general thing; but the desire to be a steamboatman kept intruding, nevertheless. I first wanted to be a cabin-boy, so that I could come out with a white apron on and shake a table-cloth over the side, where all my old comrades could see me; later I thought I would rather be the deck-hand who stood on the end of the stage-plank with the coil of rope in his hand, because he was particularly conspicuous. But these were only day-dreams—they were too heavenly to be contemplated as real possibilities. By and by one of our boys went away. He was not heard of for a long time. At last he turned up as apprentice engineer or "striker" on a steamboat. This thing shook the bottom out of all my Sunday-school teachings. That boy had been notoriously worldly, and I just the reverse; yet he was exalted to this eminence, and I left in obscurity and misery. There was nothing generous about this fellow in his greatness. He would always manage to have a rusty bolt to scrub while his boat tarried at our town, and he would sit on the inside guard and scrub it, where we all could see him and envy him and loathe him. And whenever his boat was laid up he would come home and swell around the town in his blackest and greasiest clothes, so that nobody could help remembering that he was a steamboatman; and he used all sorts of steamboat technicalities in his talk, as if he were so used to them that he forgot common people could not understand them. He would speak of the "labboard" side of a horse in an easy, natural way that would make one wish he was dead. And he was always talking about "St. Looy" like an old citizen; he would refer casually to occasions when he was "coming down Fourth Street," or when he was "passing by the Planter's House," or when there was a fire and he took a turn on the brakes of "the old Big Missouri"; and then he would go on and lie about how many towns the size of ours were burned down there that day. Two or three of the boys had long been persons of consideration among us because they had been to St. Louis once and had a vague general knowledge of its wonders, but the day of their glory was over now. They lapsed into a humble silence, and learned to disappear when the ruthless "cub"-engineer approached. This fellow had money, too, and hair oil. Also an ignorant silver watch and a showy brass watch chain. He wore a leather belt and used no suspenders. If ever a youth was cordially admired and hated by his comrades, this one was. No girl could withstand his charms. He "cut out" every boy in the village. When his boat blew up at last, it diffused a tranquil contentment among us such as we had not known for months. But when he came home the next week, alive, renowned, and appeared in church all battered up and bandaged, a shining hero, stared at and wondered over by everybody, it seemed to us that the partiality of Providence for an undeserving reptile had reached a point where it was open to criticism.

This creature's career could produce but one result, and it speedily followed. Boy after boy managed to get on the river. The minister's son became an engineer. The doctor's, and the post-master's sons became "mud clerks"; the wholesale liquor dealer's son became a barkeeper on a boat; four sons of the chief merchant, and two sons of the county judge, became pilots. Pilot was the grandest position of all. The pilot, even in those days of trivial wages, had a princely salary—from a hundred and fifty to two hundred and fifty dollars a month, and no board to pay. Two months of his wages would pay a preacher's salary for a year. Now some of us were left disconsolate. We could not get on the river—at least our parents would not let us.

So, by and by, I ran away. I said I would never come home again till I was a pilot and could come in glory. But somehow I could not manage it. I went meekly aboard a few of the boats that lay packed together like sardines at the long St. Louis wharf, and humbly enquired for the pilots, but got only a cold shoulder and short words from mates and clerks. I had to make the best of this sort of treatment for the time being, but I had comforting day-dreams of a future when I should be a great and honored pilot, with plenty of money, and could kill some of these mates and clerks and pay for them.[1]

Chapter 5: I Want to Be a Cub-Pilot

Months afterward the hope within me struggled to a reluctant death, and I found myself without an ambition. But I was ashamed to go home. I was in Cincinnati, and I set to work to map out a new career. I had been reading about the recent exploration of the river Amazon by an expedition sent out by our government. It was said that the expedition, owing to difficulties, had not thoroughly explored a part of the country lying about the head-waters, some four thousand miles from the mouth of the river. It was only about fifteen hundred miles from Cincinnati to New Orleans, where I could doubtless get a ship. I had thirty dollars left; I would go and complete the exploration of the Amazon. This was all the thought I gave to the subject. I never was great in matters of detail. I packed my valise, and took passage on an ancient tub called the *Paul Jones*, for New Orleans. For the sum of sixteen dollars I had the scarred and tarnished splendors of "her" main saloon principally to myself, for she was not a creature to attract the eye of wiser travellers.

When we presently got under way and went poking down the broad Ohio, I became a new being, and the subject of my own admiration. I was a traveller! A word never had tasted so good in my mouth before I had an exultant sense of being bound for mysterious lands and distant climes which I never have felt in so uplifting a degree since. I was in such a glorified condition that all ignoble feelings departed out of me, and I was able to look down and pity the untravelled with a compassion that had hardly a trace of contempt in it. Still, when we stopped at villages and wood-yards, I could not help lolling carelessly upon the railings of the boiler-deck to enjoy the envy of the country boys on the bank. If they did not seem to discover me, I presently sneezed to attract their attention, or moved to a position where they could not help seeing me. And as soon as I knew they saw me I gaped and stretched, and gave other signs of being mightily bored with travelling.

I kept my hat off all the time, and stayed where the wind and the sun could strike me, because I wanted to get the bronzed and weather-beaten look of an old traveller. Before the second day was half gone I experienced a joy which filled me with the purest gratitude; for I saw that the skin had begun to blister and peel off my face and neck. I wished that the boys and girls at home could see me now.

We reached Louisville in time—at least the neighborhood of it. We stuck hard and fast on the rocks in the middle of the river, and lay there four days. I was now beginning to feel a strong sense of being a part of the boat's family, a sort of infant son to the captain and younger brother to the officers. There is no estimating the pride I took in this grandeur, or the affection that began to swell and grow in me for those people. I could not know how the lordly steamboatman scorns that sort of presumption in a mere landsman. I particularly longed to acquire the least trifle of notice from the big stormy mate, and I was on the alert for an opportunity to do him a service to that end. It came at last. The riotous powwow of setting a spar was going on down on the forecastle, and I went down there and stood around in the way—or mostly skipping out of it—till the mate suddenly roared a general order for somebody to bring him a capstan bar. I sprang to his side and said: "Tell me where it is—I'll fetch it!"

If a rag-picker had offered to do a diplomatic service for the Emperor of Russia, the monarch could not have been more astounded than the mate was. He even stopped swearing. He stood and stared down at me. It took him ten seconds to scrape his disjointed remains together again. Then he said impressively: "Well, if this don't beat hell!" and turned to his work with the air of a man who had been confronted with a problem too abstruse for solution.

I crept away, and courted solitude for the rest of the day. I did not go to dinner; I stayed away from supper until everybody else had finished. I did not feel so much like a member of the boat's family now as before. However, my spirits returned, in installments, as we pursued our way down the river. I was sorry I hated the mate so, because it was not in (young) human nature not to admire him. He was huge and muscular, his face was bearded and whiskered all over; he had a red woman and a blue woman tattooed on his right arm—one on each side of a blue anchor with a red rope to it; and in the matter of profanity he was sublime. When he was getting out cargo at a landing, I was always where I could see and hear. He felt all the majesty of his great position, and made the world feel it, too. When he gave even the simplest order, he discharged it like a blast of lightning, and sent a long, reverberating peal of profanity thundering after it. I could not help contrasting the way in which the average landsman would give an order with the mate's way of doing it. If the landsman should wish the gang-plank moved a foot farther forward, he would probably say: "James, or William, one of you push that plank forward, please;" but put the mate in his place, and he would roar out: "Here, now, start that gang plank for'ard! Lively, no! *What*'re you about! Snatch it! *snatch* it! There! there! Aft again! aft again! Don't you hear me? Dash it to dash! are you going to *sleep* over it! *'Vast* heaving. 'Vast heaving, I tell you! Going to heave it clear astern? WHERE're you going with that barrel! for'ard with it 'fore I make you swallow it, you dash-dash-dash-*dashed* split between a tired mud-turtle and a crippled hearse-horse!"

I wished I could talk like that.

When the soreness of my adventure with the mate had somewhat worn off, I began timidly to make up to the humblest official connected with the boat—the night watchman. He snubbed my advances at first, but I presently ventured to offer him a new chalk pipe, and that softened him. So he allowed me to sit with him by the big bell on the hurricane deck, and in time he melted into conversation. He could not well have helped it, I hung with such homage on his words and so plainly showed that I felt honored by his notice. He told me the names of dim capes and shadowy islands as we glided by them in the solemnity of the night, under the winking stars, and by and by got to talking about himself. He seemed over-sentimental for a man whose salary was six dollars a week— or rather he might have seemed so to an older person than I. But I drank in his words hungrily, and with a faith that might have moved mountains if it had been applied judiciously. What was it to me that he was soiled and seedy and fragrant with gin? What was it to me that his grammar was bad, his construction worse, and his profanity so void of art that it was an element of weakness rather than strength in his conversation? He was a wronged man, a man who had seen trouble, and that was enough for me. As he mellowed into his plaintive history his tears dripped upon the lantern in his lap, and I cried, too, from sympathy. He said he was the son of an English nobleman—either an earl or an alderman, he could not remember which, but believed was both; his father, the nobleman, loved him, but his mother hated him from the cradle; and so while he was still a little boy he was sent to "one of them old, ancient colleges" —he couldn't remember which; and by and by his father died and his mother seized the property and "shook" him, as he phrased it. After his mother shook him, members of the nobility with whom he was acquainted used their influence to get him the position of "loblolly-boy in a ship"; and from that point my watchman threw off all trammels of date and locality and branched out into a narrative that bristled all along with incredible adventures; a narrative that was so reeking with bloodshed, and so crammed with hair-breadth escapes and the most engaging and unconscious personal villainies, that I sat speechless, enjoying, shuddering, wondering, worshipping. It was a sore blight to find out afterward that he was a low, vulgar, ignorant, sentimental, half-witted humbug, an untraveled native of the wilds of Illinois, who had absorbed wildcat literature and appropriated its marvels, until in time he had woven odds and ends of the mess into this yarn, and then gone on telling it to fledglings like me, until he had come to believe it himself.[2]

Mark Twain worked on at least fifteen steamboats, and perhaps as many as nineteen (the records are unclear). His professional career began on March 4, 1857, when he left New Orleans at the helm of the *Colonel Crossman*, under the watchful eye of the legendary river pilot Horace Bixby, who would continue guiding steamboats for another fifty-five years, two years longer than his famous protégé would live. Clemens recalled his introduction to the maritime milieu in several chapters of *Life on the Mississippi*, most notably in "Sounding," the chapter that had most to do with his famous pen name.

It was during his apprenticeship as a "cub-pilot" that Samuel Clemens began his practice of keeping notebooks. His notebooks are important sources for placing into context Mark Twain's time at sea and his writings about the sea. He referred to "my notebook (that sure index, to me, of my condition)."[3]

* * *

From *Life on the Mississippi*

Chapter 12: Sounding

When the river is very low, and one's steamboat is "drawing all the water" there is in the channel, — or a few inches more, as was often the case in the old times, — one must be painfully circumspect in his piloting. We used to have to "sound" a number of particularly bad places almost every trip when the river was at a very low stage.

Sounding is done in this way: The boat ties up at the shore, just above the shoal crossing; the pilot not on watch takes his "cub" or steersman and a picked crew of men (sometimes an officer also), and goes out in the yawl—provided the boat has not that rare and sumptuous luxury, a regularly devised "sounding-boat"—and proceeds to hunt for the best water, the pilot on duty watching his movements through a spy-glass, meantime, and in some instances assisting by signals of the boat's whistle, signifying "try higher up" or "try lower down"; for the surface of the water, like an oil-painting, is more expressive and intelligible when inspected from a little distance than very close at hand. The whistle signals are seldom necessary, however; never, perhaps, except when the wind confuses the significant ripples upon the water's surface. When the yawl has reached the shoal place, the speed is slackened, the pilot begins to sound the depth with a pole ten or twelve feet long, and the steersman at the tiller obeys the order to "hold her up to starboard;" or "let her fall off to larboard";[4] or "steady—steady as you go."

When the measurements indicate that the yawl is approaching the shoalest part of the reef, the command is given to "Ease all!" Then the men stop rowing and the yawl drifts with the current. The next order is, "Stand by with the buoy!" The moment the shallowest point is reached, the pilot delivers the order, "Let go the buoy!" and over she goes. If the pilot is not satisfied, he sounds the place again; if he finds better water higher up or lower down, he removes the buoy to that place. Being finally satisfied, he gives the order, and all the men stand their oars straight up in the air, in line; a blast from the boat's whistle indicates that the signal has been seen; then the men "give way" on their oars and lay the yawl alongside the buoy; the steamer comes creeping carefully down, is pointed straight at the buoy, husbands her power for the coming struggle, and presently, at the critical moment, turns on all her steam and goes grinding and wallowing over the buoy and the sand, and gains the deep water beyond. Or maybe she doesn't; maybe she "strikes and swings." Then she has to while away several hours (or days) sparring herself off.

Sometimes a buoy is not laid at all, but the yawl goes ahead, hunting the best water, and the steamer follows along in its wake. Often there is a deal of fun and excitement about sounding, especially if it is a glorious summer day, or a blustering night. But in winter the cold and the peril take most of the fun out of it.

A buoy is nothing but a board four or five feet long, with one end turned up; it is a reversed school-house bench, with one of the supports left and the other removed. It is anchored on the shoalest part of the reef by a rope with a heavy stone made fast to the end of it. But for the resistance of the turned-up end of the reversed bench, the current would pull the buoy under water. At night, a paper lantern with a candle in it is fastened on top of the buoy, and this can be seen a mile or more, a little glimmering spark in the waste of blackness.

Nothing delights a cub so much as an opportunity to go out sounding. There is such an air of adventure about it; often there is danger; it is so gaudy and man-of-war-like to sit up in the stern-sheets and steer a swift yawl; there is something fine about the exultant spring of the boat when an experienced old sailor crew throw their souls into the oars; it is lovely to see the white foam stream away from the bows; there is music in the rush of the water; it is deliciously exhilarating, in summer, to go speeding over the breezy expanses of the river when the world of wavelets is dancing in the sun. It is such grandeur, too, to the cub, to get a chance to give an order; for often the pilot will simply say, "Let her go about!" and leave the rest to the cub, who instantly cries, in his sternest tone of command, "Ease, starboard! Strong on the larboard! Starboard, give way! With a will, men!" The cub enjoys sounding for the further reason that the eyes of the passengers are watching all the yawl's movements with absorbing interest, if the time be daylight; and if it be night, he knows that those same wondering eyes are fastened upon the yawl's lantern as it glides out into the gloom and dims away in the remote distance.

One trip a pretty girl of sixteen spent her time in our pilot-house with her uncle and aunt, every day and all day long. I fell in love with her. So did Mr. Thornburg's cub, Tom G. Tom and I had been bosom friends until this time; but now a coolness began to arise. I told the girl a good many of my river adventures, and made myself out a good deal of a hero; Tom tried to make himself appear to be a hero, too, and succeeded to some extent, but then he always had a way of embroidering. However, virtue is its own reward, so I was a barely perceptible trifle ahead in the contest. About this time something happened which promised handsomely for me: the pilots decided to sound the crossing at the head of 21. This would occur about nine or ten o'clock at night, when the passengers would be still up; it would be Mr. Thornburg's watch, therefore my chief would have to do the sounding. We had a perfect love of a sounding-boat—long, trim, graceful, and as fleet as a greyhound; her thwarts were cushioned; she carried twelve oarsmen; one of the mates was always sent in her to transmit orders to her crew, for ours was a steamer where no end of "style" was put on.

We tied up at the shore above 21, and got ready. It was a foul night, and the river was so wide, there, that a landsman's uneducated eyes could discern no opposite shore through such a gloom. The passengers were alert and interested; every thing was satisfactory. As I hurried through the engine-room, picturesquely gotten up in storm toggery, I met Tom, and could not forbear delivering myself of a mean speech:

"Ain't *you* glad you don't have to go out sounding?"

Tom was passing on, but he quickly turned, and said:

"Now just for that, you can go and get the sounding-pole yourself. I was going after it, but I'd see you in Halifax, now, before I'd do it."

"Who wants you to get it? I don't. It's in the sounding-boat."

"It ain't, either. It's been new-painted; and it's been up on the ladies' cabin–guards two days, drying."

I flew back, and shortly arrived among the crowd of watching and wondering ladies just in time to hear the command:

"Give way, men!"

I looked over, and there was the gallant sounding-boat booming away, the unprincipled Tom presiding at the tiller, and my chief sitting by him with the sounding-pole which I had been sent on a fool's errand to fetch. Then that young girl said to me:

"Oh, how awful to have to go out in that little boat on such a night! Do you think there is any danger?"

I would rather have been stabbed. I went off, full of venom, to help in the pilot-house. By and by the boat's lantern disappeared, and after an interval a wee spark glimmered upon the face of the water a mile away. Mr. Thornburg blew the whistle in acknowledgment, backed the steamer out, and made for it. We flew along for a while, then slackened steam and went cautiously gliding toward the spark. Presently Mr. Thornburg exclaimed:

"Hello, the buoy-lantern's out!"

He stopped the engines. A moment or two later he said:

"Why, there it is again!"

So he came ahead on the engines once more, and rang for the leads. Gradually the water shoaled up, and then began to deepen again! Mr. Thornburg muttered:

"Well, I don't understand this. I believe that buoy has drifted off the reef. Seems to be a little too far to the left. No matter, it is safest to run over it, anyhow."

So, in that solid world of darkness we went creeping down on the light. Just as our bows were in the act of ploughing over it, Mr. Thornburg seized the bell-ropes, rang a startling peal, and exclaimed:

"My soul, it's the sounding-boat!"

A sudden chorus of wild alarms burst out far below—a pause— and then a sound of grinding and crashing followed. Mr. Thornburg exclaimed:

"There! the paddle-wheel has ground the sounding-boat to lucifer matches! Run! See who is killed!"

I was on the main deck in the twinkling of an eye.

My chief and the third mate and nearly all the men were safe. They had discovered their danger when it was too late to pull out of the way; then, when the great guards overshadowed them a moment later, they were prepared and knew what to do; at my chief's order they sprang at the right instant, seized the guard, and were hauled aboard. The next moment the sounding-yawl swept aft to the wheel and was struck and splintered to atoms. Two of the men and the cub Tom were missing—a fact which spread like wildfire over the boat. The passengers came flocking to the forward gangway, ladies and all, anxious-eyed, white-faced, and talked in awed voices of the dreadful thing. And often and again I heard them say, "Poor fellows! poor boy, poor boy!"

By this time the boat's yawl was manned and away, to search for the missing. Now a faint call was heard, off to the left. The yawl had disappeared in the other direction. Half the people rushed to one side to encourage the swimmer with their shouts; the other half rushed the other way to shriek to the yawl to turn about. By the callings the swimmer was approaching, but some said the sound showed failing strength.

The crowd massed themselves against the boiler-deck railings, leaning over and staring into the gloom; and every faint and fainter cry wrung from them such words as "Ah, poor fellow, poor fellow! is there *no* way to save him?"

But still the cries held out, and drew nearer, and presently the voice said pluckily:

"I can make it! Stand by with a rope!"

What a rousing cheer they gave him! The chief mate took his stand in the glare of a torch-basket, a coil of rope in his hand, and his men grouped about him. The next moment the swimmer's face appeared in the circle of light, and in another one the owner of it was hauled aboard, limp and drenched, while cheer on cheer went up. It was that devil Tom.

The yawl crew searched everywhere, but found no sign of the two men. They probably failed to catch the guard, tumbled back, and were struck by the wheel and killed. Tom had never jumped for the guard at all, but had plunged head-first into the river and dived under the wheel. It was nothing; I could have done it easy enough, and I said so; but everybody went on just the same, making a wonderful to-do over that ass, as if he had done some thing great. That girl couldn't seem to have enough of that pitiful "hero" the rest of the trip; but little I cared; I loathed her, any way.

The way we came to mistake the sounding-boat's lantern for the buoy-light was this: My chief said that after laying the buoy he fell away and watched it till it seemed to be secure; then he took up a position a hundred yards below it and a little to one side of the steamer's course, headed the sounding-boat up-stream, and waited. Having to wait some time, he and the officer got to talking; he looked up when he judged that the steamer was about on the reef; saw that the buoy was gone, but supposed that the steamer had already run over it; he went on with his talk; he noticed that the steamer was getting very close down to him, but that was the correct thing; it was her business to shave him closely, for convenience in taking him aboard; he was expecting her to sheer off, until the last moment; then it flashed upon him that she was trying to run him down, mistaking his lantern for the buoy-light; so he sang out, "Stand by to spring for the guard, men!" and the next instant the jump was made.[5]

Employment on a steamboat agreed so much with Sam Clemens that he convinced his little brother, Henry, to whom he had grown close only in recent years, to join him on the river. Henry secured a position on the bottom rung of the steamboat hierarchy, as a coal stoker, on board the *Pennsylvania*, which his brother piloted. Because of a fight with a shipmate, Sam had left the ship to go as a passenger on a different steamboat when the *Pennsylvania* blew up near Memphis. Badly burned, Henry lingered several days before dying. A vivid premonition of his brother's death had jolted Samuel awake days before the disaster took place; he'd had a dream of Henry in a coffin with a rose on his chest. The dream came true, just as he saw it. Afterward, Samuel felt personally responsible for what had happened, because he had persuaded Henry to follow him onto the river, with all its hazards. He suffered the piercing pangs of survivor guilt for the rest of his life, to judge from the traumatic memories he dictated for his posthumous autobiography in 1906. Mark Twain managed to write about it in *Life on the Mississippi*.

*   *   *

From *Life on the Mississippi*, Chapter 20

A Catastrophe

We lay three days in New Orleans, but the captain did not succeed in finding another pilot, so he proposed that I should stand a daylight watch and leave the night watches to George Ealer. But I was afraid; I had never stood a watch of any sort by myself, and I believed I should be sure to get into trouble in the head of some chute, or ground the boat in a near cut through some bar or other. Brown remained in his place, but he would not travel with me. So the captain gave me an order on the captain of the *A. T. Lacey* for a passage to St. Louis, and said he would find a new pilot there and my steersman's berth could then be resumed. The *Lacey* was to leave a couple of days after the *Pennsylvania*.

The night before the *Pennsylvania* left, Henry and I sat chatting on a freight pile on the levee till midnight. The subject of the chat, mainly, was one which I think we had not exploited before—steamboat disasters. One was then on its way to us, little as we suspected it; the water which was to make the steam which should cause it was washing past some point fifteen hundred miles up the river while we talked—but it would arrive at the right time and the right place. We doubted if persons not

clothed with authority were of much use in cases of disaster and attendant panic, still they might be of *some* use; so we decided that if a disaster
ever fell within our experience we would at least stick to the boat, and
give such minor service as chance might throw in the way. Henry remembered this, afterward, when the disaster came, and acted accordingly.

The *Lacey* started up the river two days behind the *Pennsylvania*.
We touched at Greenville, Miss., a couple of days out, and somebody
shouted:

"The *Pennsylvania* is blown up at Ship Island, and a hundred and
fifty lives lost!"

At Napoleon, Ark., the same evening, we got an extra, issued by a
Memphis paper, which gave some particulars. It mentioned my brother,
and said he was not hurt.

Further up the river we got a later extra. My brother was again mentioned, but this time as being hurt beyond help. We did not get full details
of the catastrophe until we reached Memphis. This is the sorrowful story:

It was six o'clock on a hot summer morning. The *Pennsylvania* was
creeping along, north of Ship Island, about sixty miles below Memphis,
on a half-head of steam, towing a wood-flat which was fast being emptied.
George Ealer was in the pilot-house—alone, I think; the second engineer
and a striker had the watch in the engine-room; the second mate had the
watch on deck; George Black, Mr. Wood, and my brother, clerks, were
asleep, as were also Brown and the head engineer, the carpenter, the chief
mate, and one striker; Captain Klinefelter was in the barber's chair, and
the barber was preparing to shave him. There were a good many cabin
passengers aboard, and three or four hundred deck passengers—so it
was said at the time—and not very many of them were astir. The wood
being nearly all out of the flat now, Ealer rang to "come ahead" full steam,
and the next moment four of the eight boilers exploded with a thunder-
ous crash, and the whole forward third of the boat was hoisted toward
the sky! The main part of the mass, with the chimneys, dropped upon the
boat again, a mountain of riddled and chaotic rubbish—and then, after a
little, fire broke out.

Many people were flung to considerable distances and fell in the
river; among these were Mr. Wood and my brother and the carpenter.
The carpenter was still stretched upon his mattress when he struck the

water seventy-five feet from the boat. Brown, the pilot, and George Black, chief clerk, were never seen or heard of after the explosion. The barber's chair, with Captain Klinefelter in it and unhurt, was left with its back over-hanging vacancy — everything forward of it, floor and all, had disappeared; and the stupefied barber, who was also unhurt, stood with one toe projecting over space, still stirring his lather unconsciously and saying not a word.

When George Ealer saw the chimneys plunging aloft in front of him, he knew what the matter was; so he muffled his face in the lapels of his coat, and pressed both hands there tightly to keep this protection in its place so that no steam could get to his nose or mouth. He had ample time to attend to these details while he was going up and returning. He presently landed on top of the unexploded boilers, forty feet below the former pilot-house, accompanied by his wheel and a rain of other stuff, and enveloped in a cloud of scalding steam. All of the many who breathed that steam died; none escaped. But Ealer breathed none of it. He made his way to the free air as quickly as he could; and when the steam cleared away he returned and climbed up on the boilers again, and patiently hunted out each and every one of his chessmen and the several joints of his flute.

By this time the fire was beginning to threaten. Shrieks and groans filled the air. A great many persons had been scalded, a great many crippled; the explosion had driven an iron crowbar through one man's body — I think they said he was a priest. He did not die at once, and his sufferings were very dreadful. A young French naval cadet of fifteen, son of a French admiral, was fearfully scalded, but bore his tortures manfully. Both mates were badly scalded, but they stood to their posts, nevertheless. They drew the wood-boat aft, and they and the captain fought back the frantic herd of frightened immigrants till the wounded could be brought there and placed in safety first.

When Mr. Wood and Henry fell in the water they struck out for shore, which was only a few hundred yards away; but Henry presently said he believed he was not hurt (what an unaccountable error!) and therefore would swim back to the boat and help save the wounded. So they parted and Henry returned.

By this time the fire was making fierce headway, and several persons who were imprisoned under the ruins were begging piteously for help. All efforts to conquer the fire proved fruitless, so the buckets were presently thrown aside and the officers fell to with axes and tried to cut the prisoners out. A striker was one of the captives; he said he was not injured, but could not free himself, and when he saw that the fire was likely to drive away the workers he begged that some one would shoot him, and thus save him from the more dreadful death. The fire did drive the axemen away, and they had to listen, helpless, to this poor fellow's supplications till the flames ended his miseries.

The fire drove all into the wood-flat that could be accommodated there; it was cut adrift then, and it and the burning steamer floated down the river toward Ship Island. They moored the flat at the head of the island, and there, unsheltered from the blazing sun, the half-naked occupants had to remain, without food or stimulants, or help for their hurts, during the rest of the day. A steamer came along, finally, and carried the unfortunates to Memphis, and there the most lavish assistance was at once forthcoming. By this time Henry was insensible. The physicians examined his injuries and saw that they were fatal, and naturally turned their main attention to patients who could be saved.

Forty of the wounded were placed upon pallets on the floor of a great public hall, and among these was Henry. There the ladies of Memphis came every day, with flowers, fruits, and dainties and delicacies of all kinds, and there they remained and nursed the wounded. All the physicians stood watches there, and all the medical students; and the rest of the town furnished money, or whatever else was wanted. And Memphis knew how to do all these things well; for many a disaster like the *Pennsylvania*'s had happened near her doors, and she was experienced, above all other cities on the river, in the gracious office of the Good Samaritan.

The sight I saw when I entered that large hall was new and strange to me. Two long rows of prostrate forms—more than forty in all—and every face and head a shapeless wad of loose raw cotton. It was a gruesome spectacle. I watched there six days and nights, and a very melancholy experience it was. There was one daily incident which was peculiarly depressing: this was the removal of the doomed to a chamber apart. It was done in order that the morale of the other patients might not be injuriously affected by seeing one of their number in the death-agony. The fated one was always carried out with as little stir as possible, and the stretcher was always hidden from sight by a wall of assistants; but no matter: everybody knew what that cluster of bent forms, with its muffled step and its slow movement, meant; and all eyes watched it wistfully, and a shudder went abreast of it like a wave.

I saw many poor fellows removed to the "death-room," and saw them no more afterward. But I saw our chief mate carried thither more than once. His hurts were frightful, especially his scalds. He was clothed in linseed oil and raw cotton to his waist, and resembled nothing human. He was often out of his mind; and then his pains would make him rave and shout and sometimes shriek. Then, after a period of dumb exhaustion, his disordered imagination would suddenly transform the great apartment into a forecastle, and the hurrying throng of nurses into the crew; and he would come to a sitting posture and shout, "Hump yourselves, *hump* yourselves, you petrifactions, snail-bellies, pall-bearers! going to be all *day* getting that hatful of freight out?" and supplement this explosion with a firmament-obliterating irruption of profanity which nothing could stay or stop till his crater was empty. And now and then while these frenzies possessed him, he would tear off handfuls of the cotton and expose his cooked flesh to view. It was horrible. It was bad for the others, of course—this noise and these exhibitions; so the doctors tried to give him morphine to quiet him. But, in his mind or out of it, he would not take it. He said his wife had been killed by that treacherous drug, and he would die before he would take it. He suspected that the doctors were concealing it in his ordinary medicines and in his water—so he ceased from putting either to his lips. Once, when he had been without water during two sweltering days, he took the dipper in his hand, and the sight of the limpid fluid, and the misery of his thirst, tempted him almost beyond his strength; but he mastered himself and threw it away, and after that he allowed no more to be brought near him. Three times I saw him carried to the death-room, insensible and supposed to be dying; but each time he revived, cursed his attendants, and demanded to be taken back. He lived to be mate of a steamboat again.

But he was the only one who went to the death-room and returned alive. Dr. Peyton, a principal physician, and rich in all the attributes that go to constitute high and flawless character, did all that educated judgment and trained skill could do for Henry; but, as the newspapers had said in the beginning, his hurts were past help. On the evening of the sixth day his wandering mind busied itself with matters far away, and his nerveless fingers "picked at his coverlet." His hour had struck; we bore him to the death-room, poor boy.[6]

Samuel Clemens was aboard the steamboat *Nebraska* in May 1861 when a cannonball struck its funnel, fired by one of the U.S. Navy ships blockading Memphis. After that, commercial traffic on the Mississippi ceased, and the war claimed most of the one thousand steamboats then plying the river, including most of those that Clemens had piloted.

A brief encounter with military life convinced Samuel Clemens that he was no soldier, so he "lit out for the territories" again, this time to points west. His big brother Orion had been appointed to be assistant to the territorial governor of Nevada. Sam decided the assistant would be needing an assistant.

Hawaiian Passages

After growing up on the Mississippi and then spending six years in Nevada and California, Clemens finally got to sea in 1866, when he made a transformative voyage from San Francisco to the Hawaiian Islands. That ocean passage, along with the return trip to San Francisco later in the year, changed the author's view of the world and of the experience of its animal inhabitants (including humans—Clemens saw no evidence that our species deserved special distinction), to the extent that when he turned to the task of composing his book *Roughing It*, a memoir of those footloose years, the imprint of his epic saltwater experiences—one with a steamer, one aboard a square-rigged clipper ship—is visible in his mode of expression. This imprint is like the waterline left by the surface of the sea, all along the full length of a ship's hull, a foamy demarcation, narrow but distinct, showing that this ship has closely encountered the liquidly dynamic, salty vastness of the ocean. During his Hawaiian adventure, Clemens immersed himself in that element, literally —swallowing buckets of the stuff while becoming one of the first Americans to try surfing—and figuratively, sponging up and stowing away for repeated future reference and reflection everything he saw and heard of the maritime world, from the sailors' lingo to an extended diagnosis of the untreatable multiple personality disorder of the Pacific. Sam Clemens had come under the thrall of the incomparable ocean, and his future writings would reflect this fascination, like a sailboat mirrored in the light of the rising—and the setting—sun.

The outbound trip took Clemens from the Embarcadero of San Francisco to the archipelago that Captain James Cook had dubbed the Sandwich Islands to sate his noble patron's hunger for acclaim. Clemens went aboard a "screw," a steamship with a propeller instead of a paddle wheel like those he had piloted on the Mississippi River. He reflected on the experience in chapter 67 of *Roughing It*, which relates an anecdote about some of the characters he encountered during the passage, in particular one he nicknamed "the Old Admiral."

*   *   *

From *Roughing It*, Chapter 62

The Old Admiral

After a three months' absence, I found myself in San Francisco again, without a cent. When my credit was about exhausted, (for I had become too mean and lazy, now, to work on a morning paper, and there were no vacancies on the evening journals,) I was created San Francisco correspondent of the *Enterprise*, and at the end of five months I was out of debt, but my interest in my work was gone; for my correspondence being a daily one, without rest or respite, I got unspeakably tired of it. I wanted another change. The vagabond instinct was strong upon me. Fortune favored and I got a new berth and a delightful one. It was to go down to the Sandwich Islands and write some letters for the Sacramento *Union*, an excellent journal and liberal with employés.

We sailed in the propeller *Ajax*, in the middle of winter. The almanac called it winter, distinctly enough, but the weather was a compromise between spring and summer. Six days out of port, it became summer altogether. We had some thirty passengers; among them a cheerful soul by the name of Williams, and three sea-worn old whaleship captains going down to join their vessels. These latter played euchre in the smoking room day and night, drank astonishing quantities of raw whisky without being in the least affected by it, and were the happiest people I think I ever saw. And then there was "the old Admiral—" a retired whaleman. He was a roaring, terrific combination of wind and lightning and thunder, and earnest, whole-souled profanity. But nevertheless he was tender-hearted as a girl. He was a raving, deafening, devastating typhoon, laying waste the cowering seas but with an unvexed refuge in the centre where all comers were safe and at rest. Nobody could know the "Admiral" without liking him; and in a sudden and dire emergency I think no friend of his would know which to choose—to be cursed by him or prayed for by a less efficient person.

His title of "Admiral" was more strictly "official" than any ever worn by a naval officer before or since, perhaps—for it was the voluntary offering of a whole nation, and came direct from the people themselves without any intermediate red tape—the *people* of the Sandwich Islands. It was a title that came to him freighted with affection, and honor, and appreciation of his unpretending merit. And in testimony of the genuineness of the title it was publicly ordained that an exclusive flag should be devised for him and used solely to welcome his coming and wave him God-speed in his going. From that time forth, whenever his ship was signaled in the offing, or he catted his anchor and stood out to sea, that ensign streamed from the royal halliards on the parliament house and the nation lifted their hats to it with spontaneous accord.

Yet he had never fired a gun or fought a battle in his life. When I knew him on board the *Ajax*, he was seventy-two years old and had plowed the salt water sixty-one of them. For sixteen years he had gone in and out of the harbor of Honolulu in command of a whaleship, and for sixteen more had been captain of a San Francisco and Sandwich Island passenger packet and had never had an accident or lost a vessel. The simple natives knew him for a friend who never failed them, and regarded him as children regard a father. It was a dangerous thing to oppress them when the roaring Admiral was around.

Two years before I knew the Admiral, he had retired from the sea on a competence, and had sworn a colossal nine-jointed oath that he would "never go within *smelling* distance of the salt water again as long as he lived." And he had conscientiously kept it. That is to say, *he* considered he had kept it, and it would have been more than dangerous to suggest to him, even in the gentlest way, that making eleven long sea voyages, as a passenger, during the two years that had transpired since he "retired," was only keeping the general spirit of it and not the strict letter.

The Admiral knew only one narrow line of conduct to pursue in any and all cases where there was a fight, and that was to shoulder his way straight in without an inquiry as to the rights or the merits of it, and take the part of the weaker side.—And this was the reason why he was always sure to be present at the trial of any universally execrated criminal to oppress and intimidate the jury with a vindictive pantomime of what he would do to them if he ever caught them out of the box. And this was why harried cats and outlawed dogs that knew him confidently took sanctuary under his chair in time of trouble. In the beginning he was the most frantic and bloodthirsty Union man that drew breath in the shadow of the Flag; but the instant the Southerners began to go down before the sweep of the Northern armies, he ran up the Confederate colors and from that time till the end was a rampant and inexorable secessionist.

He hated intemperance with a more uncompromising animosity than any individual I have ever met, of either sex; and he was never tired of storming against it and beseeching friends and strangers alike to be wary and drink with moderation. And yet if any creature had been guileless enough to intimate that his absorbing nine gallons of "straight" whiskey during our voyage was any fraction short of rigid or inflexible abstemiousness, in that self-same moment the old man would have spun him to the uttermost parts of the earth in the whirlwind of his wrath. Mind, I am not saying his whisky ever affected his head or his legs, for it did not, in even the slightest degree. He was a capacious container, but he did not hold enough for that. He took a level tumblerful of whisky every morning before he put his clothes on—"to sweeten his bilgewater," he said.—He took another after he got the most of his clothes on, "to settle his mind and give him his bearings." He then shaved, and put on a clean shirt; after which he recited the Lord's Prayer in a fervent, thundering bass that shook the ship to her kelson and suspended all conversation in the main cabin. Then, at this stage, being invariably "by the head," or "by the stern," or "listed to port or starboard," he took one more to "put him on an even keel so that he would mind his hellum and not miss stays and go about, every time he came up in the wind."—And now, his stateroom door swung open and the sun of his benignant face beamed redly out upon men and women and children, and he roared his "Shipmets a'hoy!" in a way that was calculated to wake the dead and precipitate the final resurrection; and forth he strode, a picture to look at and a presence to enforce attention. Stalwart and portly; not a gray hair; broadbrimmed slouch hat; semi-sailor toggery of blue navy flannel—roomy and ample; a stately expanse of shirt-front and a liberal amount of black silk neck-cloth tied with a sailor knot; large chain and imposing seals impending from his fob; awe-inspiring feet, and "a hand like the hand of Providence," as his whaling brethren expressed it; wrist-bands and sleeves pushed back half way to the elbow, out of respect for the warm weather, and exposing hairy arms, gaudy with red and blue anchors, ships, and goddesses of liberty tattooed in India ink. But these details were only secondary matters—his face was the lodestone that chained the eye. It was a sultry disk, glowing determinedly out through a weather beaten mask of mahogany, and studded with warts, seamed with scars, "blazed" all over with unfailing fresh slips of the razor; and with cheery eyes, under shaggy brows, contemplating the world from over the back of a gnarled crag of a nose that loomed vast and lonely out of the undulating immensity that spread away from its foundations. At his heels frisked the darling of his bachelor estate, his terrier "Fan," a creature no larger than a squirrel. The main part of his daily life was occupied in looking after "Fan," in a motherly way, and doctoring her for a hundred ailments which existed only in his imagination.

The Admiral seldom read newspapers; and when he did he never believed anything they said. He read nothing, and believed in nothing, but "The Old Guard," a secession periodical published in New York. He carried a dozen copies of it with him, always, and referred to them for all required information. If it was not there, he supplied it himself, out of a bountiful fancy, inventing history, names, dates, and every thing else necessary to make his point good in an argument. Consequently he was a formidable antagonist in a dispute. Whenever he swung clear of the record and began to create history, the enemy was helpless and had to surrender. Indeed, the enemy could not keep from betraying some little spark of indignation at his manufactured history—and when it came to indignation, that was the Admiral's very "best hold." He was always ready for a political argument, and if nobody started one he would do it himself. With his third retort his temper would begin to rise, and within five minutes he would be blowing a gale, and within fifteen his smoking-room audience would be utterly stormed away and the old man left solitary and alone, banging the table with his fist, kicking the chairs, and roaring a hurricane of profanity. It got so, after a while, that whenever the Admiral approached, with politics in his eye, the passengers would drop out with quiet accord, afraid to meet him; and he would camp on a deserted field.

But he found his match at last, and before a full company. At one time or another, everybody had entered the lists against him and been routed, except the quiet passenger Williams. He had never been able to get an expression of opinion out of him on politics. But now, just as the Admiral drew near the door and the company were about to slip out, Williams said:

"Admiral, are you *certain* about that circumstance concerning the clergymen you mentioned the other day?"—referring to a piece of the Admiral's manufactured history.

Every one was amazed at the man's rashness. The idea of deliberately inviting annihilation was a thing incomprehensible. The retreat came to a halt; then everybody sat down again wondering, to await the upshot of it. The Admiral himself was as surprised as any one. He paused in the door, with his red handkerchief half raised to his sweating face, and contemplated the daring reptile in the corner.

"Certain of it? Am I certain of it? Do you think I've been lying about it? What do you take me for? Anybody that don't know that circumstance, don't know anything; a child ought to know it. Read up your history! Read it up——and don't come asking a man if he's *certain* about a bit of ABC stuff that the very southern niggers know all about."

Here the Admiral's fires began to wax hot, the atmosphere thickened, the coming earthquake rumbled, he began to thunder and lighten. Within three minutes his volcano was in full irruption and he was discharging flames and ashes of indignation, belching black volumes of foul history aloft, and vomiting red-hot torrents of profanity from his crater. Meantime Williams sat silent, and apparently deeply and earnestly interested in what the old man was saying. By and by, when the lull came, he said in the most deferential way, and with the gratified air of a man who has had a mystery cleared up which had been puzzling him uncomfortably:

"Now I understand it. I always thought I knew that piece of history well enough, but was still afraid to trust it, because there was not that convincing particularity about it that one likes to have in history; but when you mentioned every name, the other day, and every date, and every little circumstance, in their just order and sequence, I said to myself, this sounds something like—this is history—this is putting it in a shape that gives a man confidence; and I said to myself afterward, I will just ask the Admiral if he is perfectly certain about the details, and if he is I will come

out and thank him for clearing this matter up for me. And that is what I
want to do now — for until you set that matter right it was nothing but just
a confusion in my mind, without head or tail to it."

Nobody ever saw the Admiral look so mollified before, and so pleased.
Nobody had ever received his bogus history as gospel before; its genuineness had always been called in question either by words or looks;
but here was a man that not only swallowed it all down, but was grateful
for the dose. He was taken a back; he hardly knew what to say; even his
profanity failed him. Now, Williams continued, modestly and earnestly:

"But Admiral, in saying that this was the first stone thrown, and that
this precipitated the war, you have overlooked a circumstance which you
are perfectly familiar with, but which has escaped your memory. Now I
grant you that what you have stated is correct in every detail — to wit: that
on the 16th of October, 1860, two Massachusetts clergymen, named Waite
and Granger, went in disguise to the house of John Moody, in Rockport,
at dead of night, and dragged forth two southern women and their two
little children, and after tarring and feathering them conveyed them to
Boston and burned them alive in the State House square; and I also grant
your proposition that this deed is what led to the secession of South Carolina on the 20th of December following. Very well." [Here the company
were pleasantly surprised to hear Williams proceed to come back at the
Admiral with his own invincible weapon — clean, pure, manufactured
history, without a word of truth in it.][1] "Very well, I say. But Admiral, why
overlook the Willis and Morgan case in South Carolina? You are too well
informed a man not to know all about that circumstance. Your arguments
and your conversations have shown you to be intimately conversant with
every detail of this national quarrel. You develop matters of history every
day that show plainly that you are no smatterer in it, content to nibble
about the surface, but a man who has searched the depths and possessed
yourself of everything that has a bearing upon the great question. Therefore, let me just recall to your mind that Willis and Morgan case — though
I see by your face that the whole thing is already passing through your
memory at this moment. On the 12th of August, 1860, two months before
the Waite and Granger affair, two South Carolina clergymen, named John
H. Morgan and Winthrop L. Willis, one a Methodist and the other an
Old School Baptist, disguised themselves, and went at midnight to the

house of a planter named Thompson—Archibald F. Thompson, Vice President under Thomas Jefferson,—and took thence, at midnight, his widowed aunt, (a Northern woman,) and her adopted child, an orphan —named Mortimer Highie, afflicted with epilepsy and suffering at the time from white swelling on one of his legs, and compelled to walk on crutches in consequence; and the two ministers, in spite of the pleadings of the victims, dragged them to the bush, tarred and feathered them, and afterward burned them at the stake in the city of Charleston. You remember perfectly well what a stir it made; you remember perfectly well that even the *Charleston Courier* stigmatized the act as being unpleasant, of questionable propriety, and scarcely justifiable, and likewise that it would not be matter of surprise if retaliation ensued. And you remember also, that this thing was the cause of the Massachusetts outrage. Who, indeed, were the two Massachusetts ministers? and who were the two Southern women they burned? I do not need to remind you, Admiral, with your intimate knowledge of history, that Waite was the nephew of the woman burned in Charleston; that Granger was her cousin in the second degree, and that the woman they burned in Boston was the wife of John H. Morgan, and the still loved but divorced wife of Winthrop L. Willis. Now, Admiral, it is only fair that you should acknowledge that the first provocation came from the Southern preachers and that the Northern ones were justified in retaliating. In your arguments you never yet have shown the least disposition to withhold a just verdict or be in anywise unfair, when authoritative history condemned your position, and therefore I have no hesitation in asking you to take the original blame from the Massachusetts ministers, in this matter, and transfer it to the South Carolina clergymen where it justly belongs."

The Admiral was conquered. This sweet spoken creature who swallowed his fraudulent history as if it were the bread of life; basked in his furious blasphemy as if it were generous sunshine; found only calm, evenhanded justice in his rampart partisanship; and flooded him with invented history so sugar-coated with flattery and deference that there was no rejecting it, was "too many" for him. He stammered some awkward, profane sentences about the———Willis and Morgan business having escaped his memory, but that he "remembered it now," and then, under pretense of giving Fan some medicine for an imaginary cough, drew out of the battle and went away, a vanquished man. Then cheers and laughter went up, and Williams, the ship's benefactor, was a hero. The news went about the vessel, champagne was ordered, and enthusiastic reception instituted in the smoking room, and everybody flocked thither to shake hands with the conqueror. The wheelman said afterward, that the Admiral stood up behind the pilot house and "ripped and cursed all to himself" till he loosened the smokestack guys and becalmed the mainsail.

The Admiral's power was broken. After that, if he began argument, somebody would bring Williams, and the old man would grow weak and begin to quiet down at once. And as soon as he was done, Williams in his dulcet, insinuating way, would invent some history (referring for proof, to the old man's own excellent memory and to copies of "The Old Guard" known not to be in his possession) that would turn the tables completely and leave the Admiral all abroad and helpless. By and by he came to so dread Williams and his gilded tongue that he would stop talking when he saw him approach, and finally ceased to mention politics altogether, and from that time forward there was entire peace and serenity in the ship.[2]

The notebook that Clemens kept on board the *Ajax* provides more detail about what the reporter experienced and observed on the eleven-day voyage in March 1866, separate from his publication of *Roughing It*.

*   *   *

From Mark Twain's Notebook

March 10 — We are making 200 miles a day. Got some sail on yesterday morning for the first time, & in afternoon crowded *every*thing on. Sea gulls chase but no catch.

Three or four of the sea-sick passengers came to lunch at noon, & several of the ladies are able to dress & sit up.

Captain reports 325 miles made in past 24 hours.

Found an old acquaintance to-day — never have been anywhere yet that I didn't find an acquaintance.

11th — Magnificent day yesterday — sea as smooth as a river ruffled by a land breeze. Occasionally the ship rolled a good deal, nevertheless. Chief

Engineer Sanford says reason is our head-winds (S.W.) smooth down
the eternal swell that is always rolling down from the N.W., but as soon as
the contrary wind dies out, the old swell rolls the ship again, even in the
calmest weather. N.W. is the prevailing wind far down through Pacific,
but dies out toward equator—then round Horn comes up the S.E. wind,
& its swell lasts up toward the line—both swells die out & leave a space
on each side of the line smooth as glass & subject to calms.

Nearly everybody out to breakfast this morning—not more than ½
doz sick now.

The old whalers aboard (Capt.s Smith, Fish & Philips—two latter
Shenandoah victims[3]—) say not more than 4 months smooth weather on
this route a year. . . .

12th—March—Very rough & rainy all afternoon—foresail shredded
last night. . . .

Lon holding on by finger-nails & leaning to roll of ship like Capt.
Cuttle.[4] . . .

2 whalers—Fish & Phillips—latter's vessel bonded—former's burned.
. . .

Capacity 60 passengers in comfort—& 40 bunks between decks.

1000 to 1200 tons with coal for full trip on—capacity.

P[i]g—Dennis.

Walking on the chickens.[5]

Restless—change pillow—turn over—roll out—tumbler fetch away
—etc. . . .

'Slops' are clothing, tobacco, &c, furnished sailors at sea & charged
against them. Sailor's advance is $40—he may find $10 for boots which
he got, $40 for boots which he didn't get, &c on return—be actually in
debt—in which case the government fee of $1 for discharging him is re-
mitted.

Long lay is the Captains & mates 10th 20th & 30th share of a whaling
voyage.

Short lay is a common seaman's 120th of the same.

Captains swindle sailors out of every dollar they can by the slop system, & every cent so saved goes to the owners. But the ungrateful owners,
by false gauges of oil, quotations of markets, false sales, pretended non-
sales & depreciation of price, &c, swindle the captains.

The consul, in buying the cargo from the sailors, reduce it some by putting it on gold basis, by leakage, shrinkage, margin for depreciation from ruling rates, &c, reduce the value of the cargo ⅔.

'Pulling' is the arrest of Capt by seamen for ill treatment.

Portuguese greenies often put on short lay of 300th—go to sea—learn how been swindled—desert first opportunity to ship offers more.

Roughest night of the voyage last night—ship rolled heavily.

Still rougher this morning till 11 o'ck, when course was altered to W., which eased her up considerably.

Settee fetched away at breakfast, & precipitated 4 heavy men on their backs.

Rev. Mr. Thurston, Capt Smith & family (Lon) Ye Ancient Mariner —Sea Monster—Capt Cuttle—'Don't like gale holding on so close to change of moon—if holds 48 hours will hang on through the quarter.'

'If wind don't haul around with sun won't have fair wind—no fair wind comes but comes with the sun.'

Yarns of force of sea—68 pounders on [Saint] Helena, forty ft. above water, in calm—*Great Repub[lic]* decks broke in—15,000 tons of 30-ton rocks moved back 300 yards & left in winrow—decks stripped lean with gentle sea—27 stancions, &c.[6]

13th—Tuesday—Very rough again all night—had head winds & had to take in all sail—made poor run—weather fine this morning, but still head winds, & there being not a rag of canvas to steady the ship, she rolls disagreeably, though the sea is not rough.

14th—Wednesday—Good weather. I have suffered from something like mumps for past 2 days.

15th—Thursday. Dress by the latitude and longitude—Capt & Chf Eng came out in full summer rig to-day because by the sextant we in lat. 26° though the weather don't justify it.

Mumps—mumps—mumps—it was so decided to-day—a d—d disease that children have—I suppose I am to take a new disease to the Islands & depopulate them, as all white men have done heretofore.

Mr. Sanford Ch Eng been in US service 16 years—been in 7 battles in Mex & 6 in America.

Mr. Baxter, Mate, been on gunboat in the war, too. & Captain Godfrey. Heavily timbered, strong bolted ship.

3 watches, repeated of 8 bells each—each beginning at 12 o'clock & ending at 12. 1st watch morning—12 to 4—2d, 4 to 8—3d, 8 to 12. . . .

16th March—Friday—They say we shall be in sight of land to-morrow at noon. Good weather and smooth sea for the past 2 days.

Dennis the hog was killed yesterday and served for breakfast this morning.

The water begins to taste of the casks. . . .

'Ship time'—(taken with the sextant reckoning every day at noon.)

Ye whalers at Euchre: 'Who hove that ace on there?' 'He kep' heavin' 'em down so fast I couldn't tell noth'n 'tall 'bout it.' 'Here goes for a euchre—by G—I'll make a point or break a rope-yarn.' 'Call small odd suit "blubber."' 'Now what'd you trump that for? You're sailin' too close to the wind—there, I know'd it—royals, stuns'ls—everything, gone to h—l.' 'That's my ace!' '—no t'aint—it's mine—you hove the King—' 'Not by a d—d sight!—rot my copper if I hove the King—leave it to Johnny here if I did.'

Whaler drink—¾ of tumblerfull.

Capt. Smith secesh.[7] . . .

1 Stewardess.—Captains always doctors.

Night of 17th—Never could swear to being in the tropics by the weather till to-night—hot as hell in the state rooms. Magnificent breezy starlight & new moon on deck—everybody out.

18th—8 A.M. Sunday—Land in sight on left—like a couple of vague whales lying in blue mist under the distant horizon.

Oahu glinting in the sun through light mist—20 miles away.

This is the most magnificent, balmy atmosphere in the world—ought to take dead man out of grave. . . .

Harp engine laid horizontally—normal condition vertical—gives great compactness & leaves no portion of machinery above the water line —*Ajax* was built for gun boat.

Temperature in fire-room (no ventilation) 148°. Firemen only live about 5 years, & then probably don't mind hell much.

Screw 13 inches diameter, 70 feet long—flukes 13 feet diameter, 22½ feet.

Running past Diamond Head on about 100 feet of water—beautiful light blue color—see shadows of bottom sometimes—water very transparent—water shames the pale heavens with the splendor of its brilliant blue.[8]

On board an interisland hauler suitably named *Boomerang*, Clemens set out from Oahu to tour the Big Island:

* * *

From *Roughing It*, Chapter 69

Bound for Hawaii (a hundred and fifty miles distant,) to visit the great volcano and behold the other notable things which distinguish that island above the remainder of the group, we sailed from Honolulu on a certain Saturday afternoon, in the good schooner *Boomerang*.

The *Boomerang* was about as long as two street cars, and about as wide as one. She was so small (though she was larger than the majority of the inter-island coasters) that when I stood on her deck I felt but little smaller than the Colossus of Rhodes must have felt when he had a man-of-war under him. I could reach the water when she lay over under a strong breeze. When the Captain and my comrade (a Mr. Billings), myself and four other persons were all assembled on the little after portion of the deck which is sacred to the cabin passengers, it was full—there was not room for any more quality folks. Another section of the deck, twice as large as ours, was full of natives of both sexes, with their customary dogs, mats, blankets, pipes, calabashes of poi, fleas, and other luxuries and baggage of minor importance. As soon as we set sail the natives all lay down on the deck as thick as negroes in a slave-pen, and smoked, conversed, and spit on each other, and were truly sociable.

The little low-ceiled cabin below was rather larger than a hearse, and as dark as a vault. It had two coffins on each side—I mean two bunks. A small table, capable of accommodating three persons at dinner, stood against the forward bulkhead, and over it hung the dingiest whale oil lantern that ever peopled the obscurity of a dungeon with ghostly shapes. The floor room unoccupied was not extensive. One might swing a cat in it, perhaps, but not a long cat. The hold forward of the bulkhead had but little freight in it, and from morning till night a portly old rooster, with a voice like Balaam's ass, and the same disposition to use it, strutted up and down in that part of the vessel and crowed. He usually took dinner at six o'clock, and then, after an hour devoted to meditation, he mounted a barrel and crowed a good part of the night. He got hoarser all the time, but he scorned to allow any personal consideration to interfere with his duty, and kept up his labors in defiance of threatened diphtheria.

Sleeping was out of the question when he was on watch. He was a source of genuine aggravation and annoyance. It was worse than useless to shout at him or apply offensive epithets to him—he only took these things for applause, and strained himself to make more noise. Occasionally, during the day, I threw potatoes at him through an aperture in the bulkhead, but he only dodged and went on crowing.

The first night, as I lay in my coffin, idly watching the dim lamp swinging to the rolling of the ship, and snuffing the nauseous odors of bilge water, I felt something gallop over me. I turned out promptly. However, I turned in again when I found it was only a rat. Presently something galloped over me once more. I knew it was not a rat this time, and I thought it might be a centipede, because the Captain had killed one on deck in the afternoon. I turned out. The first glance at the pillow showed me a repulsive sentinel perched upon each end of it—cockroaches as large as peach leaves—fellows with long, quivering antennae and fiery, malignant eyes. They were grating their teeth like tobacco worms, and appeared to be dissatisfied about something. I had often heard that these reptiles were in the habit of eating off sleeping sailors' toe nails down to the quick, and I would not get in the bunk any more. I lay down on the floor. But a rat came and bothered me, and shortly afterward a procession of cockroaches arrived and camped in my hair. In a few moments the rooster was crowing with uncommon spirit and a party of fleas were throwing double somersaults about my person in the wildest disorder, and taking a bite every time they struck. I was beginning to feel really annoyed. I got up and put my clothes on and went on deck.

The above is not overdrawn; it is a truthful sketch of inter-island schooner life. There is no such thing as keeping a vessel in elegant condition, when she carries molasses and Kanakas.

It was compensation for my sufferings to come unexpectedly upon so beautiful a scene as met my eye—to step suddenly out of the sepulchral gloom of the cabin and stand under the strong light of the moon—in the centre, as it were, of a glittering sea of liquid silver—to see the broad sails straining in the gale, the ship heeled over on her side, the angry foam hissing past her lee bulwarks, and sparkling sheets of spray dashing high over her bows and raining upon her decks; to brace myself and hang fast to the first object that presented itself, with hat jammed down and coat tails whipping in the breeze, and feel that exhilaration that thrills in one's hair and quivers down his back bone when he knows that every inch of canvas is drawing and the vessel cleaving through the waves at her utmost speed. There was no darkness, no dimness, no obscurity there. All was brightness, every object was vividly defined. Every prostrate Kanaka; every coil of rope; every calabash of poi; every puppy; every seam in the flooring; every bolthead; every object; however minute, showed sharp and distinct in its every outline; and the shadow of the broad mainsail lay black as a pall upon the deck, leaving Billings's white upturned face glorified and his body in a total eclipse.[9]

Of all the activities Clemens pursued in Hawaii—horseback riding in the jungles of Oahu, climbing the active volcano Kilauea on the Big Island of Hawaii, watching Hawaiian girls bathing nude, chasing the "multitudes of cats"—the most unusual was surfing. Aside from brief descriptions from the last voyage of Captain James Cook, no one prior to Mark Twain had ever described for a general audience this water sport that would generate its own unique transnational culture on the way to becoming a global phenomenon. That passage, which is something like a sacred text for devotees of the waves, appears in chapter 73 of *Roughing It*:

*   *   *

From *Roughing It*, Chapter 73

The native canoe is an irresponsible looking contrivance. I cannot think of anything to liken it to but a boy's sled runner hollowed out, and that does not quite convey the correct idea. It is about fifteen feet long, high and pointed at both ends, is a foot and a half or two feet deep, and so narrow that if you wedged a fat man into it you might not get him out again. It sits on top of the water like a duck, but it has an outrigger and does not upset easily, if you keep still. This outrigger is formed of two long bent sticks like plow handles, which project from one side, and to their outer ends is bound a curved beam composed of an extremely light wood, which skims along the surface of the water and thus saves you from an upset on that side, while the outrigger's weight is not so easily lifted as to make an upset on the other side a thing to be greatly feared. Still, until one gets used to sitting perched upon this knife-blade, he is apt to reason within himself that it would be more comfortable if there were just an outrigger or so on the other side also.

I had the bow seat, and Billings sat amidships and faced the Kanaka, who occupied the stern of the craft and did the paddling. With the first stroke the trim shell of a thing shot out from the shore like an arrow. There was not much to see. While we were on the shallow water of the reef, it was pastime to look down into the limpid depths at the large bunches of branching coral—the unique shrubbery of the sea. We lost that, though, when we got out into the dead blue water of the deep. But we had the picture of the surf, then, dashing angrily against the crag-bound shore and sending a foaming spray high into the air. There was interest in this beetling border, too, for it was honey-combed with quaint caves and arches and tunnels, and had a rude semblance of the dilapidated architecture of ruined keeps and castles rising out of the restless sea. When this novelty ceased to be a novelty, we turned our eyes shoreward and gazed at the long mountain with its rich green forests stretching up into the curtaining clouds, and at the specks of houses in the rearward distance and the diminished schooner riding sleepily at anchor. And when these grew tiresome we dashed boldly into the midst of a school of huge, beastly porpoises engaged at their eternal game of arching over a wave and disappearing, and then doing it over again and keeping it up—always circling over, in that way, like so many well-submerged wheels. But the porpoises wheeled themselves away, and then we were thrown upon our own resources. It did not take many minutes to discover that the sun was blazing like a bonfire, and that the weather was of a melting temperature. It had a drowsing effect, too.

In one place we came upon a large company of naked natives, of both sexes and all ages, amusing themselves with the national pastime of surf-bathing. Each heathen would paddle three or four hundred yards out to sea, (taking a short board with him), then face the shore and wait for a particularly prodigious billow to come along; at the right moment he would fling his board upon its foamy crest and himself upon the board, and here he would come whizzing by like a bombshell! It did not seem that a lightning express train could shoot along at a more hair-lifting speed. I tried surf-bathing once, subsequently, but made a failure of it. I got the board placed right, and at the right moment, too; but missed the connection myself. — The board struck the shore in three quarters of a second, without any cargo, and I struck the bottom about the same time, with a couple of barrels of water in me. None but natives ever master the art of surf-bathing thoroughly.[10]

3

Pacific Perils

The Wreck of the Clipper Ship *Hornet*

Mark Twain scored his first major byline by a grisly fluke. His lengthy day-by-day account of how the suffering survivors of the shipwrecked first-class clipper *Hornet* drifted for six weeks before reaching Hawaii caused a minor sensation. Clemens's access to these survivors was due to the nigh-on-divine intercession of Anson Burlingame, the U.S. diplomat who played the seminal role in cultivating Sino-American relations. When news reached Honolulu that the *Hornet*'s lifeboat had come ashore, carrying its sad cargo of sentient skeletons, Clemens was at home, flat on his stomach—not his back!—suffering from infected saddle sores after excessive exploration of the exotic island's rugged interior on a horse. He was very fortunate to have befriended Burlingame, the eminent visitor, who arranged for the scoop-seeking correspondent to be carried on a stretcher to the hospital where the survivors had been taken. Clemens interviewed them, dashed off the story overnight, and took it to the dock in the morning, just in the nick of time to catch a schooner setting sail for San Francisco. Someone with "a strong hand," probably a stevedore, heaved the papery bundle from the wharf across the widening watery gap onto the deck of the vessel, where it landed safely, to be borne off to the pages of the *Sacramento Union*.

The newspaper printed the story on July 19, 1866, and other presses around the country, and then around the world, picked it up in the days and weeks to come, while Clemens was at sea, on his way back to California. Three of the *Hornet* survivors—the captain and the well-educated Ferguson brothers—were his shipmates for the slow passage aboard the often becalmed clipper *Smyrniote*, giving the author ample time for further interviews with them. The three even allowed him to read and transcribe the written records—the captain's log and the brothers' personal journals—that they had maintained during their ordeal. Twain added the details he gleaned from these conversations and documents to his newspaper report, expanding it into a full-length article. He submitted the piece first to *Harper's Weekly*, one of America's most popular publications at the time, which published a version on September 29, 1866 (Fig. 1). Then *Harper's New Monthly Magazine* published the full narrative in installments over three issues, November 1866 to January 1867, under the title "43 Days in an Open Boat." That now obscure piece of the author's extensive journalistic reportage established him as a professional writer before he could rely on fiction (which was his genius). Bracketed text in the article below is Twain's.

*   *   *

From *Harper's Weekly*

Forty-Three Days in an Open Boat:
Compiled from Personal Diaries

The superb clipper ship Hornet, Captain Josiah Mitchell, sailed out of New York harbor about the first week in January, 1866, bound for San Francisco. She had a quick passage around the Horn, and experienced no ill luck of any kind until just after crossing the equator, upward bound, in the Pacific. Then, on the morning of the 3rd of May, she took fire and was burned up, and the crew and passengers, with ten days' provisions saved from the vessel, found themselves adrift in three open boats.

Each boat had a compass, a quadrant, a copy of *Bowditch's Navigator*, and a *Nautical Almanac*, and the Captain's and chief mate's boats had chronometers. There were 31 men, all told. The Captain took an account of stock, with the following result: four hams, nearly thirty pounds of salt pork, half-box of raisins, one hundred pounds of bread, twelve two-pound cans of oysters, clams, and assorted meats, a keg containing four pounds of butter, twelve gallons of water in a forty-gallon "scuttle-butt," four one-gallon demi-johns full of water, three bottles of brandy (the property of the passengers), some pipes, matches, and a hundred pounds of tobacco. No medicines. Of course the whole party had to go on short rations at once.

The Captain kept a "log," and so did each of the two passengers, Sam-

FIGURE 1. While in Hawaii in 1866, Mark Twain reported on the
burning and sinking of the clipper ship *Hornet* and the sufferings of
its handful of survivors, a story that *Harper's Weekly* published,
with this illustration, giving him his first national headline.
"'Burning of the California Clipper *Hornet*, One Thousand Miles from Land,' sketched by Mr. Weir,"
Harper's Weekly, September 29, 1866, 616. Courtesy of the Roorda/Doyle Collection.

uel and Henry Ferguson, aged 28 and 18 respectively—young gentlemen
making their first sea voyage. The plain, matter-of-fact journal of the elder
Ferguson was as interesting to me as a novel, notwithstanding I knew all
the circumstances of the desperate voyage in the open boat before I read
it. I give it entire, adding extracts from the other logs occasionally. . . .

Samuel Ferguson's Diary

May 3.—At 7 A.M., fire broke out down booby hatch. The boats got off
safe, and all hands. Compute our latitude at 2° 20′ N., and longitude 112°
10′ W. The ship burned very rapidly. Two hours after the fire broke out
the main-mast fell over the side, and dragged the mizzen-topmast with
it. Saved nothing but what we had on, except our over-coats. Got in as
much provisions and water as time would allow. Staid by the burning

ship all day and night. Divided forces—fourteen in the long-boat, and nine and eight men in the two quarter-boats. Our boat—the long-boat—was in command of Captain Mitchell, and the other boats were in charge of the first and second mates. Rations, one half-biscuit for breakfast; one biscuit and some canned meat for dinner; and half a biscuit for tea, with a few swallows of water at each meal.

May 4.—The ship burned all night very brightly; and hopes are that some ship has seen the light, and is bearing down upon us. None seen, however, this forenoon: so we have determined to go together north and a little west to some islands in 18° to 19° N. latitude, and 114° to 115° W. longitude, hoping in the mean time to be picked up by some ship. The ship sank suddenly at about 5 A.M. We find the sun very hot and scorching; but all try to keep out of it as much as we can. The men stand it so far well, though we have three or four on board who have been sick and disabled for some time. Though we have had none yet, we hope, in this latitude, to have plenty of showers, which will work two ways, however; as they must wet our provisions, and also kill the wind. Our course to-day has been north-by-east. Our water rations are increased while we are in the "Doldrums," where we have too frequent showers.

May 5.—Last night was a very unpleasant one; it rained very hard, and it was mighty hard stowage. We all got some sleep. To-day has been overcast, so we have not suffered from the burning sun as we otherwise should. We caught a good deal of water last night, and have now more than we had when we left the ship. The Captain, my brother Henry, myself, the third mate, and nine men lead in the long-boat, which have most sail (*Hornet*'s main-top-gallant studding-sail), tows the other two—the first mate's coming next, and the second mate's last. We made a good run till about midnight, when the wind lessened a good deal. So far every thing goes on as well as can be expected. The men are in good spirits, though we all have a pretty hard time. We were enabled to keep on our course until showers and squalls headed us off.

Sunday, May 6.—This morning began very stormy and squally; it rained very hard, and one time the sea was very wicked—the waves broken and dangerous—what sailors call a "cobbling" sea. Every body became soaked, of course; bread got wet—with fresh water, however. Wind very light until one P.M.; then a rain squall. We keep on the look-out all the time for a sail. In the evening it rained again, making every thing very disagreeable. This boat is a very disagreeable one. What with a large water-cask, the bag of bread, and the bags belonging to the men, there is hardly any room left. We naturally thought often of all at home, and were glad to remember that it was Sacrament Sunday, and that prayers would go up from our friends for us, although they know not our peril. We read and said our prayers as best we could for the rain. Not much wind. First part of the night very rainy and uncomfortable.

May 7. — Henry got the best sleep last night he had yet; the Captain also got a few good cat-naps, the first he has had during the four days and nights since we lost the ship. Wind light until seven or eight o'clock, when it freshened up and gave us a high and cobbling sea — much worse than any we have seen in a good while. The other boats get on well, and are much better sea-boats than the chunk we are in — not that I have any reason to complain of her action. Upon consultation the Captain thought best to steer more easterly to an island called Clipperton Rock, which is decidedly the nearest. Suppose we do not find it, we shall still stand in the highway of ships, and also make a good deal of easting, by which we are better able to make the isles further north, they being in latitude 18° to 20° N., and longitude 111° to 131′ W. About ten o'clock we headed east-northeast, and hope to find Clipperton Island in latitude 10° 28′, and longitude 109° 19′. The bread department of our provisions is decidedly our weak point. The Captain places no reliance upon the chronometers on account of their constant disarrangement by the plunging of the boat; but he means to take sights now and then, as they keep together tolerably well.

May 8. — Last night a series of calms and light breezes, during which we had wind in all directions; rained, but not hard, till morning, when about six it began and kept it up pretty regularly — wet every thing and every body again. No wind all day. About noon it cleared off and came out hot. Second mate's boat desiring to row, we went to the rear and each boat took to the "white-ash" — that is, to the oars. Saw plenty of dolphins, but could not catch any. I think we are all beginning more and more to realize the awful situation we are in. It often takes a ship a week to get through the Doldrums — how much longer, then, such a craft as ours, which can not sail within seven to eight points of the wind. We are so crowded that we can not stretch ourselves out for a good sleep, but have to take it in any way we can get it. I am glad I managed to get aboard my three bottles of brandy—it will do us good service.

May 9.—Last night was a pleasant one—no rain of any account—so most of the day was spent in drying our wet clothes and blankets. Early in the evening the second mate's boat took the lead, rowing, when shortly a breeze sprang up, and they made sail, continuing to row. We reefed our sail and set it, and so soon caught up that we took the lead; then shook out the reef. We have been highly favored in being able to keep together so well. The sun is very hot indeed, and gave me a warning to keep out of it as much as possible, in a very peculiar doubling of the sight when looking with both eyes, while with either one the vision was unmarred. Looking with both eyes the horizon crossed thus: X. Lying down in the shade of the sail soon banished the trouble, however, and I am all right now. Henry keeps well, but broods over our troubles more than I wish he did. Caught to-day two dolphins; had part of one cooked in a pan; it tasted well. Turned in about 7½ o'clock and slept pretty well till 12; then turned out to give Henry a chance. Had a good breeze and no rain. The Captain believed the compass out of the way, but the long invisible North Star came out—a welcome sight—and indorsed the compass.

May 10.—Latitude 7° 0′ 3″ N.; longitude 111° 32′ W. Drifting in the calms all day. Even as the Captain says, all romance has long since vanished, and I think most of us are beginning to look the fact of our awful situation full in the face. We are still in a good place to be picked up, but seem to make little or nothing on our course toward the isles. We are so cramped up here that it makes it more trying than all else. They are not as provident as they should be in the third [second] mate's boat. They have eaten up all the canned meats brought from the ship, and now are growing discontented. The men in the first mate's boat are careful and contented, however. The chronometers are going, but differ somewhat, and so they can not be depended upon. We have been mercifully guarded against the destructive effects of these sudden and violent squalls. We have all the water we want. To-day Joe caught some more dolphins and a small turtle. Charley cooked a portion of the former.

May 11.—Latitude 7°; longitude 110° 0′ 3″. Standing still! Or worse; we lost more last night than we made yesterday. Caught some little rain, but not enough to fill up the water-butts. The sun in the middle of the day is very powerful, and makes it necessary to cover one's head. To-day the mate's boat caught a turtle; so we have some meat, though we have to eat it raw. The cock that was rescued and pitched into the boat while the ship was on fire still lives, and crows with the breaking of dawn, cheering us all a good deal. The second mate's boat again want water to-day, showing that they overdrink their allowance. The Captain spoke pretty sharply to them. From appearances they ought to be able to catch enough to-night. Have no reported sights of sails yet. In this latitude the horizon is filled with little upright clouds that look very much like ships. The men keep up well in our boat, and the Captain serves out two table-spoonfuls of brandy and water—half and half—to our crew. I offered one bottle of the brandy to the chief mate, but he declined, saying he could keep the after-boat quiet, and we had not enough for all.

May 12.—A good rain last night and we caught a good deal, though not enough to fill up our tank, pails, etc. Our object is to get out of these Doldrums, but it seems as if we can not do it. To-day we have had it very variable, and hope we are on the northern edge, though we are not much above 7°. This morning we all thought we had made out a sail; but it was one of those deceiving clouds. Rained a good deal to-day, making all hands wet and uncomfortable; we filled up pretty nearly all our water-pots, however. I hope we may have a fine night, for the Captain certainly wants rest, and while there is any danger of squalls, or danger of any kind, he is always on hand. I never would have believed that open boats such as ours, with their loads, could live in some of the seas we have had. We are all right so far, and as comfortable as can be expected. I feel the fatigue of the lack of exercise, together with the insufficiency of food, consider-ably. Henry seems to bear up pretty well, though looking at times pretty miserable.

Sunday, May 13.—Last night was one of the finest nights we have had —no rains or squalls, though a variable set of winds. This morning finds us all pretty cheerful. During the night the cry of "A ship!" brought us to our feet, but it proved to be only a star rising out of the water. Thought often of those at home to-day, and of the disappointment they will feel next Sunday at not hearing from us by telegraph from San Francisco. To-day our rations were reduced to a quarter of a biscuit a meal, with about half a pint of water. We hope to catch more turtles and fish to eke out our small stores. The men, I am sorry to say, are improvident; they don't waste what they have, but would take three times as much as is necessary, if they could get it, and eat it instead of keeping it.

May 14.—To-day very showery, though last night was the most comfortable we have had. In the afternoon had a regular thunder-storm, which toward night seemed to close in around us on every side, making it very dark and squally. With great gratitude we saw the clouds break and stars once more appear. Our situation is becoming more and more desperate, for we have very little steady wind to make northing, and every day diminishes our small stock of provisions. We want to get to 18° N., and make some of the islands put down as lying thereabouts, but will have the northeast trades to contend against; they would be a good steady breeze, but with our sail and boat I doubt if we could sail within eight points of the wind—certainly not while towing the other boats. We have one large compass, and the second mate another; my little compass that H— gave me I have loaned to the first mate. The time must soon come when we must separate.

May 15.—From 10 P.M. last night we had a more comfortable night, though every thing was in a perfect sop. Wind baffling and very light—made but little progress. Spirits keep up, and I trust all will be well; but it is a terrible thing for us all so cramped and with no change of clothes. Sun out again hot; drying our wet things, but making it very scorching. We manage to head about north, but make very little progress. One blessing we have is a continued supply of water, which, as we must soon take the trades, is very important. The Captain took a longitude sight this morning, but noon was too cloudy for latitude. This afternoon wind headed us off to nearly E., and threatened squalls and showers late in the evening. Joe caught another dolphin to-day. In his maw we found one flying-fish and two skip-jacks. Had a visit from a land bird to-day, which perched on the yard for a while. This shows that we cannot be far from Clipperton Rock, but whether we shall make it or not is very doubtful.

May 16.—Last night was a very quiet and comfortable one as regards rain, though our limited space makes it very hard sleeping for any length of time. We all keep well as yet, thank God, but are growing weaker. To-day we have a wind from the northeast, which we hope will settle down to a good steady trade, and take us either to the islands or across some vessel's track. The first mate's crew are in good spirits, but they have lived very close and are pretty weak. The cock still lives, and daily carols forth his praise. We have yet eaten neither of the turtles; when we do we must eat them raw, for want of means to cook them. No more fish caught to-day. Bids fair for a rainy night, which I do not mind if we can fill up our water-butts.

[In Henry's log is mentioned that on the 17th one of those dire spectres of the deep—a waterspout—stalked by them, and they trembled for their lives. With accustomed brevity and expressiveness he observes that "it might have been a fine sight from a ship." Captain Mitchell's log for this day gives this item: "Only half bushel of bread crumbs left."]

May 17.—Was stopped writing last evening by the rain, which continued steadily all night, with a heavy and dangerous sea. All day yesterday till 2 P.M. rained steadily, and a more uncomfortable set of wretches one cannot imagine. To-day, however, we are drying a little. To-day we were fortunate enough to catch a dolphin and a bonita—the latter, in its distress, took shelter under our rudder from a large sword-fish that was hovering around, and which we dared not, for our lives, try to catch or even molest. To-day we have been two weeks in these egg-shells, and it certainly seems as if we are to be saved. God grant that an end to our captivity may soon be sent. The men in all the boats seem pretty well—the feeblest of the sick ones (not able, for a long time, to stand his watch on board the ship) is wonderfully recovered. A great increase of birds about us this morning.

["Passed a most awful night. Rained hard nearly all the time, and blew in squalls, accompanied by terrific thunder and lightning, from all points of the compass."—Henry's log.

"Most awful night I ever witnessed."—Captain's log.]

May 18.—Latitude 11° 11'. Last night no rain of any consequence; had a pretty good night. Drifted about till 2 A.M., when we got a good breeze, which gave us our course. Mate came aboard to-day and reports all well with him but Peter, who has again got the fever, poor fellow! The third boat cooked the turtle the second boat caught, and mate reports the meat first-rate. We talk of separating, and must soon do so—we can tow one boat, but not two. It seems too bad, but it must be done for the safety of the whole. At first I never dreamed, but now hardly shut my eyes for a cat-nap without conjuring up something or other — to be accounted for by weakness, I suppose. Very likely we would have been in to San Francisco to-morrow or next day, had not our disaster happened. I should like to have sent B —[1] the telegram for her birthday. At 2 A.M. we took a brisk little breeze from southwest, which allowed us to run our course north by east.

May 19. — Calm last night — rested pretty well. This morning Captain called up the two quarter-boats, and said one would have to go off on its own hook. Second mate would not go, so the first mate took his boat, and with six of the second mate's men who volunteered to go, with two of his own (in all nine), started early, and by 5 P.M. were out of sight to windward. Was very sorry to have the mate leave us; but all considered it for the best. This morning we have had a most scorching and burning sun, making it almost intolerable. Very calm all day to about 4 P.M., when a slight breeze sprang up. It did not last very long, however. The mate's boat nowhere to be seen this morning. I hope he was more successful in catching water than we were. Water will now be a scarce article, for as we get out of the Doldrums we shall only get showers now and then in the trades. This life is telling severely on my strength. Henry holds out first-rate.

Sunday, May 20. — Latitude 12° 0′ 9″. Very little rain last night — none that we could save to put in the cask. No breeze to speak of. It is very strange that we do not get the trades, which usually come at 8° to 10°. We all watch anxiously for a sail, but as yet have only had visions of ships that came to naught — the semblance without the substance. God grant that the time is not far distant when we shall be picked up, for that is my greatest hope! The turtle which Joe caught served us for dinner yesterday and to-day, and very good it was. No fish about us to-day. We are daily in hopes of catching something, for it helps out our stores wonderfully. The second mate, this afternoon, succeeded in catching a "booby" — a bird as large as a wild duck. As they have no other meat it will go well.

May 21. — Fine breeze all night, about east — quite as much as we could well stand. It soon brought up a sea, but we made a good night's work of it. No rain to-day; more squally, and the wind not steady. The second mate has been fortunate enough to catch three more boobies, and gave us one. For dinner to-day we had half a can of mince-meat divided up and served round, which strengthened us somewhat. Just after dinner, during a little squall and rolling very much, we sprung our mast so badly that it had to be taken down, cut off, and reshipped. The sail also was altered. We may now be said to be on our trade-wind. Our rigging, like ourselves, is rather weak, however. I believe I have not before stated that, in getting this long-boat off the ship's deck, a large hole was stove on the starboard side of the keel; it has been calked the best we could, but still we have to keep one man baling all the while. One of the quarter-boats also had an oar-handle stove through her. We have headed to-day about northwest, which is perhaps well, for we hope we have easting enough to make some of the isles; if not, we are in better position to be picked up.

May 22.—Last night wind headed us off, so that part of the time we had to steer east-southeast, and then west-northwest, and so on. This morning we were all startled by a cry of "Sail ho." Sure enough, we could see it! And for a time we cut adrift from the second mate's boat, and steered so as to attract its attention. This was about half past five A.M. After sailing in a state of high excitement for almost twenty minutes, we made it out to be the chief mate's boat. Of course we were glad to see them and have them report all well; but still it was a bitter disappointment to us all. Now that we are in the trades it seems impossible to make northing enough to strike the isles. We have determined to do the best we can, and get in the route of vessels. Such being the determination, it became necessary to cast off the other boat, which, after a good deal of unpleasantness, was done, we again dividing water and stores, and taking Cox into our boat. This makes our number fifteen. The second mate's crew wanted to all get in with us and cast the other boat adrift. It was a very painful separation. This afternoon caught a booby.

May 23.—A good breeze all night, allowing us to head about northwest or a little better. Took a longitude observation this morning, but the sun was overclouded at noon, so we could make out neither latitude or longitude. Our chances as we go west increase in regard to being picked up, but each day our scanty fare is so much reduced. Without the fish, turtle, and birds sent us, I do not know how we should have got along. The other day I offered to read prayers morning and evening for the Captain, and last night commenced. The men, although of various nationalities and religions, are very attentive, and always uncovered. May God grant my weak endeavor its issue! Sea much gone down, and altogether a comfortable day; wind regular trade, allowing us to head about northwest. Sun obscured nearly all day. We want a few good showers to fill up our cask, now twice heavily drawn upon in supplying the departing boats. These, however, I hope and trust will be sent in good time. We as yet suffer little from thirst, having as a ration about half a tumbler a meal; besides, since the trades set in it is not so hot or languid. No boobies nor fish to-day. I am afraid our chance for fish after this is small, as few here bite at a trolling hook, and we have a fresh wind almost all the time. Turtles will be scarce also. However, I hope for birds.

May 24.—Latitude 14° 18′ N. Headed about northwest all day. In the afternoon heavy sea, with promise of a bad night. No birds or fish. Can of oysters for dinner, which gave five oysters apiece and three spoonfuls of juice which, with an eighth of a biscuit,[2] made our allowance, with about a gill of water. Such is our fare. God have mercy upon us all! We are all plainly getting weaker—there is no blinding ourselves to that sorrowful truth. Our best hope is to the westward, in the track of ships, and let go the isles, as we waste twice the time tacking for them. Such is the captain's notion. Ah, how I wish I had striven to get the rest of my whisky! A spoonful of brandy with water has a marked effect upon us all. All the evening had a heavy and cobbling sea.

May 25.—Last night was a very hard one till about 4 A.M., the sea breaking over our weather side, making every thing wet and uncomfortable; nor was the day any better. I think hardly any one managed to keep entirely dry. Sun not fully out all day. Tried, but could get no observation. These are splendid trades for a ship, but too much for our crank craft. My cramped position makes lying one way any length of time almost impossible, and one is sore almost all over. Plenty of flying-fish about, but none disposed to come aboard. Passed at some distance a spar, but not near enough to see what it was. Saw also some whales blow. Weather misty, with very fine rain, which is penetrating. Good prospect of just such another night as last. Great difference noticeable in the men in regard to close steering and keeping a dry boat. Though our meals are very slight and poor, men were never eager for them or appreciated them better than we do.

May 26.—Latitude 15° 50′. Last night much more comfortable than the one before this. Occasionally we took some water. In the first watch (the watches are kept up, four six-hour watches in a day) a large flying-fish came aboard, and at about 4 A.M. we caught a booby, which will do for our dinners to-day. Both fish and flesh we have to eat raw, after drying or baking in the sun (which has been so far a good hot one). The men grow weaker, and, I think, despondent; they say very little, though. We can not do better with the boat than sail within eight points of the wind, particularly as the trades bring considerable sea, which aids to head us off. This beating is out of the question. It seems our best chance to get in and lie in the track of ships, with the hope that some one will run near enough our speck to see it. I fear for the other two boats, for the sea we had Thursday night and Friday was very hard for them. I hope they stood west, and are picked up.

Sunday, May 27.—Latitude 16° 0′ 5″; longitude, by chronometer, 117° 22′. Our fourth Sunday! When we left the ship we reckoned on having about ten days' supplies, and now we hope to be able, by rigid economy, to make them last another week if possible. Last night the sea was comparatively quiet, but the wind headed us off to about west-northwest. Tried this morning to read the full service to myself, with the communion, but found it too much; am too weak, and get sleepy and can not give strict attention; so I put off half until this afternoon. I trust God will hear the prayers gone up for us at home to-day, and graciously answer them by sending us succor and help in this our season of deep distress. The ship was fired by carelessly drawing some varnish with an open lamp in hand, the barrel of varnish being in the "booby-hatch," where are stored spare sails, rigging, etc. Orders had been given to have it on deck to open.

May 28.—Wind light and sea smooth last night, so that all hands, I hope, got a good six hours' rest. This day wind freshened, enabling us to head about northwest. A good day for seeing a ship, but none to be seen. I still feel pretty well, but my legs are very weak. Henry bears up and keeps strength the best of any aboard, I think, thank God! My earnest prayer is that he may be saved, at any rate, and restored.

May 29.—Good breeze last night, and not very rough after nine o'clock. The moon is of great benefit to us and a cheering comrade. I am sorry it is now on the wane. To-day we changed to two meals a day, thereby to lengthen out our scanty stores as long as possible. We are all wonderfully well and strong, comparatively speaking, thanks to God and the good fare we had on board the ship. All the men are hearty and strong: even the ones that were down sick are well, except poor Peter, who had to be left to the second mate's boat. The two boats are ere this saved, or I fear for them. We have here a man who might have been a duke had not political troubles banished him from Denmark. He is one of our best men; have to-day quite enjoyed a chat with him. The rest, including "Harry" (Frenchman), seem rather callous to their condition. All seem attentive to our morning and evening prayers, which Henry reads, his voice being strongest. There is no complaining or swearing aboard, which is a great comfort. Henry and I have quiet little evening chats, which are of great comfort and consolation to us, even though they are on very painful subjects. Latitude 16° 44′ north, longitude (chron.) 119° 20′.

["Reduced ration to a quarter of a biscuit a day to each man. Two quarts of bread crumbs left, one-third of a ham, three small cans of oysters, and twenty gallons of water."—Captain's log.]

May 30.—Latitude 17° 17′. Last night a comparatively quiet one. Had a good breeze, which enabled us to head about north-northwest. The result shows for itself in our latitude to-day; made over thirty-three miles of northing since yesterday's observation. Shipped but little water, so all hands did some sleeping. This noon, upon general agreement, we have changed our course to west by north. Our reasons are good: We are just in the latitude of a group of islands—the "American Group"—though a long way east of them; our prevailing wind (trade) is from the northeast; our chance is equally good of seeing vessels, and lastly, by sailing "free" we do not waste time, which, as our provisions are very low, is a great object. It is a hard scratch and a long six hundred and fifty miles, but is, all in all, our best course. It is perfectly useless to try to beat to windward with this boat, so the other isles (the Revillagiegado Group) are of no account to us. Our ration at 9 A.M. yesterday was a piece of ham two inches square, and about as thin as it could be cut, and one-eighth of a biscuit, five oysters (which constitute one-fifteenth of a can), one and a half tablespoonsful of the juice, and a gill of water. Our stores, however, will not stand even two such meals a day as the above. We have got to reduce the rations further, for our bread is almost gone. We have now left: 1

can of oysters, about 3 pounds of raisins, one can of "soup-and-bouillé," less than half a ham, and about 3 pints of biscuit crumbs. God help us and provide for us. Somehow I feel much encouraged by this change of course we have inaugurated to-day.

May 31. — Very little to chronicle to-day. Last night was cold, but not very wet. Made good headway all the twenty-four hours. God grant us deliverance soon, in the shape of a ship, or if not, strength to reach the "American Group" of islands. This A.M. the bread-bag was found open and some bread missing. We dislike to suspect anyone of such a rascally act, but there is no question that this grave crime had been committed. Two days will certainly finish the remaining morsels. Day obscured until about 3 P.M., when the wind and sea always seem to increase, but afterward generally subside somewhat. We have kept an anxious look-out for vessels all day, but it was all for naught. The hope was vain. The Captain has lost his glasses, and therefore cannot read our pocket prayer-books as much as I think he would like, though he is not familiar with them. He is a good man, and has been kind to us, almost fatherly. He says if he had been offered the command of the ship sooner, he would have brought his two daughters with him. Naturally enough, he is now devoutly thankful he did not.

["Two meals a day: of fourteen raisins and a piece of cracker the size of a cent, for tea; and a gill of water, and a piece of ham and a piece of bread, each the size of a cent, for breakfast." — Captain's log.]

June 1. — Last night and to-day sea very high and cobbling, breaking over and making us all cold and wet. Weather squally, and there is no doubt that only careful management, with God's protecting care, preserved us through both the night and day; and really it is most marvelous how every morsel that passes our lips is blessed to us. It makes me think daily of the miracle of the loaves and fishes. Henry keeps up wonderfully, which is a great consolation to me. I somehow have great confidence, and hope that our afflictions will soon be ended, though we are running rapidly across the track of both outward and inward bound vessels, and away from them; our chief hope is a whaler, man-of-war, or some American ship. The isles we are steering for, are put down in Bowditch, but on the map are said to be doubtful. God grant that they may be there.

["Hardest day yet." — Captain's log.]

June 2.—Latitude 18° 9′. Last night much like previous one—squally and cloudy, with slight showers of rain and a heavy sea. This morning much the same; toward noon, however, the sea went down somewhat, and although it is still high, it is a great deal more comfortable. The sun, also, was out a good part of the time, which has not been the case for a day or two. It is a great blessing, as it dries us. The charitable breeze keeps off thirst wonderfully, so that we even save water out of our scanty allowances. We see very few birds now except "Mother Cary's chickens;" occasionally a "boatswain," and some sea-birds that keep continually darting about just over the tops of the waves. I can not help thinking of the cheerful and comfortable time we had aboard the *Hornet*.

["Two day's scanty supplies left; ten rations of water apiece and a little morsel of bread. But the sun shines, and God is merciful."—Captain's log.]

Sunday, June 3.—Latitude 17° 54′. Heavy sea all night, and from 4 A.M. very wet, the sea breaking over us in frequent sluices, and soaking every thing aft, particularly. All day the sea has been very high, and it is a wonder that we are not swamped. Heaven grant that it may go down this evening! Our suspense and condition are getting terrible. I managed this morning to crawl, more than step, to the forward end of the boat, and was surprised to find I was so weak, especially in the legs and knees. The sun has been out again, and I have dried some things, and hope for a better night.

June 4.—Latitude 17° 6′; longitude 131° 30′. Shipped hardly any seas last night, and to-day the sea has gone down somewhat, although it is still too high for comfort, as we have an occasional reminder that water is wet. The sun has been out all day, and so we have had a good drying. I have been trying for the past ten or twelve days to get a pair of drawers dry enough to put on, and to-day I have succeeded. I mention this to show the state in which we have lived. If our chronometer is any where near right, we ought to see the American Isles to-morrow or next day. If they are not there, we have only the chance, for a few days, of a stray ship, for we can not eke out the provisions more than five or six days longer, and our strength is failing very fast. I was much surprised to-day to note how my legs have wasted away above my knees; they are hardly thicker than my upper arm used to be. Still I trust in God's infinite mercy, and feel sure He will do what is best for us. To survive, as we have done, thirty-two days in an open boat, with only about ten day's fair provisions for thirty-one men in the first place, and these twice divided subsequently, is more than mere unassisted human art and strength could have accomplished or endured.

["Bread and raisins all gone."—Captain's log.

"Men growing dreadfully discontented, and awful grumbling and unpleasant talking is arising. God save us from all strife of men; and if we must die now, take us himself and not embitter our bitter death still more."—Henry's log.]

June 5.—Quiet night and pretty comfortable day, though our sail and block show signs of failing, and need taking down—which latter is something of a job, as it requires the climbing of the mast. We also had news from forward, there being discontent and some threatening complaints of unfair allowances, etc., all as unreasonable as foolish; still these things bid us be on our guard. I am getting miserably weak, but try to keep up the best I can. If we can not find those isles we can only try to make northwest and get in the track of Sandwich Island bound vessels, living as best we can in the mean time. To-day we changed to one meal, and that at about noon, with a small ration of water at 8 or 9 A.M., another at 12 P.M., and a third at 5 or 6 P.M.

["Nothing left but a little piece of ham and a gill of water, all around."—Captain's log.

Note secretly passed by Henry to his brother:

"Cox told me last night there is getting to be a good deal of ugly talk among the men against the Captain and us aft. Harry, Jack and Fred especially. They say that the Captain is the cause of it all—that he did not try to save the ship at all, nor to get provisions, and even would not let the men put in the some they had, and that partiality is shown us in apportioning our rations aft. Jack asked Cox the other day if he would starve first or eat human flesh. Cox answered he would starve. Jack then told him it would be only killing himself. If we do not find these islands we would do well to prepare for anything. Harry is the loudest of them all."

Reply—"We can depend on Charley, I think, and Thomas and Cox, can we not?"

Second note—"I guess so, and very likely on Peter—but there is no telling. Charley and Cox are certain. There is nothing definite said or hinted as yet, as I understand Cox; but starving men are the same as maniacs. It would be well to keep watch on your pistol, so as to have it and the cartridges safe from theft."

Henry's log, June 5. — "Dreadful forebodings. God spare us all from such horrors! Some of the men getting to talk a good deal. Nothing to write down. Heart very sad.

Henry's log, June 6. — "Passed some sea-weed, and something that looked like the trunk of an old tree, but no birds; beginning to be afraid islands not there. To-day it was said to Captain, in the hearing of all, that some of the men would not shrink, when a man was dead, from using the flesh, though they would not kill. Horrible! God give us all full use of our reason, and spare us from such things! 'From plague, pestilence, and famine, from battle and murder — and from sudden death: good Lord deliver us!'"]

June 6. — Latitude 16° 30′; longitude (chron.) 134°. Dry night, and wind steady enough to require no change in sail; but this A.M. an attempt to lower it proved abortive. First, the third mate tried and got up the block, and fastened a temporary arrangement to reeve the halyards through, but had to come down, weak and almost fainting, before finishing; then Joe tried, and after twice ascending, fixed it and brought down the block; but it was very exhausting work, and afterward he was good for nothing all day. The claw-iron which we are trying to make serve for the broken block works, however, very indifferently; and will, I am afraid, soon cut the rope. It is very necessary to get every thing connected with the sail in good, easy running order before we get too weak to do any thing with it.

["Only three meals left." — Captain's log.]

June 7. — Latitude 16° 35′ N.; longitude 136° 30′ W. Night wet and uncomfortable. To-day shows us pretty conclusively that the American Isles are not here, though we have had some signs that looked like them. At noon we decided to abandon looking any further for them, and to-night haul a little more northerly, so as to get in the way of Sandwich Island vessels, which, fortunately, come down pretty well this way — say to latitude 19° to 20° to get the benefit of the trade-winds. Of course all the westing we have made is gain, and I hope the chronometer is wrong in our favor, for I do not see how any such delicate instrument can keep good time with the constant jarring and thumping we get from the sea. With the strong trade we have, I hope that a week from Sunday will put us in sight of the Sandwich Islands, if we are not saved before that time by being picked up.

June 8.—My cough troubled me a good deal last night, and therefore I got hardly any sleep at all. Still I make out pretty well, and should not complain. Yesterday the third mate mended the block, and this P.M. she sailed, after some difficulty, was got down, and Harry got to the top of the mast and rove the halyards through after some hardship, so that it now works easy and well. This getting up the mast is no easy matter at any time with the sea we have, and is very exhausting in our present state. We have made good time and course to-day. Heading her up, however, makes the boat ship seas, and keeps us all wet; however, it can not be helped. Writing is a rather precarious thing these times. Our meal to-day for the fifteen consists of half a can of "soup-and-bouillé"—the other half is re-served for to-morrow. Henry still keeps up grandly, and is a great favorite. God grant he may be spared!

["A better feeling prevails among the men."—Captain's log.]

June 9.—Latitude 17° 53′. Finished to-day, I may say, our whole stock of provisions. We have only left lower end of ham-bone, with some of the outer rind and skin on. In regard to the water, however, I think we have got ten days' supply at our present rate of allowance. This, with what nourishment we can get from boot-legs and such chewable matter, we hope will enable us to weather it out till we get to the Sandwich Islands, or, sailing in the mean time in the track of vessels thither bound, be picked up. My hope is the latter—for in all human probability I can not stand the other. Still, we have been marvelously protected, and God, I hope, will preserve us all in His own good time and way. The men are getting weaker, but are still quiet and orderly.

Sunday, June 10.—Latitude 18° 40′, longitude 142° 34′. A pretty good night last night, with some wettings, and again another beautiful Sunday. I can not but think how we should all enjoy it at home, and what a con-trast is here! How terrible their suspense must begin to be! God grant it may be relieved before very long, and He certainly seems to be with us in every thing we do, and has preserved this boat miraculously; for since we left the ship we have sailed considerably over three thousand miles, which, taking into consideration our meager stock of provisions, is almost unprecedented. As yet I do not feel the stint of food so much as I do that of water. Even Henry, who is naturally a great water-drinker, can save half of his allowance from time to time, when I can not. My diseased throat may have something to do with that, however.[3]

Henry Ferguson's Log

Sunday, June 10. — Our ham-bone has given us a taste of food to-day, and we have got left a little meat and the remainder of the bone for to-morrow. Certainly never was there such a sweet knuckle-bone, or one which was so thoroughly appreciated. I do not know that I feel any worse than I did last Sunday, notwithstanding the reduction of diet; and I trust that we may all have strength given us to sustain the sufferings and hardships of the coming week. We estimate that we are within 700 miles of the Sandwich Islands, and that our average, daily, is somewhat over 100 miles, so that our hopes have some foundation in reason. Heaven send we may all live to reach land!

June 11. — Ate the meat and rind of our ham-bone, and have the bone and the greasy cloth from around the ham left to eat to-morrow. God send us birds or fish, and let us not perish of hunger, or be brought to the dreadful alternative of feeding on human flesh! As I feel now, I do not think any thing could persuade me; but you can not tell what you will do when you are reduced by hunger and your mind wandering. I hope and pray we can make out to reach the Islands before we get to this strait; but we have one or two pretty desperate men aboard, though they are quiet enough now. It is my firm trust and belief that we are going to be saved.

["All food gone." — Captain's log.]

June 12. — Stiff breeze, and we are fairly flying — dead ahead of it — and toward the Islands. Good hopes, but the prospects of hunger are awful. Ate ham-bone to-day. It is the Captain's birthday — he is 54 years old to-day.

June 13. — The ham-rags are not gone yet, and the boot-legs, we find, are very palatable after we get the salt out of them. A little smoke, I think, does some little good; but I don't know.

June 14. — Hunger does not pain us as much, but we are dreadful weak. Our water is getting frightfully low. God grant we may see land soon!

Nothing to eat—but feel better than I did yesterday. Toward evening saw a magnificent double-rainbow—the first we had seen. Captain said, "Cheer up, boys, it's a prophecy!—it's the bow of promise!"

June 15.—God be forever praised for His infinite mercy to us! Land in sight! Rapidly neared it, and soon we were sure of it. . . . Two noble Kanakas swam out and took the boat ashore. We were joyfully received by two white men—Mr. Jones and his steward Charley—and a crowd of native men, women, and children. They treated us splendidly—aided us, and carried us up the bank, and brought us water, poi, bananas, and green cocoa-nuts; but the white men took care of us, and prevented those who would have eaten too much from doing so. Every body overjoyed to see us, and all sympathy expressed in faces, deeds, and words. We were then helped up to the house, and help we needed. Mr. Jones and his steward, Charley, are the only white men here. Treated us splendidly. Gave us first about a teaspoonful of spirits in water, and then to each a cup of hot tea with a little bread. Takes care of us. Gave us later another cup of tea —and bread the same—and then let us go to rest. It is the happiest day of my life. God, in his mercy, has heard our prayer, and we are saved. . . . Everybody is so kind. Words can not tell—

June 16.—Mr. Jones gave us a delightful bed, and we surely had a good night's rest—but not sleep—we were too happy to sleep. They gave the Captain a little room, and the same to Sam and me, and gave the sitting-room to the men. We enjoyed the night, but did not sleep—would keep the reality, and not let it turn to a delusion—dreaded that we might wake up and find ourselves in the boat again.

They have told their story, and in their own language. I hardly know which to admire most—the steady persistence and faithfulness with which they kept up their journals through such a weary time, or the unwavering hopefulness they showed from first to last, in the face of the seeming hopelessness of rescue.

They wanted to "doctor" the diaries a little, but it did not appear to me that any emendations were necessary; a careful and elegantly composed log-book, gotten up in the midst of thirst, starvation, and a stormy sea, would seem so strikingly unnatural that its genuineness might reasonably be questioned.

The men were so carefully nursed where they landed (at Laupahoe-hoe, on the island of Hawaii) that all except one seaman were able to walk about within ten days afterward. Yet in some cases there has been no action of their bowels for twenty and thirty days, and in one case, for forty-four days!

With ten days' provisions Captain Mitchell performed this extraordinary voyage of forty-three days and eight hours in an open boat (sailing 4000 miles in reality and 3360 by direct courses), and brought every man safe to land. Each individual day of those six weeks bears its testimony to his watchfulness, his prudence, his cool courage, his foresight, perseverance, and fidelity to his duty, and his rare intelligence. In him are the elements of greatness.

This strange voyage, in its entirety, is an eloquent witness of the watchful presence of an all-powerful Providence, and as such its record carries with it a lesson that can not be valueless. This presence was distinctly manifested on two occasions at least. Henry mentions the fact of the boat going directly before the wind toward the island on that last day. It was getting late. They had to make land that day or perish. They struck boldly for the shore, and when they had got pretty well in they lowered the sail, and afterward, not liking the appearance of the reef, tried to hoist it again and retreat, but they were too feeble to accomplish it, and beheld themselves drifting helplessly upon the rocks after all their toils and hardships. And it was all the better. They swept through an almost imperceptible opening in the coral reef and were saved. There was not another place within thirty-five miles where they could have got to the land or found a human habitation. Every where else a precipice more than a thousand feet high comes down like a wall to the sea, with forty fathoms of water at its base, and not even bordered by a strip of ground wide enough for a man to stand upon. The other case is that of Cox. The mate's boat had bidden the Captain's good-by and departed, but came back directly and the Captain was requested to receive a man. Cox came on board, and was the only man who warned the Captain and the passengers afterward, when the conspirators had sworn their lives away.

Before closing, a few words ought to be said about the conspiracy. The Captain says that for many days he had known that a murderous discontent was brewing by the distraught air of some of the men and the guilty look of others, and so he staid on guard—slept no more—kept his hatchet hid and close at hand.

At this time the famishing, ravenous men were cutting boots, handkerchiefs and shirts into bits and eating them. They had done so for days. They were even eating the staves of the butter-cask. They were wild with hunger. They were in a manner insane, and in the judgment of no just and merciful man responsible for their words or deeds. They afterward dreaded, in Honolulu, that the Captain and passengers would take legal measures against them because of their murderous conspiracy; but their fears were without foundation. These gentlemen well understood the case, and only pitied the men. They insisted for some time that I should leave out all mention of the conspiracy from their published journals. That the men were frenzied is shown by the fact that they told Cox, in a whispered conference at night, that the Captain had all the ship's money in the boat—"a million dollars in gold and silver!"—just about enough to sink such a craft. They were afraid of Ferguson's pistol and the Captain's hatchet, and laid many a plan for getting hold of these weapons. They told Cox they would divide the money with him if he kept quiet and helped, but they would kill him if he exposed them. He refused to join the conspiracy, and they said he should die; and so, after that, day after day and night after night, he did not go to sleep, but kept watch upon them in fear for his life. The Captain and his passengers remained under arms, and watched also, but talked pleasantly, and gave no sign that they knew what was in the men's minds. The Captain spoke now and then of his strength holding out being a necessity, since only he could use the chart and the quadrant and find the land.

By way of conclusion it may be well enough to say that up to the present time no tidings have been received of the poor fellows in the missing boats. It seems almost idle, now, to hope that they are saved.

Honolulu, Sandwich Islands, July 2, 1866.[4]

From Hawaii to New York

Mark Twain returned to California under sail in the late summer of 1866, aboard "the elegant A 1 New York built, first class clipper *Smyrniote*," as an advertisement for the Hawaiian Packet Line described the vessel. He spent much of the twenty-five-day voyage becalmed. He commented on the voyage briefly at the outset of chapter 78 of *Roughing It*. Clemens went on at greater length in his notebook.

* * *

From *Roughing It*, Chapter 78

After half a year's luxurious vagrancy in the islands, I took shipping in a sailing vessel, and regretfully returned to San Francisco—a voyage in every way delightful, but without an incident: unless lying two long weeks in a dead calm, eighteen hundred miles from the nearest land, may rank as an incident. Schools of whales grew so tame that day after day they played about the ship among the porpoises and the sharks without the least apparent fear of us, and we pelted them with empty bottles for lack of better sport. Twenty-four hours afterward these bottles would be still lying on the glassy water under our noses, showing that the ship had not moved out of her place in all that time. The calm was absolutely breathless, and the surface of the sea absolutely without a wrinkle. For a whole day and part of a night we lay so close to another ship that had drifted to our vicinity, that we carried on conversations with her passengers, introduced each other by name, and became pretty intimately acquainted with people we had never heard of before, and have never heard of since. This was the only vessel we saw during the whole lonely voyage.

We had fifteen passengers, and to show how hard pressed they were at last for occupation and amusement, I will mention that the gentlemen gave a good part of their time every day, during the calm, to trying to sit on an empty champagne bottle (lying on its side), and thread a needle without touching their heels to the deck, or falling over; and the ladies sat in the shade of the mainsail, and watched the enterprise with absorbing interest. We were at sea five Sundays; and yet, but for the almanac, we never would have known but that all the other days were Sundays too.[1]

* * *

From Mark Twain's Notebook

Honolulu, July 18/66. Have got my passport from the Royal d—d Hawaiian Collector of Customs & paid a dollar for it, & tomorrow we sail for America in the good ship *Smyrniote*, Lovett, master—& I have got a devilish saddle-boil to sit on for the first two weeks at sea. . . .

Honolulu, July 19, 1866. The *Comet* . . . left at 2 P.M., with great firing of cannon, & went to wind'ard (unusual)—we left peaceably in the *Smyrniote* at 4:30 (*Comet* out of sight) & went in same direction. Now we shall see who beats to San Francisco.

Made 110 miles up to noon of Friday 20th, but were then only 10 miles from Oahu, having gone clear around the island.

On 21st made 179 miles.

Sunday, 4th day out—lat. 28.12. long. 157.42—distance 200 miles in the last 24 hours.

Monday, July 23—5th day out—lat. 31.34—longitude 157.30—distance 202 miles. . . .

Tuesday, July 24—6th day out—lat. 34.31 N. long. 157.40 W. Distance 180 miles. Had calms several times. Are we never going to make any longitude? The trades are weakening—it is time we struck the China winds about midnight—say in lat. 36.

Ship *California* loaded with grain at San F for China.—grain very scarce in Australia & China & very plenty in Cal. . . .

25th July—lat. 29 N.—I was genuinely glad, this evening, to welcome the first *twilight* I have seen in 6 years,

No twilight in the S. Islands, California or Washoe. . . .

Damon[2]—Oh—don't swear, friend, don't swear—that won't mend the matter.

Whaler—Brother Damon it's all very well for you to say don't swear, & it's all right too—I don't say nothing against it—but don't you know that if you was to ship a crew of sailors for Heaven & was to stop at Hell two hours and half for provisions, some d—d son of a gun would run away.

Thursday 26—Got 50 miles opposite San Francisco & at noon started back & are now running south-east—almost calm—1700 miles at sea. . . .

Friday 27—We are just barely moving to-day in a general direction southeast toward San F—though last night we stood stock still for hours, pieces of banana skins thrown to the great sea-birds swimming in our wake floating perfectly still in the sluggish water. In the last 24 hours we have made but 38 miles—made most of that drifting sideways. Position at noon, 38.55 N. 157.37 W. . . .

Tuesday & Friday bean day; Saturday fish day; Monday & Thursday duck (or duff?) days. At 7 bells in the evening dog watch pump ship.[3]

The sea is fully level as the Mississippi—at least as smooth as the river when ruffled by a very light breeze & swelling with a few dying steamboat waves.

We see *nothing* on this wide, wide, lonely ocean—nothing but some large sea-birds, sometimes a dolphin, & occasionally a Mother Cary's chicken—these latter persisting in flying low, indicating calm weather—the sailors say they only bring tidings of the coming storm when they fly *high*. . . .

The monotony of this calm! One can only tell the days of the week by the food—duff on Sunday, beans Tuesdays & Fridays, Salt Fish on Saturday, &c. . . .

Had an eye like an albatross. . . .

A land bird came & hovered over the ship a while to-day—he is a long way from home—thought of the old song—"Bird at Sea." . . .

Splendidly-colored lunar rainbow to-night.

Fishing for goneys, but hooks too large—the birds bite freely, however. . . .

Caught 2 goneys—they are all the same size—they measured 7 feet 1 inch from tip to tip of wings.

They made a wooden clog fast to him & let him go—a pitiful advantage for "god-like" man to take of a helpless bird.

Get photographs of the *Hornets*.[4]

The bird looked reproachfully upon them with his great human eyes while they did him this wrong.

Saturday, 28 May [*sic*]—38.46—156.36—48 miles—had *sternway* awhile. . . .

Sunday, July 29. Overcast, breezy and *very* pleasant on deck. All hands on deck immediately after breakfast. Rev. Franklin S. Rising preached, & the passengers formed choir. . . .

Sunday, July 29[5]—lat. 38.43, long. 154.55—Distance 80 miles. . . .

Romantic to see fine ship go to sea—sailor goes round the world but never into it,[6] & is simple & ignorant as a child & knows nothing about it—is as green at 50 as a farmer's boy. . . .

Monday, July 30—This is the fifth day of dead, almost motionless calm—a man can walk a crack in the deck, the ship lies so still. I enjoy it, and believe all hands do except the d—d baby.

Aug. 1—Lat. 38.50 N. Long. 150.56 W.—Distance 100 miles.

Off sounding in fair weather.

Close-hauled—Brail up the mizzen & mizzen-staysail, let go the main-sheet, so as the sail will shiver, put the helm a-lee & brace the mizzen topsail square, so it'll back, you know. You keep the head-sails & the jib & staysails just as they were before, you understand, & haul taut & belay the lee-braces. When she's nearly lost her headway but is still coming to the wind, you heave the lead & you heave it quick, too—cussed quick, as you might say.

Would you mind saying that over again if it ain't too much trouble.

(Repeat.)

Well, yes, I sh[d] say so.

Going Large—(Another method, w[h] is preferable.) Brace the head-sails square, haul down the jib & staysails, without stirring the aftersails, & put the helm a-lee

Oh, yes, that is much preferable, I sh[d] think. . . .

Aug. 3—The calm continues. Magnificent weather. Men all turned to boys. Play boyish games on the poop & quarter-deck. Lay small object on fife-rail of mainmast—shut one eye, walk 3 steps & strike at it with fore-finger. Lay small object on deck, walk 7 steps blindfolded & try to find it. Kneel—elbows against knees, hands extended in front along deck; place object against ends of fingers—then clasp hands behind back & try to pick it up with teeth & rise up from knees. Tie string around main-brace, turn back to it—blindfold—walk 5 steps—turn round 3 times—return & put finger on string. Tying of all kinds sailors knots. Go aloft. . . .

Sailors walk with hands somewhat spread and palms turned backward.

Sunday, Aug 5, 1866—Everybody cheerful—at daylight saw the *Comet* in the distance on our lee—it is pleasant in this tremendous solitude to have company. . . .

Wednesday, Aug. 8—800 miles west of San Francisco the calm is over & we have got a strong breeze. *This* sort of life on the ocean wave will do—the ship is flying like a bird—she tears the sea into seething foam —& yet the ocean is quiet and sunny—so steady is the ship that I could walk a crack. . . .

The calm is no more. There are 3 vessels in sight. It is so sociable to have them hovering about us in this limitless world of waters. It is sunny and pleasant, but blowing hard. Every rag about the ship is spread to the breeze & she is speeding over the sea like a bird. There is a very large brig right astern of us with all her canvas set & chasing us at her very best. She came up fast while the winds were light, but now it is hard to tell whether she gains or not. We can see the people on her forecastle with the glass. The race is very exciting.

Further along: She is to the setting sun—looks sharply cut & black as coal against a background of fire & floating on a sea of blood.

Aug. 13—San Francisco—Home again. No—*not* home again—in prison again—and all the wild sense of freedom gone. The city seems so cramped, & so dreary with toil & care & business anxiety. God help me, I wish I were at sea again![7]

Back on the West Coast, Mark Twain spun his Hawaiian escapade into a lucrative crowd-drawing lecture that he delivered across California and Nevada for weeks. Then he took his act east. It had taken him and Orion three hard weeks to make the dangerous 1,700-mile land crossing to Nevada to join the staff of the territorial governor; then, later, Sam got to know the route over the Sierra Nevada to San Francisco. The return trip would be easier in some ways and even more perilous in others. It began on December 15, 1866, on board the "opposition steamer" *America*, meaning a vessel of the Nicaragua-crossing Accessory Transit Company of Cornelius Vanderbilt, competitor to the dominant Panama-crossing line, the Pacific Mail Steamship

Company. The voyage from San Francisco to San Juan del Sur, Nicaragua, lasted two memorable weeks for Sam Clemens; memorable because the ship was commanded by Captain Edgar "Ned" Wakeman, who became Mark Twain's iconic captain. He is the subject of an entire chapter in *Roughing It*. Mark Twain wrote about him for the first time in his letters published in a San Francisco newspaper, the *Daily Alta California*, excerpts from which follow.

* * *

From the *Alta California* Letters

Steamship America, at sea, 900 miles south of San Francisco . . .

All the afternoon, yesterday, two or three hundred passengers paced the promenade deck, and so quiet was the sea that not half a dozen of them succumbed to sickness. But at 8 or 9 at night the wind began to rise, and from that time it steadily increased in violence until, at midnight, it was blowing a hurricane. There was a tremendous sea running, and the night was so pitch dark that a man standing on the deck would find by voices at his elbow that other persons were almost touching him, when he imagined himself alone. On deck, above the lashing of the waves, and the roaring of the winds, the shouting of the captain and his officers, and the hurried tramping of the men were scarcely to be heard.

The steerage passengers were at once imprisoned below, and the hatches battened down and canvassed over; the ship was by the head, and the seas were sweeping over the bows every now and then; every man under the ship's pay—officers, cabin crew and all—were set to work to break cargo and move it aft; a large quantity of flour was transferred to the stern, and the large boats on the after-guard were pumped full of water. These precautions eased the ship's head and saved her. It was well that the hatches were down snug before the terrific squall struck us, just after midnight, else either of the three fearful seas that swept over the ship then in quick succession must have poured thousands of tons of water into her and sent her to the bottom.

As it was, the vessel was in peril enough. She was tossed about like a plaything—climbed a lofty billow, paused a moment on the crest, and then plunged down into the gulf on the other side; climbed the next wave, and while one held his breath in anticipation of the ghastly dive and the deadly sinking notion in the chest that always accompanies it, a prodigious wave would spring upon her from some side angle, and send her stunned and staggering, broadside on, like a man struck with a club! And then the officers floundered in water up to their hip, and shouted orders that came aft reduced to hoarse, confused whispers by the howling blast! Then the gunwale, a solid timber as thick as a man's thigh, snapped like a pipe—stern-away went twenty feet of the starboard bulwarks forward—down came a dozen stanchions with a clatter—crash went a deluge of water booming aft through steerage and forward-cabin, carrying stools, carpet-sacks, boxes, boots, valises, and a rattling smash-up of queens-ware and crockery along with it—and on the reeling floor, amid the shrieking of the cordage and the roaring of the midnight winds and the thundering of the midnight sea down on their knees in the slush went two hundred and fifty of the ungodliest of all the ungodly crowds that ever lumbered a ship yet, to pray!

Such consternation as there was aboard this ship you have not seen in ten years, perhaps. Poor fellows, some of them were well nigh beside themselves. A man from one of the back settlements knelt down, in the middle of the forward cabin, with an arm clasping a stanchion to enable him to maintain his position; and there he knelt and prayed fervently, till an oil-skin carpet sack came washing by him, and he grabbed it—found it was not his—set it adrift again—and went on praying; and so he went on, supplicating for succor and prospecting for carpet sacks, till sea-sickness got him, and he had to drop all other considerations and attend to bailing out his stomach. But it may be said of this stranger that he meant well, and held his grip as well as any man could have done it. And any man of judgment cannot but think well of his modesty in only relying on Providence to save the ship, but looking out for his carpet sack himself. If we would always do our share many things would be accomplished that never are accomplished.

It was a heavy storm—the heaviest Captain Wakeman has seen on this coast in seventeen years, except one—and the heaviest another old sea captain (among our passengers) of twenty-eight years' experience, ever saw in his life. [N.B. Is there always an old skipper aboard who never saw such a storm before?][8] It proved the *America* to be a staunch and reliable vessel, however, and her commander a thoroughly competent officer, and these things will render the passengers more satisfied and confident hereafter in case we have another storm.[9]

On board steamer *Columbia*, at sea . . .
The Captain
Midnight—I have been listening to some of Captain Wakeman's stunning forecastle yarns, and I will do him the credit to say he knows how to tell them. With his strong, cheery voice, animated countenance, quaint phraseology, defiance of grammar and extraordinary vim in the matter of gesture and emphasis, he makes a most effective story out of very unpromising materials. There is a contagion about his whole-souled jollity that the chief mourner at a funeral could not resist. He is fifty years old, and as rough as a bear in voice and action, and yet as kind-hearted and tender as a woman. He is a burly, hairy, sunburned, stormy-voiced old salt, who mixes strange oaths with incomprehensible sailor phraseology and the gentlest and most touching pathos, and is tattooed from head to foot like a Fejee islander. His tongue is forever going when he has got no business on his hands, and though he knows nothing of policy or the ways of the world, he can cheer up any company of passengers that ever travelled in a ship, and keep them cheered up. He never drinks a drop, never gambles, and never swears where a lady or a child may chance to hear him—but with all things consonant with the occasion he sometimes soars into flights of fancy swearing that fill the listener with admiration.[10]

Steamer *Columbia*, at sea . . .
Sunday, December 23d.—Last night was magnificent—cool, balmy, breezy, an easy sea on, and all things so flooded with moonlight that each wave of the ocean, each rope and spar of the ship, and each face and form about the decks were almost as plain to the sight as if it were noonday. The six individuals who sing (think of it—only six persons out of five hundred who make the slightest pretensions to vocal talent!) organized themselves into a choir and practiced several hymns until a late hour —for we are to have religious services today. After that they sang "Dog Tray," and "Marching Through Georgia," and "What is Home Without a Mother," and other venerable melodies, and a few wretched volunteers

joined in and completed the villainy of the performance. Home without a mother may not amount to much, but there is no use in aggravating the thing with such a tune as that. And the idea of resurrecting that infamous Dog Tray at this day. That choir sang everything they ought not to have sung except one, and I trembled to think the surroundings would yet suggest it. I refer to the song called "Roll On, Silver Moon." If they had attempted that outrage I would have scuttled the ship. I can stand a good deal, but I cannot stand everything. I would rather perish than lose my reason. Altogether, ours is a very poor choir. I will remark here, that although I hummed a tune occasionally, and whistled some, I was not requested to sing.

This is a beautiful morning and all parties seem as light-hearted and happy as children. In fact the pastimes of the gentlemen on the promenade deck in the shade of the awnings, for their own and the ladies' amusement, have an entirely boyish cast about them. Two men are playing "mumble-peg" with absorbing interest; a large party are trying to see which shall be able to walk ten steps, blindfolded, and place a hat on the compass; a colonel, who greatly distinguished himself in the war, is trying to sit on a champagne bottle, with feet crossed, arms folded, and thread a darning needle without falling over—the bottle lying on its side, of course, and pointing straight astern, while he faces towards the ship's head—he has just accomplished it, after the ninth attempt, and received a boisterous round of applause—some consolation for the bursts of laughter that greeted his failures. All are engaged in this sort of nonsense, (Isaac, the Israelite, included,) except the youth they call "Shape." With hat perched jauntily on one side of his head, and hands thrust into his coat pockets, he promenades the deck fore and aft, and admires his legs. They say he is a little "cracked," I don't know—the idea may have originated with Miss Slimmens of the "Thunderclap."[11]

Being a little under the weather, I have intruded into the Captain's room, along with the veteran Sleet, a skipper of thirty years standing, going home on furlough from his ship. The forenoon is waning fast. Enter Captain Waxman, sweating and puffing from over-exertion, and says he has "tore up the whole ship" (he scorns grammar when his mind is seething with business,) has "tore up the whole ship" to build a pulpit at the after compass and rig benches and chairs athwart the quarter-deck and fetch up the organ from below and get everything shipshape for the parson—

"And—the passengers," said he, "as soon as they found they were going to be sermonized, they've up anchors and gone to sea—clean gone and deserted—there ain't a baker's dozen left on the after deck! They're worse than the rats in Hon—here, you velvet-head! you son of Afric's sunny clime! go forrard and tell the mate to let her go a couple of points free—in Honolulu. Me and old Josephus—he was a Jew, and got rich as Creosote in San Francisco afterwards—we were going home passengers from the Sandwich Islands, in a bran-new brig, on her third voyage, and our trunks were down below—he went with me—laid over one vessel to do it—because he warn't no sailor, and he liked to be convoyed by a man that was—felt safer, you understand—and the brig was sliding out between the buoy, and her headline was paying out ashore—there was a wood-pile right where it was made fast on the pier—when up come the biggest rat—as big as any ordinary cat, he was—and darted out on that line and cantered for the shore!—and up come another! and another! and another! and away they galloped over that hawser, each one treading on t'other's tail, till they were so thick you couldn't see a thread of the cable, and there was a procession of 'em three hundred yards long over the levee like a streak of pismires,[12] and the Kanakas, some throwing sticks from that wood-pile and chunks of lava and coral at 'em and knocking 'em endways every shot—but do you suppose it made any difference to them rats?—not a particle—not a particle on earth, bless you—they'd smelt trouble!—they'd smelt it by their unearthly, supernatural instinct! —they wanted to go, and they never let up till the last rat was ashore out of that bran-new beautiful brig!

"I called a Kanaka, with his boat, and he hove alongside and shinned up a rope and stood, off and on for orders, and says I:

"'Do you see that trunk down there?'

"'Ai.'

"'Well, yank it out of there and snake it ashore quicker'n you can wink. Lively, now!'

"Solomon, the Jew—what did I say his cussed name was? Anyhow, he says:

"'What are you doing, Captain?'

"'Doing! Why, I'm a taking my trunk ashore—that's about what I'm a doing.'

"'Taking your trunk ashore? Why, bless us, what is that for?'

"'What is it for?' says I, 'do you see them rats a leaving this ship? She's doomed, sir! she's doomed past retribution! Burnt brandy wouldn't save her, sir. She'll never finish this voyage—she'll never be heard of again, sir.'

"Solomon says—'Boy, take that other trunk ashore, too.'

"And don't you know, that bran new beautiful brig sailed out of Honolulu without a rat on board, and was never seen again by mortal man, sir! It's so—as sure as you're born, it's so. We shipped in an old tub that was so rotten that you had to walk easy on her main deck to keep from going through—so crazy, sir, that in our berths, when there was a sea on, the timbers overhead worked backwards and forwards eleven inches in their sockets—just for the world like an old wicker basket, sir—and the rats were as big as a greyhound, and a lean one, sir; and they bit the buttons off our coats, and chawed our toe-nails off while we slept; and there were so many of them that in a gale once they all scampered to the starboard side when we were going about, and put her down the wrong way, so that she missed stays, and come monstrous near foundering. But she went through safe, I tell you, because she had rats aboard." [After this marvellous chapter of personal history the Captain rushed out in a business frenzy, and rushed back again in the course of a couple of minutes.][13]

"Everything's set—the passengers are back again and stowed, and the parson's all ready to cat his anchor and get under way—everybody ready and waiting on that bloody choir that was practicing and squawking and blatting all night, and now ain't come to time when their watch is called."[14]

[Out again, and back in something like a minute.][15]

"D—n that choir! They're like the fellow's sow—had to haul her ears off to get her up to the trough, and then had to pull her tail out to get her away again. But rats!—don't tell me nothing about the talent of rats! It's been noticed, sir!—notes has been taken of it, sir! and their judgment is better than a human's, sir! Didn't I hear old Ben Wilson, mate of the *Empress of the Seas*—as fine a sailor and as lovely a ship as ever rode a gale—didn't I hear him tell how, seventeen years ago, when he was laying at Liverpool docks empty—empty as a jug—and a full Indiaman right alongside, full of provisions, and corn, and everything a rat might prefer, and going to sail next day—how in the middle of the night the rats all left her and crossed his decks and went ashore—everyone of 'em—every bloody one of 'em, sir!—and finally—it was moonlight—he saw a muss going on by the capstan of that other ship, and he slipped around, and there was a dozen old rats laying their heads together and chattering about something and looking down the forrard hatch every now and then, and finally they appeared to have got their minds made up, and one of 'em went aft and got a scrap of old stuns'l half a foot square, and they bored holes in the corners with their teeth, and bent on some long pieces of spun-yarn—made a sort of a little hammock of it, you understand—and then they lowered away gently for a while and stopped—and directly they begun heaving again, and up out of that forrard hatch, in full view of the mate, who was watching 'em all the time, up comes that little hammock with a poor, old, decrepit sick rat on it, all gone in with the consumption!—and they lugged him ashore, and they all went up town to the very last rat—and that ship sailed the next day for India, or Cape o' Good Hope, or somewheres, and the mate of the *Empress* didn't sail for as much as three weeks, and up to that time that ship hadn't been heard from, sir! Drat that choir! I must go and start 'em out—this sort of thing won't do!"[16]

On board steamer *Columbia*, at sea . . .
A Legend from the Captain
We have been sailing placidly along the coast of Guatemala all day—a broad, low land, densely clad in a green, tropical vegetation, among which the cocoanut tree is prominent; occasionally we see a thatched native hut. In full view are three noble mountains—tall, symmetrical cones, with sides furrowed with wrinkle-like valleys veiled in a dreamy, purple mist that is charming to the eye, and summits swathed in a grand turban of rolling clouds. They say these are volcanoes, but we cannot see any smoke. No matter—it is a fairy landscape that is very pleasant to look upon.

"Do you see that ship anchored yonder?"

The young lady addressed said she did see the ship.

"Well," said Captain W., "she's a whaler. She's trying out oil. The first

time I ever was along here was seventeen years ago. I didn't know anything about whaling then, bless you. It was in the night, just after dark,
and just where you see that ship there now, I saw a ship all on fire! I laid-
to immediately and ordered out a boat's crew, and says, 'Pull, boys, for
your life! Don't miss a stroke—don't you lose a minute! Tell the Captain
not to lose his grip. I'll lay here a week and give him all the help I can,
and then I'll take him and his crew to California, and do the very best I
know how by 'em.' Well, we lay-to and waited and waited—all the passengers on deck and anxious for the boat to come back with the awful
news. But nine o'clock, no boat; ship still burning, and glaring out on
the black ocean like a sun dropped out of the sky. Ten o'clock—no boat;
passengers beginning to get tired, and two or three quit and went to bed.
Eleven—no boat; and one by one they sidled off to roost—give it up, you
see—all gone but me and one solitary motherly old soul—me marching
slow up and down the deck and she gazing out across the water at the
burning ship. We were just so until half-past 11, and then we heard the
sound of oars. We closed up to the railing and stood by for them. Pretty
soon the boat ranged up alongside—I tell you I felt awful—something
made me hanker to look down into that boat, and yet something held
me back. The officer of the boat reported: 'The ship ain't burning, sir;
(I felt relieved then;) he says he's in big luck—is full of oil, and ready for
home, and so they're cooking doughnuts in the fat and having a grand
blow-out, illumination and jollification. But he's uncommon thankful for
the good intentions you've shown, and hopes you'll accept this lot of A 1
sea-turkles.' The old woman leaned over the rail and shaded her eyes
from the lantern with her hand, and she see them varmints flopping their
flippers about in the boat and she says:
    "'For land's sake!—I've sot here, and sot here, and sot here all this
blessed night cal'latin' you'd fetch a boat-load of sorrowful roasted
corpses, and now it ain't nothing but a lot of nasty cussed mud-turkles
—it's a dern thieving shame, that's my opinion of it!'"[17]

It took the passengers two difficult days to cross Lake Nicaragua and putter down the
San Juan River through blanketlike rainstorms and cumulus clouds of biting insects.
They celebrated the first day of 1867 with a view of Greytown, Nicaragua, on the
miasmic Miskito Coast (fitting moniker), where the steamship *San Francisco* was to
be their deliverance. Or so they thought . . .

Steamer San Francisco

At sea, January 1st.

Under Way Again

All this morning the surf-boats were busy bringing New York passengers ashore from the steamer *San Francisco*, and carrying us out to take their places—and all in the midst of a heavy sea and a drenching rain. We took our places in the surf-boat at 8 A.M., and with the first stroke of the oars we were soaked to the skin. Yet it was very pleasant. It was quite a picture to get a misty and momentary glimpse of the boat ahead of us through the driving rain, as it rose high upon the crest of a lofty wave, and then sank down, leaving nothing visible in all the wide horizon but the rainy sea.

It was dreary enough on the ship when we got there, squatting around on the wet promenade deck watching baggage and looking soaked, woe-begone and disconsolate. We were well satisfied, though, for the boat loads that were leaving the vessel every moment were bound for vastly drearier quarters. We sailed at noon.

Our Confounded Choir

Midnight—There goes that choir again:

"God save the good ship as onward she flies!
We're homeward bound! homeward bound!"

That is well enough—I like that. But usually they do sing the wretched-est old songs in the world. Think of them sitting up there, under these jeweled skies, with all the ocean around them glistening with white-caps, piping "Just Before the Battle, Mother!" and "Johnny Comes Marching Home!" and "Lily Dale!" and "Dog Tray." When they sing hymns they do well enough and make good music, but perdition catch their other efforts! "Homeward Bound" and the "Larboard Watch Ahoy!" nobody objects to, because they are in keeping with our surroundings—but what in the nation is there in common between the shoreless sea, the gemmed and arching heavens, the crested billows, the stately ship ploughing her gallant way and leaving a highway of fire behind her, the thousand thoughtful eyes gazing out upon the ocean, lost in dreams of the homes that shall soon bless their sight again—and Dog Tray! Why is Dog Tray to be intruded upon circumstances of such moral and physical sublimity as these? What has Dog Tray got to do with such matters? Confound Dog Tray! . . .

The West Sou'-Wester

We had a rare good time on the *San Francisco*. The old Captain was jolly, and a gentleman—formerly a Lieutenant Commander in the navy. The Purser was a long, gangly, first-rate fellow—perfect gentleman—and told the oldest, rattiest, last-century stories, and told them with the worst grace! We had a very jolly time. The cholera was in the ship, medicines were nearly out, and we had to be jolly. It wouldn't do to get melancholy for a moment. Brown and Smith (my room-mates) invented a harmless tropical drink (I thought I had tasted it before) which they named "west-sou'-wester;" and every day, before each meal, all the boys were drummed forward to take it.

It was built thus:

White sugar .... lbs. ¾
Ice .... lbs. 1½
Limes .... dozen 1
Lemon 1
Orange 1
Brandy .... bot. ½

Put in ¾ gal. ice-pitcher, and fill up with water.

The smoking room was always full of lovers, teething babies and sea-sick women, and so Brown and I had to take it turn about getting sick every night. The idea of this was, so that we might have a large ship's lantern in our state-room instead of the dingy little spark of a swinging lamp usually provided for passengers, and which must be blown out promptly at ten o'clock. Only sick people can have ship-lanterns, and burn them as long as they want to see how the medicine operates, and play seven-up. We never worried much about the medicine—we let it operate or not, just as it came handy, because it wasn't anything but west-sou'-westers anyhow—but we used to be very regular about getting the room crammed full of cigar-smoke and boys, and listening to the purser's infamous old stories, and playing pitch seven-up till midnight.

The Monkey

The monkey was a well-spring of joy—one of the passengers got him at Greytown and kept him in a locker near our room on the upper deck —and we used to get him as tight as a brick occasionally, on a banana soaked in cherry brandy, and then it was fun to see him reel away and scamper up the rigging and miscalculate his jumps and fall thirty feet and catch by his tail on another rope and save himself. He was dressed up by the ladies in a gray Scotch cap and pantaloons, gray coat with cuffs and collar of brilliant red and gold, and a belt and wooden dagger, and was as comical and happy-spirited a scoundrel as ever lived. He was never idle —never still; always prospecting and rummaging in state-rooms or galloping up the rigging to the very masthead. The gale, and the quivering mast, and the plunging ship, were nonsense to him on his dizzy perch. One morning when he was tight and the weather was cool, he went and got into bed with a sick woman who was asleep—drew the covers down carefully, one after the other, watching her face all the time with his sharp eyes—then turned back the sheet and sprung in! He nestled snugly up to the lady, keeping up his low, gratified squeak all the time, and drew up the bedclothes till nothing of him was visible but the brim of his cap and the end of his gray nose. His squeaking woke the woman and she looked once at the diminutive old face on her pillow, and then she screamed like a locomotive and sprang out of bed. The next moment the monkey was at the masthead, infinitely worse scared than she was. . . .

The Cholera

Most of the steerage passengers ate quantities of fruit on the Isthmus and drank *aguadiente*—a dangerous combination, even for a native—and we had hardly got to sea before the effects of their imprudence appeared. In my log I find these entries:

"January 2d.—Two cases cholera in the steerage reported this morning."

"4 P.M.—Surgeon has just reported to the Captain that 'two of the cases are mighty bad, and the third awful bad.' So there is a new one, it seems."

"9:10 P.M.—One of the sick men died a few minutes ago, and was at once sheeted and thrown overboard. Rev. Mr. Fackler read the prayers."

"Midnight.—Another patient at the point of death—they are filling him up with brandy. These are sad times."

"1 A.M.—The man is dead."

"2 A.M.—He is overboard. Expedition has to be used in our circumstances."

"January 4th.—Off coast of Cuba. Another man died this morning—of cholera, everybody in the ship said, of course—but it was not. Old case of consumption."

"January 5th.—We are to put in at Key West, Florida, to-day, for coal, so they say, but no doubt it is to cool down the fright of the passengers as well. Some are lively, but others are in a terrible way. Seven cases sickness yesterday—one a first cabin passenger."

"Noon.—Another man said to be dying of cholera—the young man they call 'Shape.'"

"Half a dozen on the sick list now. The blockheads let the diarrhoea run two or three days, and then, getting scared, they run to the surgeon and hope to be cured. And they lie like all possessed—swear they have just been taken, when the doctor knows better by their symptoms. He asked a patient the other day if he had any money to get some brandy with?—said 'no,' and so the ship had to furnish it—when the man died they found forty-five dollars in his pocket. May be it was all the money the poor fellow had, but then he needn't have spoken falsely about it when the chances were all in favor of his going to the bottom anyway, and then he wouldn't want it."

"'Shape' been walking the deck in stocking feet at midnight last night—getting wet—exposing himself—going to die, they say."

"The disease has got into the second cabin at last, and one case in first cabin. The consternation is so great among some of the passengers, that several are going to get off at Key West (if quarantine regulations permit it) and go north overland."

"The Captain and the Surgeon go through with the regular daily inspection of every nook and corner and state-room in the ship, as usual. It is a good regulation, and more than ever necessary now."

"Shape is dead—sick about twelve hours."

"2 P.M.—The Episcopal clergyman, Rev. Mr. Fackler, is taken—bad diarrhoea and griping. He has buried all the dead, and he is a good-hearted man and it always affected him so to see those poor fellows plunge into the sea. Pure distress of mind has made him sick—nothing else. He started out to read prayers over 'Shape,' and when he came in sight of the sheeted corpse he fainted and fell down by the capstan."

"All hands looking anxiously forward to the cool weather we shall strike twenty-four hours hence, to drive away the sickness."

"4 P.M.—The Minister has got a fit—convulsions of some kind. They are nursing him well; everybody likes him and respects him."

"Just heard the Captain give the order to Purser to put up a sign, in letters large enough for all to read: 'No charge for medical attendance whatever.' It is a good idea—we have found some more like that fellow that died and didn't want to buy brandy."

"5:30 P.M.—As the boys came to the room, one after the other, I observed a marked change in their demeanor. They report that the Minister —only sick such a short time—is already very low; and that a hospital has been fitted up in the steerage and he removed thither. Verily the ship is fast becoming a floating hospital herself—not a single hour passes but brings its new sensation—its melancholy tidings. If ever a group of earnest countenances assemble on any part of the deck, you will see everybody flock there—they know there is some more news of dire import. When I think of poor 'Shape' and the preacher, both so well when I saw them yesterday, it makes me feel gloomy. Since the last two hours, all laughter, all cheerfulness, have died out of the ship. A settled sadness is upon the faces of the passengers."

"The last arrival says the Minister is dying. The passengers are fearfully exercised, and with considerable reason, for we are about to have our fifth death in five days, and the sixth of the voyage."

"That bolt-head broke several days ago, and we lost two hours while it was being mended. It broke again the next day, and we lost three or four hours. It broke again this afternoon, and again we lay like a log on the water (head wind,) for three or four hours more. These things distress the passengers beyond measure. They are scared about the epidemic and so impatient to get along that a stoppage of an hour seems a week to them, and gets them nervous and excited. One or two insist that we are 'out of luck,' and that we are all going to the very dickens, wherever that may be. Good many patients in the hospital. One well man is in a terrible way—can't bear the idea of dying and being buried at sea—as if his dead carcass would be more comfortable being eaten by grub-worms than sharks. Has got sixty-eight articles on cholera and its treatment—does nothing but read them. He tried hard to get the Captain to promise not to throw him overboard in case he died—offered him a hundred dollars. He is determined to quit the ship at Key West, and so are twenty or thirty others."

"January 6th.—At two o'clock this morning, the Rev. Mr. Fackler died, and half an hour afterwards we landed at Key West. It is Sunday. Two of us attended Episcopal service here, and retired when they prepared to take the sacrament, and left a request at the pastor's house that he would preach the funeral sermon. We visited the cemetery in the edge of town, and then, supposing there was plenty of time, strolled through the principal streets and took some notes. When we got to the ship, it being a little after one o'clock, they said the funeral was already over."[18]

The Gulf Stream

January 8th—Man named Belmayne died to-day of dropsy, and was buried at sea.

The temperature of the Gulf Stream here (they try it every two hours for the information of the Navy Department) is 76°, atmosphere 72°. We are comfortable enough now, while we are in this fluid stove, but when we leave it at Cape Hatteras it will be terribly cold. The speed of the Stream varies from one-third of a mile to three and one-half miles an hour. We have been making 210 to 220 miles a day heretofore, but in this current we can turn off 250, 260 and 275 miles.

The ship has beautiful charts, compiled by Lieut. Maury, which are crammed with shoals, currents, lights, buoys, soundings, and winds, and calms and storms—black figures for soundings, and bright spots for beacons, and so on, and an interminable tangle, like a spider's web, of red lines denoting the tracks of hundreds of ships whose logs were sent to Maury—everything mapped out so accurately that a man might know what water he had, what current, what beacon he was near, what style of wind he might expect, and from which direction, on any particular day in the year, at any given point on the world's broad surface. 'They that go down to the sea in ships see the wonders of the great deep'—but this modern navigation out-wonders any wonder the scriptural writers dreamt of. To see a man stand in the night, when everything looks alike —far out in the midst of a boundless sea—and measure from one star to another and tell to a dot right where the ship is—tell the very spot the little insignificant speck occupies on a vast expanse of land and sea twenty-five thousand miles in circumference! Verily, with his imperial intellect and his deep-searching wisdom, man is almost a God!

In the strongest current of the Gulf Stream at 4 o'clock this morning, off Jupiter Inlet—3½ miles an hour. Numerous bets we wouldn't make 250 miles—made 271 in the 24 hours ending at noon. The current for the next 24 hours will not be so strong.

January 10th.—At noon shall be off Hatteras, 26 days out from San Francisco. We shall leave this warming pan of a Gulf Stream to-day, and then it will cease to be genial summer weather and become wintry cold. We already see the signs—they put feather-beds and blankets on the berths this morning. It is warm, now, and raining.

Eight sick—five diarrhoea—two better—three convalescent.

Passing out of the Gulf Stream rapidly. At 2 P.M., temperature of the water had fallen seven degrees in half an hour—from 72° down to 65°. Already the day is turning cold, and one after another the boys adjourn from the deck a moment and then come back with overcoats on. At 2:30, temperature of water two degrees lower—viz., 63°. At 3, it was 61°. It fell eleven degrees in an hour and a half. Then we passed out, and the weather turned bitter cold."

Safe at Last in "the States"

We swore the ship through at quarantine, which was right—she hadn't had any real cholera on board since we left Greytown—and at 8 o'clock this morning we stood in the biting air of the upper deck and sailed by the snow-covered, wintry looking residences on Staten Island—recognized Castle Garden—beheld the vast city spread out beyond, encircled with its palisade of masts, and adorned with its hundred steeples—saw the steam-tug and ferry-boats swarming through the floating ice, instinct with a frenzied energy, as we passed the river—and in a little while we were ashore and safe housed at the Metropolitan.

After comparing notes, all decided that the voyage had been exceedingly pleasant, notwithstanding its little drawbacks, and that we would like very well to leave the cholera ashore and take the trip over again.

The Nicaragua Steamship Company are building three splendid new steamers, all of them fast and commodious—and six weeks hence the first one will start around the Horn to do duty on the other side. They claim that she will be able to make fifteen knots right along with twenty pounds of steam. I would like to go in one of their new ships and see that beautiful scenery on the Lake and San Juan River again.[19]

The Innocents Afloat

he Innocents Abroad established Mark Twain as a professional writer, after his peripatetic, if not to say prodigal, young adulthood. It was an immediate best-seller and grew into an international sensation, which made Twain famous. While he was alive, the name Mark Twain was more closely associated with *The Innocents Abroad* than with any other work; thirty years after it came out, rowdy people in lecture audiences were still appreciatively shouting to him the leitmotif tagline of the book: "Is he dead?" Since then several, if not most, of his many other books have eclipsed *The Innocents Abroad* in fame — *The Adventures of Tom Sawyer*, *The Prince and the Pauper* (a fact that would make him cringe but delight his wife), *Life on the Mississippi*, and especially *The Adventures of Huckleberry Finn*, which is considered his masterpiece, and has sold more than twenty million copies since its first edition in 1884. But during Mark Twain's lifetime, far more copies of *The Innocents Abroad* sold than did copies of the controversial *Huck*, or of any other work in the epochal artist's oeuvre. The saltiest bits of *Innocents* follow here.

*   *   *

The Voyage Out

Chapter 2

Occasionally, during the following month, I dropped in at 117 Wall Street to inquire how the repairing and refurnishing of the vessel was coming on, how additions to the passenger list were averaging, how many people the committee were decreeing not "select" every day and banishing in sorrow and tribulation. I was glad to know that we were to have a little printing press on board and issue a daily newspaper of our own. I was glad to learn that our piano, our parlor organ, and our melodeon were to be the best instruments of the kind that could be had in the market. I was proud to observe that among our excursionists were three ministers of the gospel, eight doctors, sixteen or eighteen ladies, several military and naval chieftains with sounding titles, an ample crop of "Professors" of various kinds, and a gentleman who had "COMMISSIONER OF THE UNITED STATES OF AMERICA TO EUROPE, ASIA, AND AFRICA" thundering after his name in one awful blast! I had carefully prepared myself to take rather a back seat in that ship because of the uncommonly select material that would alone be permitted to pass through the camel's eye of that committee on credentials; I had schooled myself to expect an imposing array of military and naval heroes and to have to set that back seat still further back in consequence of it maybe; but I state frankly that I was all unprepared for *this* crusher.

I fell under that titular avalanche a torn and blighted thing. I said that if that potentate *must* go over in our ship, why, I supposed he must—but that to my thinking, when the United States considered it necessary to send a dignitary of that tonnage across the ocean, it would be in better taste, and safer, to take him apart and cart him over in sections in several ships.

Ah, if I had only known then that he was only a common mortal, and that his mission had nothing more overpowering about it than the collecting of seeds and uncommon yams and extraordinary cabbages and peculiar bullfrogs for that poor, useless, innocent, mildewed old fossil the Smithsonian Institute, I would have felt *so* much relieved.

During that memorable month I basked in the happiness of being for once in my life drifting with the tide of a great popular movement. Everybody was going to Europe—I, too, was going to Europe. Everybody was going to the famous Paris Exposition—I, too, was going to the Paris Exposition. The steamship lines were carrying Americans out of the various ports of the country at the rate of four or five thousand a week in the aggregate. If I met a dozen individuals during that month who were not going to Europe shortly, I have no distinct remembrance of it now. I walked about the city a good deal with a young Mr. Blucher, who was booked for the excursion. He was confiding, good-natured, unsophisticated, companionable; but he was not a man to set the river on fire. He had the most extraordinary notions about this European exodus and came at last to consider the whole nation as packing up for emigration to France. We stepped into a store on Broadway one day, where he bought a handkerchief, and when the man could not make change, Mr. B. said:

"Never mind, I'll hand it to you in Paris."

"But I am not going to Paris."

"How is—what did I understand you to say?"

"I said I am not going to Paris."

"Not going to *Paris*! Not g— well, then, where in the nation *are* you going to?"

"Nowhere at all."

"Not anywhere whatsoever?—not any place on earth but this?"

"Not any place at all but just this—stay here all summer."

My comrade took his purchase and walked out of the store without a word—walked out with an injured look upon his countenance. Up the street apiece he broke silence and said impressively: "It was a lie—that is my opinion of it!"

In the fullness of time the ship was ready to receive her passengers. I was introduced to the young gentleman who was to be my roommate, and found him to be intelligent, cheerful of spirit, unselfish, full of generous impulses, patient, considerate, and wonderfully good-natured. Not any passenger that sailed in the *Quaker City* will withhold his endorsement of what I have just said. We selected a stateroom forward of the wheel, on the starboard side, "below decks." It had two berths in it, a dismal dead-light, a sink with a washbowl in it, and a long, sumptuously cushioned locker, which was to do service as a sofa—partly—and partly as a hiding place for our things. Notwithstanding all this furniture, there was still room to turn around in, but not to swing a cat in, at least with entire security to the cat. However, the room was large, for a ship's stateroom, and was in every way satisfactory.

The vessel was appointed to sail on a certain Saturday early in June.

A little after noon on that distinguished Saturday I reached the ship and went on board. All was bustle and confusion. (I have seen that remark before somewhere.) The pier was crowded with carriages and men; passengers were arriving and hurrying on board; the vessel's decks were encumbered with trunks and valises; groups of excursionists, arrayed in unattractive traveling costumes, were moping about in a drizzling rain and looking as droopy and woebegone as so many molting chickens. The gallant flag was up, but it was under the spell, too, and hung limp and disheartened by the mast. Altogether, it was the bluest, bluest spectacle! It was a pleasure excursion—there was no gainsaying that, because the program said so—it was so nominated in the bond—but it surely hadn't the general aspect of one.

Finally, above the banging, and rumbling, and shouting, and hissing of steam rang the order to "cast off!"—a sudden rush to the gangways—a scampering ashore of visitors—a revolution of the wheels, and we were off—the picnic was begun! Two very mild cheers went up from the dripping crowd on the pier; we answered them gently from the slippery decks; the flag made an effort to wave, and failed; the "battery of guns" spake not—the ammunition was out.

We steamed down to the foot of the harbor and came to anchor. It was still raining. And not only raining, but storming. "Outside" we could see, ourselves, that there was a tremendous sea on. We must lie still, in the calm harbor, till the storm should abate. Our passengers hailed from fifteen states; only a few of them had ever been to sea before; manifestly it would not do to pit them against a full-blown tempest until they had got their sea-legs on. Toward evening the two steam tugs that had accompanied us with a rollicking champagne-party of young New Yorkers on board who wished to bid farewell to one of our number in due and ancient form departed, and we were alone on the deep. On deep five fathoms, and anchored fast to the bottom. And out in the solemn rain, at that. This was pleasuring with a vengeance.

It was an appropriate relief when the gong sounded for prayer meeting. The first Saturday night of any other pleasure excursion might have been devoted to whist and dancing; but I submit it to the unprejudiced mind if it would have been in good taste for *us* to engage in such frivolities, considering what we had gone through and the frame of mind we were in. We would have shone at a wake, but not at anything more festive.

However, there is always a cheering influence about the sea; and in my berth that night, rocked by the measured swell of the waves and lulled by the murmur of the distant surf, I soon passed tranquilly out of all consciousness of the dreary experiences of the day and damaging premonitions of the future.

Chapter 3

All day Sunday at anchor. The storm had gone down a great deal, but the sea had not. It was still piling its frothy hills high in the air "outside," as we could plainly see with the glasses. We could not properly begin a pleasure excursion on Sunday; we could not offer untried stomachs to so pitiless a sea as that. We must lie still till Monday. And we did. But we had repetitions of church and prayer-meetings; and so, of course, we were just as eligibly situated as we could have been any where.

I was up early that Sabbath morning and was early to breakfast. I felt a perfectly natural desire to have a good, long, unprejudiced look at the passengers at a time when they should be free from self-consciousness—which is at breakfast, when such a moment occurs in the lives of human beings at all.

I was greatly surprised to see so many elderly people—I might almost say, so many venerable people. A glance at the long lines of heads was apt to make one think it was *all* gray. But it was not. There was a tolerably fair sprinkling of young folks, and another fair sprinkling of gentlemen and ladies who were non-committal as to age, being neither actually old or absolutely young.

The next morning, we weighed anchor and went to sea. It was a great happiness to get away after this dragging, dispiriting delay. I thought there never was such gladness in the air before, such brightness in the sun, such beauty in the sea. I was satisfied with the picnic then and with all its belongings. All my malicious instincts were dead within me; and as America faded out of sight, I think a spirit of charity rose up in their place that was as boundless, for the time being, as the broad ocean that was heaving its billows about us. I wished to express my feelings—I wished to lift up my voice and sing; but I did not know anything to sing, and so I was obliged to give up the idea. It was no loss to the ship, though, perhaps.

It was breezy and pleasant, but the sea was still very rough. One could not promenade without risking his neck; at one moment the bowsprit was taking a deadly aim at the sun in midheaven, and at the next it was trying to harpoon a shark in the bottom of the ocean. What a weird sensation it is to feel the stern of a ship sinking swiftly from under you and see the bow climbing high away among the clouds! One's safest course that day was to clasp a railing and hang on; walking was too precarious a pastime.

By some happy fortune I was not seasick.—That was a thing to be proud of. I had not always escaped before. If there is one thing in the world that will make a man peculiarly and insufferably self-conceited, it is to have his stomach behave itself, the first day at sea, when nearly all his comrades are seasick. Soon a venerable fossil, shawled to the chin and bandaged like a mummy, appeared at the door of the after deck-house, and the next lurch of the ship shot him into my arms. I said:

"Good-morning, Sir. It is a fine day."

He put his hand on his stomach and said, "*Oh*, my!" and then staggered away and fell over the coop of a skylight.

Presently another old gentleman was projected from the same door with great violence. I said:

"Calm yourself, Sir—There is no hurry. It is a fine day, Sir."

He, also, put his hand on his stomach and said "*Oh*, my!" and reeled away.

In a little while another veteran was discharged abruptly from the same door, clawing at the air for a saving support. I said:

"Good morning, Sir. It is a fine day for pleasuring. You were about to say—"

"*Oh*, my!"

I thought so. I anticipated *him*, anyhow. I stayed there and was bombarded with old gentlemen for an hour, perhaps; and all I got out of any of them was "*Oh*, my!"

I went away then in a thoughtful mood. I said, this is a good pleasure excursion. I like it. The passengers are not garrulous, but still they are sociable. I like those old people, but somehow they all seem to have the "Oh, my" rather bad.

I knew what was the matter with them. They were seasick. And I was glad of it. We all like to see people seasick when we are not, ourselves. Playing whist by the cabin lamps when it is storming outside is pleasant; walking the quarterdeck in the moonlight is pleasant; smoking in the breezy foretop is pleasant when one is not afraid to go up there; but these are all feeble and commonplace compared with the joy of seeing people suffering the miseries of seasickness.

I picked up a good deal of information during the afternoon. At one time I was climbing up the quarterdeck when the vessel's stern was in the sky; I was smoking a cigar and feeling passably comfortable. Somebody ejaculated:

"Come, now, *that* won't answer. Read the sign up there—NO SMOKING ABAFT THE WHEEL!"

It was Captain Duncan, chief of the expedition. I went forward, of course. I saw a long spyglass lying on a desk in one of the upper-deck state-rooms back of the pilot-house and reached after it—there was a ship in the distance.

"Ah, ah—hands off! Come out of that!"

I came out of that. I said to a deck-sweep—but in a low voice:

"Who is that overgrown pirate with the whiskers and the discordant voice?"

"It's Captain Bursley—executive officer—sailing master."

I loitered about awhile, and then, for want of something better to do, fell to carving a railing with my knife. Somebody said, in an insinuating, admonitory voice:

"Now, *say*—my friend—don't you know any better than to be whittling the ship all to pieces that way? *You* ought to know better than that."

I went back and found the deck sweep.

"Who is that smooth-faced, animated outrage yonder in the fine clothes?"

"That's Captain L—, the owner of the ship—he's one of the main bosses."

In the course of time I brought up on the starboard side of the pilot-house and found a sextant lying on a bench. Now, I said, they "take the sun" through this thing; I should think I might see that vessel through it. I had hardly got it to my eye when someone touched me on the shoulder and said deprecatingly:

"I'll have to get you to give that to me, Sir. If there's anything you'd like to know about taking the sun, I'd as soon tell you as not—but I don't like to trust anybody with that instrument. If you want any figuring done —Aye, aye, sir!"

He was gone to answer a call from the other side. I sought the deck-sweep.

"Who is that spider-legged gorilla yonder with the sanctimonious countenance?"

"It's Captain Jones, sir—the chief mate."

"Well. This goes clear away ahead of anything I ever heard of before. Do you—now I ask you as a man and a brother—*do* you think I could venture to throw a rock here in any given direction without hitting a captain of this ship?"

"Well, sir, I don't know—I think likely you'd fetch the captain of the watch may be, because he's a-standing right yonder in the way."

I went below—meditating and a little downhearted. I thought, if five cooks can spoil a broth, what may not five captains do with a pleasure excursion.

Chapter 4

We plowed along bravely for a week or more, and without any conflict of jurisdiction among the captains worth mentioning. The passengers soon learned to accommodate themselves to their new circumstances, and life in the ship became nearly as systematically monotonous as the routine of a barrack. I do not mean that it was dull, for it was not entirely so by any means—but there was a good deal of sameness about it. As is always the fashion at sea, the passengers shortly began to pick up sailor terms —a sign that they were beginning to feel at home. Half-past six was no longer half-past six to these pilgrims from New England, the South, and the Mississippi Valley, it was "seven bells"; eight, twelve, and four o'clock were "eight bells"; the captain did not take the longitude at nine o'clock, but at "two bells." They spoke glibly of the "after cabin," the "for'rard cabin," "port and starboard" and the "fo'castle."

At seven bells the first gong rang; at eight there was breakfast, for such as were not too seasick to eat it. After that all the well people walked arm-in-arm up and down the long promenade deck, enjoying the fine summer mornings, and the seasick ones crawled out and propped themselves up in the lee of the paddle-boxes and ate their dismal tea and toast, and looked wretched. From eleven o'clock until luncheon, and from luncheon until dinner at six in the evening, the employments and amusements were various. Some reading was done, and much smoking and sewing, though not by the same parties; there were the monsters of the deep to be looked after and wondered at; strange ships had to be scrutinized through opera-glasses, and sage decisions arrived at concerning them; and more than that, everybody took a personal interest in seeing that the flag was run up and politely dipped three times in response to the salutes of those strangers; in the smoking room there were always parties of gentlemen playing euchre, draughts and dominoes, especially dominoes, that delightfully harmless game; and down on the main deck, "for'rard"—for'rard of the chicken-coops and the cattle—we had what was called "horse billiards." Horse billiards is a fine game. It affords good, active exercise, hilarity, and consuming excitement. It is a mixture of "hop-scotch" and shuffleboard played with a crutch. A large hop-scotch diagram is marked out on the deck with chalk, and each compartment numbered. You stand off three or four steps, with some broad wooden disks before you on the deck, and these you send forward with a vigorous thrust of a long crutch. If a disk stops on a chalk line, it does not count anything. If it stops in division No. 7, it counts 7; in 5, it counts 5, and so on. The game is 100, and four can play at a time. That game would be very simple played on a stationary floor, but with us, to play it well required science. We had to allow for the reeling of the ship to the right or the left. Very often one made calculations for a heel to the right and the ship did not go that way. The consequence was that that disk missed the whole hopscotch plan a yard or two, and then there was humiliation on one side and laughter on the other.

When it rained the passengers had to stay in the house, of course—or at least the cabins—and amuse themselves with games, reading, looking out of the windows at the very familiar billows, and talking gossip.

By 7 o'clock in the evening, dinner was about over; an hour's promenade on the upper deck followed; then the gong sounded and a large majority of the party repaired to the after cabin (upper), a handsome saloon fifty or sixty feet long, for prayers. The unregenerated called this saloon the "Synagogue." The devotions consisted only of two hymns from the Plymouth Collection and a short prayer, and seldom occupied more than fifteen minutes. The hymns were accompanied by parlor-organ music when the sea was smooth enough to allow a performer to sit at the instrument without being lashed to his chair.

After prayers the Synagogue shortly took the semblance of a writing

school. The like of that picture was never seen in a ship before. Behind
the long dining tables on either side of the saloon, and scattered from one
end to the other of the latter, some twenty or thirty gentlemen and ladies
sat them down under the swaying lamps and for two or three hours wrote
diligently in their journals. Alas! that journals so voluminously begun
should come to so lame and impotent a conclusion as most of them did!
I doubt if there is a single pilgrim of all that host but can show a hundred
fair pages of journal concerning the first twenty days' voyaging in the
Quaker City, and I am morally certain that not ten of the party can show
twenty pages of journal for the succeeding twenty thousand miles of voyaging! At certain periods it becomes the dearest ambition of a man to
keep a faithful record of his performances in a book; and he dashes at this
work with an enthusiasm that imposes on him the notion that keeping a
journal is the veriest pastime in the world, and the pleasantest. But if he
only lives twenty-one days, he will find out that only those rare natures
that are made up of pluck, endurance, devotion to duty for duty's sake,
and invincible determination may hope to venture upon so tremendous
an enterprise as the keeping of a journal and not sustain a shameful defeat.

One of our favorite youths, Jack, a splendid young fellow with a head
full of good sense, and a pair of legs that were a wonder to look upon in
the way of length and straightness and slimness, used to report progress
every morning in the most glowing and spirited way, and say:

"Oh, I'm coming along bully!" (he was a little given to slang in his
happier moods.) "I wrote ten pages in my journal last night—and you
know I wrote nine the night before and twelve the night before that. Why,
it's only fun!"

"What do you find to put in it, Jack?"

"Oh, everything. Latitude and longitude, noon every day; and how
many miles we made last twenty-four hours; and all the domino games
I beat and horse billiards; and whales and sharks and porpoises; and
the text of the sermon Sundays (because that'll tell at home, you know);
and the ships we saluted and what nation they were; and which way the
wind was, and whether there was a heavy sea, and what sail we carried,
though we don't ever carry *any*, principally, going against a head wind
always—wonder what is the reason of that?—and how many lies Moult
has told—Oh, every thing! I've got everything down. My father told me

to keep that journal. Father wouldn't take a thousand dollars for it when I get it done."

"No, Jack; it will be worth more than a thousand dollars—when you get it done."

"Do you?—no, but do you think it will, though?

"Yes, it will be worth at least as much as a thousand dollars—when you get it done. May be more."

"Well, I about half think so, myself. It ain't no slouch of a journal."

But it shortly became a most lamentable "slouch of a journal." One night in Paris, after a hard day's toil in sightseeing, I said:

"Now I'll go and stroll around the cafés awhile, Jack, and give you a chance to write up your journal, old fellow."

His countenance lost its fire. He said:

"Well, no, you needn't mind. I think I won't run that journal anymore. It is awful tedious. Do you know—I reckon I'm as much as four thousand pages behind hand. I haven't got any France in it at all. First I thought I'd leave France out and start fresh. But that wouldn't do, *would* it? The governor would say, 'Hello, here—didn't see anything in France? *That* cat wouldn't fight, you know. First I thought I'd copy France out of the guide-book, like old Badger in the for'rard cabin, who's writing a book, but there's more than three hundred pages of it. Oh, *I* don't think a journal's any use—do you? They're only a bother, *ain't* they?"

"Yes, a journal that is incomplete isn't of much use, but a journal properly kept is worth a thousand dollars—when you've got it done."

"A thousand!—well, I should think so. *I* wouldn't finish it for a million."

His experience was only the experience of the majority of that industrious night school in the cabin. If you wish to inflict a heartless and malignant punishment upon a young person, pledge him to keep a journal a year.

A good many expedients were resorted to to keep the excursionists amused and satisfied. A club was formed, of all the passengers, which met in the writing school after prayers and read aloud about the countries we were approaching and discussed the information so obtained. . . .

On several starlight nights we danced on the upper deck, under the awnings, and made something of a ball-room display of brilliancy by hanging a number of ship's lanterns to the stanchions. Our music consisted of the well-mixed strains of a melodeon which was a little asthmatic and apt to catch its breath where it ought to come out strong, a clarinet which was a little unreliable on the high keys and rather melancholy on the low ones, and a disreputable accordion that had a leak somewhere and breathed louder than it squawked—a more elegant term does not occur to me just now. However, the dancing was infinitely worse than the music. When the ship rolled to starboard the whole platoon of dancers came charging down to starboard with it, and brought up in mass at the rail; and when it rolled to port they went floundering down to port with the same unanimity of sentiment. Waltzers spun around precariously for a matter of fifteen seconds and then went scurrying down to the rail as if they meant to go overboard. The Virginia reel, as performed on board the *Quaker City*, had more genuine reel about it than any reel I ever saw before, and was as full of interest to the spectator as it was full of desperate chances and hairbreadth escapes to the participant. We gave up dancing, finally.

We celebrated a lady's birthday anniversary with toasts, speeches, a poem, and so forth. We also had a mock trial. No ship ever went to sea that hadn't a mock trial on board. The purser was accused of stealing an overcoat from stateroom No. 10. A judge was appointed; also clerks, a crier of the court, constables, sheriffs; counsel for the State and for the defendant; witnesses were subpoenaed, and a jury empaneled after much challenging. The witnesses were stupid and unreliable and contradictory, as witnesses always are. The counsels were eloquent, argumentative, and vindictively abusive of each other, as was characteristic and proper. The case was at last submitted and duly finished by the judge with an absurd decision and a ridiculous sentence.

The acting of charades was tried on several evenings by the young gentlemen and ladies, in the cabins, and proved the most distinguished success of all the amusement experiments.

An attempt was made to organize a debating club, but it was a failure. There was no oratorical talent in the ship.

We all enjoyed ourselves—I think I can safely say that, but it was in a rather quiet way. We very, very seldom played the piano; we played the flute and the clarinet together, and made good music, too, what there was

of it, but we always played the same old tune; it was a very pretty tune
—how well I remember it—I wonder when I shall ever get rid of it. We
never played either the melodeon or the organ except at devotions—but
I am too fast: young Albert *did* know part of a tune something about "O
Something-or-Other How Sweet It Is to Know That He's His What's-
His-Name" (I do not remember the exact title of it, but it was very plaintive and full of sentiment); Albert played that pretty much all the time
until we contracted with him to restrain himself. But nobody ever sang by
moonlight on the upper deck, and the congregational singing at church
and prayers was not of a superior order of architecture. I put up with
it as long as I could and then joined in and tried to improve it, but this
encouraged young George to join in too, and that made a failure of it;
because George's voice was just "turning," and when he was singing a
dismal sort of bass it was apt to fly off the handle and startle everybody
with a most discordant cackle on the upper notes. George didn't know
the tunes, either, which was also a drawback to his performances. I said:

"Come, now, George, *don't* improvise. It looks too egotistical. It will
provoke remark. Just stick to 'Coronation,' like the others. It is a good
tune—*you* can't improve it any, just off-hand, in this way."

"Why, I'm not trying to improve it—and I *am* singing like the others
—just as it is in the notes."

And he honestly thought he was, too; and so he had no one to blame
but himself when his voice caught on the center occasionally and gave
him the lockjaw.

There were those among the unregenerated who attributed the un-
ceasing head-winds to our distressing choir-music. There were those
who said openly that it was taking chances enough to have such ghastly
music going on, even when it was at its best; and that to exaggerate the
crime by letting George help was simply flying in the face of Providence.
These said that the choir would keep up their lacerating attempts at
melody until they would bring down a storm some day that would sink
the ship.

There were even grumblers at the prayers. The executive officer said
the pilgrims had no charity:

"There they are, down there every night at eight bells, praying for fair
winds—when they know as well as I do that this is the only ship going

east this time of the year, but there's a thousand coming west—what's a fair wind for us is a *head* wind to them—the Almighty's blowing a fair wind for a thousand vessels, and this tribe wants him to turn it clear around so as to accommodate *one*—and she a steamship at that! It ain't good sense, it ain't good reason, it ain't good Christianity, it ain't common human charity. Avast with such nonsense!"

Chapter 5

Taking it "by and large," as the sailors say, we had a pleasant ten days' run from New York to the Azores islands—not a fast run, for the distance is only twenty-four hundred miles, but a right pleasant one in the main. True, we had head winds *all* the time, and several stormy experiences which sent fifty percent of the passengers to bed sick and made the ship look dismal and deserted—stormy experiences that all will remember who weathered them on the tumbling deck and caught the vast sheets of spray that every now and then sprang high in the air from the weather bow and swept the ship like a thunder-shower; but for the most part we had balmy summer weather and nights that were even finer than the days. We had the phenomenon of a full moon located just in the same spot in the heavens at the same hour every night. The reason of this singular conduct on the part of the moon did not occur to us at first, but it did afterward when we reflected that we were gaining about twenty minutes every day because we were going east so fast—we gained just about enough every day to keep along with the moon. It was becoming an old moon to the friends we had left behind us, but to us Joshuas it stood still in the same place and remained always the same. . . .

We saw the usual sharks, blackfish, porpoises, &c., of course, and by and by large schools of Portuguese men-of-war were added to the regular list of sea wonders. Some of them were white and some of a brilliant carmine color. The nautilus is nothing but a transparent web of jelly that spreads itself to catch the wind, and has fleshy-looking strings a foot or two long dangling from it to keep it steady in the water. It is an accomplished sailor and has good sailor judgment. It reefs its sail when a storm threatens or the wind blows pretty hard, and furls it entirely and goes down when a gale blows. Ordinarily it keeps its sail wet and in good sailing order by turning over and dipping it in the water for a moment. Seamen say the nautilus is only found in these waters between the 35th and 45th parallels of latitude.

At three o'clock on the morning of the twenty-first of June, we were awakened and notified that the Azores islands were in sight. I said I did not take any interest in islands at three o'clock in the morning. But another persecutor came, and then another and another, and finally believing that the general enthusiasm would permit no one to slumber in peace, I got up and went sleepily on deck. It was five and a half o'clock now, and a raw, blustering morning. The passengers were huddled about the smokestacks and fortified behind ventilators, and all were wrapped in wintry costumes and looking sleepy and unhappy in the pitiless gale and the drenching spray.[1]

Chapter 7

A week of buffeting a tempestuous and relentless sea; a week of seasickness and deserted cabins; of lonely quarterdecks drenched with spray —spray so ambitious that it even coated the smokestacks thick with a white crust of salt to their very tops; a week of shivering in the shelter of the lifeboats and deckhouses by day and blowing suffocating "clouds" and boisterously performing at dominoes in the smoking room at night.

And the last night of the seven was the stormiest of all. There was no thunder, no noise but the pounding bows of the ship, the keen whistling of the gale through the cordage, and the rush of the seething waters. But the vessel climbed aloft as if she would climb to heaven—then paused an instant that seemed a century and plunged headlong down again, as from a precipice. The sheeted sprays drenched the decks like rain. The blackness of darkness was everywhere. At long intervals a flash of lightning clove it with a quivering line of fire that revealed a heaving world of water where was nothing before, kindled the dusky cordage to glittering silver, and lit up the faces of the men with a ghastly luster!

Fear drove many on deck that were used to avoiding the night winds and the spray. Some thought the vessel could not live through the night, and it seemed less dreadful to stand out in the midst of the wild tempest and *see* the peril that threatened than to be shut up in the sepulchral cabins, under the dim lamps, and imagine the horrors that were abroad on the ocean. And once out—once where they could see the ship struggling in the strong grasp of the storm—once where they could hear the shriek of the winds and face the driving spray and look out upon the majestic picture the lightnings disclosed, they were prisoners to a fierce fascination they could not resist, and so remained. It was a wild night—a very, very long one.

Everybody was sent scampering to the deck at seven o'clock this lovely morning of the thirtieth of June with the glad news that land was in sight! It was a rare thing and a joyful, to see *all* the ship's family abroad once more, albeit the happiness that sat upon every countenance could only partly conceal the ravages which that long siege of storms had wrought there. But dull eyes soon sparkled with pleasure, pallid cheeks flushed again, and frames weakened by sickness gathered new life from the quickening influences of the bright, fresh morning. Yea, and from a still more potent influence: the worn castaways were to see the blessed land again!—and to see it was to bring back that motherland that was in all their thoughts.

Within the hour we were fairly within the Straits of Gibraltar, the tall yellow-splotched hills of Africa on our right, with their bases veiled in a blue haze and their summits swathed in clouds—the same being according to Scripture, which says that "clouds and darkness are over the land." The words were spoken of this particular portion of Africa, I believe. On our left were the granite-ribbed domes of old Spain. The strait is only thirteen miles wide in its narrowest part.

At short intervals along the Spanish shore were quaint-looking old stone towers—Moorish, we thought—but learned better afterwards. In former times the Morocco rascals used to coast along the Spanish Main in their boats till a safe opportunity seemed to present itself, and then dart in and capture a Spanish village and carry off all the pretty women they could find. It was a pleasant business, and was very popular. The Spaniards built these watchtowers on the hills to enable them to keep a sharper lookout on the Moroccan speculators.

The picture on the other hand was very beautiful to eyes weary of the changeless sea, and by and by the ship's company grew wonderfully cheerful. But while we stood admiring the cloud-capped peaks and the lowlands robed in misty gloom a finer picture burst upon us and chained every eye like a magnet—a stately ship, with canvas piled on canvas till she was one towering mass of bellying sail! She came speeding over the sea like a great bird. Africa and Spain were forgotten. All homage was for the beautiful stranger. While everybody gazed she swept superbly by and flung the Stars and Stripes to the breeze! Quicker than thought, hats and handkerchiefs flashed in the air, and a cheer went up! She was beautiful before—she was radiant now. Many a one on our decks knew then for the first time how tame a sight his country's flag is at home compared to what it is in a foreign land. To see it is to see a vision of home itself and all its idols, and feel a thrill that would stir a very river of sluggish blood!

We were approaching the famed Pillars of Hercules, and already the African one, "Ape's Hill," a grand old mountain with summit streaked with granite ledges, was in sight. The other, the great Rock of Gibraltar, was yet to come. The ancients considered the Pillars of Hercules the head of navigation and the end of the world. The information the ancients didn't have was very voluminous. Even the prophets wrote book after book and epistle after epistle, yet never once hinted at the existence of a great continent on our side of the water; yet they must have known it was there, I should think.[2]

*   *   *

The Mediterranean

Chapter 10

We passed the Fourth of July on board the *Quaker City*, in mid-ocean. It was in all respects a characteristic Mediterranean day—faultlessly beautiful. A cloudless sky; a refreshing summer wind; a radiant sunshine that glinted cheerily from dancing wavelets instead of crested mountains of water; a sea beneath us that was so wonderfully blue, so richly, brilliantly blue, that it overcame the dullest sensibilities with the spell of its fascination.

They even have fine sunsets on the Mediterranean—a thing that is certainly rare in most quarters of the globe. The evening we sailed away from Gibraltar, that hard-featured rock was swimming in a creamy mist so rich, so soft, so enchantingly vague and dreamy, that even the Oracle, that serene, that inspired, that overpowering humbug, scorned the dinner gong and tarried to worship!

He said: "Well, that's gorgis, ain't it! They don't have none of them things in our parts, *do* they? I consider that them effects is on account of the superior refragability, as you may say, of the sun's diramic combination with the lymphatic forces of the perihelion of Jubiter. What should you think?" . . .

But I digress. The thunder of our two brave cannon announced the Fourth of July, at daylight, to all who were awake. But many of us got our information at a later hour, from the almanac. All the flags were sent aloft except half a dozen that were needed to decorate portions of the ship below, and in a short time the vessel assumed a holiday appearance. During the morning, meetings were held and all manner of committees set to work on the celebration ceremonies. In the afternoon, the ship's company assembled aft, on deck, under the awnings; the flute, the asthmatic melodeon, and the consumptive clarinet crippled "The Star-Spangled Banner," the choir chased it to cover, and George came in with a peculiarly lacerating screech on the final note and slaughtered it. Nobody mourned.

We carried out the corpse on three cheers (that joke was not intentional and I do not endorse it), and then the President, throned behind a cable locker with a national flag spread over it, announced the "Reader," who rose up and read that same old Declaration of Independence which we have all listened to so often without paying any attention to what it said; and after that the President piped the Orator of the Day to quarters and he made that same old speech about our national greatness which we so religiously believe and so fervently applaud. Now came the choir into court again, with the complaining instruments, and assaulted "Hail Columbia"; and when victory hung wavering in the scale, George returned with his dreadful wild-goose stop turned on and the choir won, of course. A minister pronounced the benediction, and the patriotic little gathering disbanded. The Fourth of July was safe, as far as the Mediterranean was concerned.

At dinner in the evening, a well-written original poem was recited with spirit by one of the ship's captains, and thirteen regular toasts were washed down with several baskets of champagne. The speeches were

bad—execrable almost without exception. In fact, without *any* exception
but one. Captain Duncan made a good speech; he made the only good
speech of the evening. He said:

"LADIES AND GENTLEMEN: May we all live to a green old age and be
prosperous and happy. Steward, bring up another basket of champagne."

It was regarded as a very able effort.

The festivities, so to speak, closed with another of those miraculous
balls on the promenade deck. We were not used to dancing on an even
keel, though, and it was only a questionable success. But take it all together, it was a bright, cheerful, pleasant Fourth.

Toward nightfall the next evening, we steamed into the great artificial
harbor of this noble city of Marseilles, and saw the dying sunlight gild its
clustering spires and ramparts, and flood its leagues of environing ver-
dure with a mellow radiance that touched with an added charm the white
villas that flecked the landscape far and near.[3]

At that point, the passengers split into groups to make inland excursions. We rejoin
the narrator once everyone has returned to the ship.

Chapter 32

Home, again! For the first time, in many weeks, the ship's entire family met and shook hands on the quarter-deck. They had gathered from
many points of the compass and from many lands, but not one was missing; there was no tale of sickness or death among the flock to dampen
the pleasure of the reunion. Once more there was a full audience on deck
to listen to the sailors' chorus as they got the anchor up, and to wave an
adieu to the land as we sped away from Naples. The seats were full at
dinner again, the domino parties were complete, and the life and bustle
on the upper deck in the fine moonlight at night was like old times—old
times that had been gone weeks only, but yet they were weeks so crowded
with incident, adventure and excitement, that they seemed almost like
years. There was no lack of cheerfulness on board the *Quaker City*. For
once, her title was a misnomer.

At seven in the evening, with the western horizon all golden from
the sunken sun, and specked with distant ships, the full moon sailing
high over head, the dark blue of the sea under foot, and a strange sort

of twilight affected by all these different lights and colors around us and about us, we sighted superb Stromboli. With what majesty the monarch held his lonely state above the level sea! Distance clothed him in a purple gloom, and added a veil of shimmering mist that so softened his rugged features that we seemed to see him through a web of silver gauze. His torch was out; his fires were smoldering; a tall column of smoke that rose up and lost itself in the growing moonlight was all the sign he gave that he was a living Autocrat of the Sea and not the spectre of a dead one.

At two in the morning we swept through the Straits of Messina, and so bright was the moonlight that Italy on the one hand and Sicily on the other seemed almost as distinctly visible as though we looked at them from the middle of a street we were traversing. The city of Messina, milk-white, and starred and spangled all over with gaslights, was a fairy spectacle. A great party of us were on deck smoking and making a noise, and waiting to see famous Scylla and Charybdis. And presently the Oracle stepped out with his eternal spy-glass and squared himself on the deck like another Colossus of Rhodes. It was a surprise to see him abroad at such an hour. Nobody supposed he cared anything about an old fable like that of Scylla and Charybdis. One of the boys said:

"Hello, doctor, what are you doing up here at this time of night?—What do you want to see this place for?"

"What do *I* want to see this place for? Young man, little do you know me, or you wouldn't ask such a question. I wish to see *all* the places that's mentioned in the Bible."

"Stuff—this place isn't mentioned in the Bible."

"It ain't mentioned in the Bible!—*this* place ain't—well now, what place *is* this, since you know so much about it?"

"Why it's Scylla and Charybdis."

"Scylla and Cha—confound it, I thought it was Sodom and Gomorrah!"

And he closed up his glass and went below. The above is the ship story. Its plausibility is marred a little by the fact that the Oracle was not a biblical student, and did not spend much of his time instructing himself about Scriptural localities.—They say the Oracle complains, in this hot weather, lately, that the only beverage in the ship that is passable, is the butter. He did not mean butter, of course, but inasmuch as that article remains in a melted state now since we are out of ice, it is fair to give him the credit of getting one long word in the right place, anyhow, for once in his life. He said, in Rome, that the Pope was a noble-looking old man, but he never *did* think much of his *Iliad*.

We spent one pleasant day skirting along the Isles of Greece. They are very mountainous. Their prevailing tints are gray and brown, approaching to red. Little white villages surrounded by trees, nestle in the valleys or roost upon the lofty perpendicular seawalls.

We had one fine sunset—a rich carmine flush that suffused the western sky and cast a ruddy glow far over the sea.—Fine sunsets seem to be rare in this part of the world—or at least, striking ones. They are soft, sensuous, lovely—they are exquisite, refined, effeminate, but we have seen no sunsets here yet like the gorgeous conflagrations that flame in the track of the sinking sun in our high northern latitudes.[4]

Chapter 57

It was worth a kingdom to be at sea again. It was a relief to drop all anxiety whatsoever—all questions as to where we should go; how long we should stay; whether it were worth while to go or not; all anxieties about the condition of the horses; all such questions as "Shall we *ever* get to water?" "Shall we *ever* lunch?" "Ferguson, how many *more* million miles have we got to creep under this awful sun before we camp?"[5] It was a relief to cast all these torturing little anxieties far away—ropes of steel they were, and every one with a separate and distinct strain on it—and feel the temporary contentment that is born of the banishment of all care and responsibility. We did not look at the compass: we did not care, now, where the ship went to, so that she went out of sight of land as quickly as possible. When I travel again, I wish to go in a pleasure ship. No amount of money could have purchased for us, in a strange vessel and among unfamiliar faces, the perfect satisfaction and the sense of being *at home* again which we experienced when we stepped on board the *Quaker City*, —*our own ship*—after this wearisome pilgrimage. It is a something we have felt always when we returned to her, and a something we had no desire to sell.

We took off our blue woollen shirts, our spurs, and heavy boots, our sanguinary revolvers and our buckskin-seated pantaloons, and got

shaved and came out in Christian costume once more. All but Jack, who
changed all other articles of his dress, but clung to his traveling pantaloons. They still preserved their ample buckskin seat intact; and so his
short pea jacket and his long, thin legs assisted to make him a picturesque
object whenever he stood on the forecastle looking abroad upon the
ocean over the bows. At such times his father's last injunction suggested
itself to me. He said:

"Jack, my boy, you are about to go among a brilliant company of gentlemen and ladies, who are refined and cultivated, and thoroughly accomplished in the manners and customs of good society. Listen to their
conversation, study their habits of life, and learn. Be polite and obliging
to all, and considerate towards every one's opinions, failings and prejudices. Command the just respect of all your fellow-voyagers, even though
you fail to win their friendly regard. And Jack—don't you ever dare,
while you live, appear in public on those decks in fair weather, in a costume unbecoming your mother's drawing-room!'"

It would have been worth any price if the father of this hopeful
youth could have stepped on board some time, and seen him standing
high on the forecastle, pea jacket, tasseled red fez, buckskin patch and
all, placidly contemplating the ocean—a rare spectacle for any body's
drawing-room.[6]

Chapter 59

We were at sea now, for a very long voyage—we were to pass through the
entire length of the Levant; through the entire length of the Mediterranean proper, also, and then cross the full width of the Atlantic—a voyage
of several weeks. We naturally settled down into a very slow, stay-at-home
manner of life, and resolved to be quiet, exemplary people, and roam no
more for twenty or thirty days. No more, at least, than from stem to stern
of the ship. It was a very comfortable prospect, though, for we were tired
and needed a long rest.

We were all lazy and satisfied, now, as the meager entries in my notebook (that sure index, to me, of my condition,) prove. What a stupid
thing a note-book gets to be at sea, any way. Please observe the style:

"Sunday—Services, as usual, at four bells. Services at night, also.
No cards."

"Monday—Beautiful day, but rained hard. The cattle purchased at Alexandria for beef ought to be shingled. Or else fattened. The water stands in deep puddles in the depressions forward of their after shoulders. Also here and there all over their backs. It is well they are not cows—it would soak in and ruin the milk. The poor devil eagle[7]——from Syria looks miserable and droopy in the rain, perched on the forward capstan. He appears to have his own opinion of a sea voyage, and if it were put into language and the language solidified, it would probably essentially dam the widest river in the world."

"Tuesday—Somewhere in the neighborhood of the island of Malta. Can not stop there. Cholera. Weather very stormy. Many passengers seasick and invisible."

"Wednesday—Weather still very savage. Storm blew two land birds to sea, and they came on board. A hawk was blown off, also. He circled round and round the ship, wanting to light, but afraid of the people. He was so tired, though, that he had to light, at last, or perish. He stopped in the foretop, repeatedly, and was as often blown away by the wind. At last Harry caught him. Sea full of flying-fish. They rise in flocks of three hundred and flash along above the tops of the waves a distance of two or three hundred feet, then fall and disappear."

"Thursday—Anchored off Algiers, Africa. Beautiful city, beautiful green hilly landscape behind it. Staid half a day and left. Not permitted to land, though we showed a clean bill of health. They were afraid of Egyptian plague and cholera."

"Friday—Morning, dominoes. Afternoon, dominoes. Evening, promenading the decks. Afterwards, charades."

"Saturday—Morning, dominoes. Afternoon, dominoes. Evening, promenading the decks. Afterwards, dominoes."

"Sunday—Morning service, four bells. Evening service, eight bells. Monotony till midnight.—Whereupon, dominoes."

"Monday—Morning, dominoes. Afternoon, dominoes. Evening, promenading the decks. Afterwards, charades and a lecture from Dr. C. Dominoes."

"No date—Anchored off the picturesque city of Cagliari, Sardinia. Staid till midnight, but not permitted to land by these infamous foreigners. They smell inodorously—they do not wash—they dare not risk cholera."

"Thursday—Anchored off the beautiful cathedral city of Malaga, Spain.—Went ashore in the captain's boat—not ashore, either, for they would not let us land. Quarantine. Shipped my newspaper correspondence, which they took with tongs, dipped it in sea water, clipped it full of holes, and then fumigated it with villainous vapors till it smelt like a Spaniard. Inquired about chances to run the blockade and visit the Alhambra at Granada. Too risky—they might hang a body. Set sail—middle of afternoon.

"And so on, and so on, and so forth, for several days. Finally, anchored off Gibraltar, which looks familiar and home-like."[8]

* * *

Returning, Remembering

[From Chapter 60]
The old-fashioned ship-life had returned, now that we were no longer in sight of land. For days and days it continued just the same, one day being exactly like another, and, to me, every one of them pleasant. At last we anchored in the open roadstead of Funchal, in the beautiful islands we call the Madeiras.

The mountains looked surpassingly lovely, clad as they were in living green; ribbed with lava ridges; flecked with white cottages; riven by deep chasms purple with shade; the great slopes dashed with sunshine and mottled with shadows flung from the drifting squadrons of the sky, and the superb picture fitly crowned by towering peaks whose fronts were swept by the trailing fringes of the clouds.

But we could not land. We staid all day and looked, we abused the man who invented quarantine, we held half a dozen mass-meetings and crammed them full of interrupted speeches, motions that fell still-born, amendments that came to nought and resolutions that died from sheer exhaustion in trying to get before the house. At night we set sail.

We averaged four mass-meetings a week for the voyage—we seemed always in labor in this way, and yet so often fallaciously that whenever at long intervals we were safely delivered of a resolution, it was cause for public rejoicing, and we hoisted the flag and fired a salute.

Days passed—and nights; and then the beautiful Bermudas rose out of the sea, we entered the tortuous channel, steamed hither and thither among the bright summer islands, and rested at last under the flag of England and were welcome. We were not a nightmare here, where were civilization and intelligence in place of Spanish and Italian superstition, dirt and dread of cholera. A few days among the breezy groves, the flower gardens, the coral caves, and the lovely vistas of blue water that went curving in and out, disappearing and anon again appearing through jungle walls of brilliant foliage, restored the energies dulled by long drowsing on the ocean, and fitted us for our final cruise—our little run of a thousand miles to New York—America—HOME.

We bade good-bye to "our friends the Bermudians," as our programme hath it—the majority of those we were most intimate with were negroes—and courted the great deep again. I said the majority. We knew more negroes than white people, because we had a deal of washing to be done, but we made some most excellent friends among the whites, whom it will be a pleasant duty to hold long in grateful remembrance. We sailed, and from that hour all idling ceased. Such another system of overhauling, general littering of cabins and packing of trunks we had not seen since we let go the anchor in the harbor of Beirout. Every body was busy. Lists of all purchases had to be made out, and values attached, to facilitate matters at the custom-house. Purchases bought by bulk in partnership had to be equitably divided, outstanding debts canceled, accounts compared, and trunks, boxes and packages labeled. All day long the bustle and confusion continued.

And now came our first accident. A passenger was running through a gangway, between decks, one stormy night, when he caught his foot in the iron staple of a door that had been heedlessly left off a hatchway, and the bones of his leg broke at the ankle. It was our first serious misfortune. We had traveled much more than twenty thousand miles, by land and sea, in many trying climates, without a single hurt, without a serious case of sickness and without a death among five and sixty passengers. Our good fortune had been wonderful. A sailor had jumped overboard at Constantinople one night, and was seen no more, but it was suspected that his object was to desert, and there was a slim chance, at least, that he reached the shore. But the passenger list was complete. There was no name missing from the register.

At last, one pleasant morning, we steamed up the harbor of New York, all on deck, all dressed in Christian garb—by special order, for there was a latent disposition in some quarters to come out as Turks—and amid a waving of handkerchiefs from welcoming friends, the glad pilgrims noted the shiver of the decks that told that ship and pier had joined hands again and the long, strange cruise was over. Amen.[9]

Conclusion

Nearly one year has flown since this notable pilgrimage was ended; and as I sit here at home in San Francisco thinking, I am moved to confess that day by day the mass of my memories of the excursion have grown more and more pleasant as the disagreeable incidents of travel which encumbered them flitted one by one out of my mind—and now, if the *Quaker City* were weighing her anchor to sail away on the very same cruise again, nothing could gratify me more than to be a passenger. With the same captain and even the same pilgrims, the same sinners. I was on excellent terms with eight or nine of the excursionists (they are my staunch friends yet,) and was even on speaking terms with the rest of the sixty-five. I have been at sea quite enough to know that that was a very good average. Because a long sea-voyage not only brings out all the mean traits one has, and exaggerates them, but raises up others which he never suspected he possessed, and even creates new ones. A twelve months' voyage at sea would make of an ordinary man a very miracle of meanness. On the other hand, if a man has good qualities, the spirit seldom moves him to exhibit them on shipboard, at least with any sort of emphasis. Now I am satisfied that our pilgrims are pleasant old people on shore; I am also satisfied that at sea on a second voyage they would be pleasanter, somewhat, than they were on our grand excursion, and so I say without hesitation that I would be glad enough to sail with them again. I could at least enjoy life with my handful of old friends. They could enjoy life with *their* cliques as well—passengers invariably divide up into cliques, on *all* ships.

And I will say, here, that I would rather travel with an excursion party of Methuselahs than have to be changing ships and comrades constantly, as people do who travel in the ordinary way. Those latter are always grieving over some *other* ship they have known and lost, and over *other* comrades whom diverging routes have separated from them. They learn to love a ship just in time to change it for another, and they become attached to a pleasant traveling companion only to lose him. They have that most dismal experience of being in a strange vessel, among strange people who care nothing about them, and of undergoing the customary bullying by strange officers and the insolence of strange servants, repeated over and over again within the compass of every month. They have also that other misery of packing and unpacking trunks—of running the distressing gauntlet of custom-houses—of the anxieties attendant upon getting a mass of baggage from point to point on land in safety. I had rather sail with a whole brigade of patriarchs than suffer so. We never packed our trunks but twice—when we sailed from New York, and when we returned to it. Whenever we made a land journey, we estimated how many days we should be gone and what amount of clothing we should need, figured it down to a mathematical nicety, packed a valise or two accordingly, and left the trunks on board. We chose our comrades from among our old, tried friends, and started. We were never dependent upon strangers for companionship. We often had occasion to pity Americans whom we found traveling drearily among strangers with no friends to exchange pains and pleasures with. Whenever we were coming back from a land journey, our eyes sought one thing in the distance first—the ship—and when we saw it riding at anchor with the flag apeak, we felt as a returning wanderer feels when he sees his home. When we stepped on board, our cares vanished, our troubles were at an end—for the ship was home to us. We always had the same familiar old state-room to go to, and feel safe and at peace and comfortable again.

I have no fault to find with the manner in which our excursion was conducted. Its programme was faithfully carried out—a thing which surprised me, for great enterprises usually promise vastly more than they perform. It would be well if such an excursion could be gotten up every year and the system regularly inaugurated. Travel is fatal to prejudice, bigotry and narrow-mindedness, and many of our people need it sorely on these accounts. Broad, wholesome, charitable views of men and things can not be acquired by vegetating in one little corner of the earth all one's lifetime.[10]

The most important moment of the whole excursion for Samuel Clemens was when his shipboard buddy Charly Langdon introduced him to his sister, Olivia—via a photograph! Clemens was smitten by the image of this young woman with delicate features, as he would vividly and repeatedly recall in later years. He met "Livy" Langdon in person on New Year's Eve 1867, when they attended a reading by Charles Dickens at New York's Steinway Hall. Clemens courted her with a barrage of love letters, such as only he could have written, and won her heart with his words. Her parents, the wealthiest people in Elmira, New York, lived in the city's largest house, where Sam became a frequent guest, overcoming the couple's initial disapproval of his profession, his smoking, and what they had heard of his rowdy past in the West, until they approved their daughter's marriage to him. Samuel Clemens and Olivia Langdon announced their engagement in February 1869, and they married at the Langdon mansion one year later.

6

Back to California, and Back

efore he could publish *The Innocents Abroad*, Mark Twain had to secure the copyright for his letters to the *Alta California*, since the newspaper held the rights and had the legal leeway to collect and publish the letters without the additions and revisions that the author urgently intended to make. That urgency drove Clemens from New York back to California. He boarded the Pacific Mail Steamship Company's *Henry Chauncey* on March 11, 1868, for the leg of the trip to the port of Aspinwall, in the state of Panama, Republic of Colombia (now Colón, Republic of Panama). From there, he took the Panama Railway across the isthmus, covering the distance in three hours, which the veteran traveler considered an immense improvement over the two days it had taken him to traverse the dangerous Nicaragua route in January 1867. On the Pacific side, he took the *Sacramento* to reach San Francisco on April 2, completing a three-week voyage. His old haunts awakened fond memories, and the welcome he received amounted to a personal victory lap. In a mood of pugilistic confidence, he accomplished his mission by May, coming away with full permission to use his own words, a signal victory won during the infancy of copyright law, the vagaries of which would cost Samuel Clemens a fortune from the pirating of the works of Mark Twain.

Clemens retraced his steps from San Francisco to New York City via Panama, this time on the steamer *Montana*, going through the Golden Gate for the last time in his life on July 6. He enjoyed the social life on this vessel, as this published letter testifies.

* * *

From the *Alta California* Letters

The Proper Time to Sail

Editors *Alta*: I think the middle of summer must be the pleasantest season of the year to come East by sea. Going down to the Isthmus in the *Montana*, in the very geographical centre of July, we had smooth water and cool breezes all the time. We enjoyed life very well. We could not easily have done otherwise. There were a hundred and eighty-five quiet, orderly passengers, and ten or fifteen who were willing to be cheerful. These latter were equally divided into a stag party and a Dorcas Society. The stag party held its court on the after guard, and the Dorcas Society, presided over by a gentleman, amused itself in the little social hall amidships. There was considerable talent on the after guard, and some of our little private entertainments were exceedingly creditable. Read one of our programmes — It speaks for itself:

PORT GUARD THEATRE.
New Bill, New Scenery, New Cast.
Powerful Combination.
Dazzling Array of Talent.

The management take pleasure in informing the public that on this evening, July 10, will be presented, for the first time on any ship, the thrilling tragedy of the

COUNTRY SCHOOL EXHIBITION.
Programme:
Dominie, Mr. J. L.

Oration — You'd Scarce expect one of my age .... Mr. G. W.
Recitation — The Boy Stood on the Burning Deck, with his
    Baggage Checked for Troy .... Mr. M.
Duett — Give me Three Grains of Corn,
    Mother .... Messrs. L. & H.
Composition — The Cow .... "M. T."
Declamation — Patrick Henry on War .... Mr. R. R.
Poem — Mary Had a little Lamb .... Mr. O. G.
Chorus — Old John Brown had One little Injun .... School

Instrumental Duett—Comb and Jewsharp......Messrs. J. B. & J. T.
Poem—Twinkle, twinkle, little Star ....Mr. H. M. T.
Recitation—Not a leaf stirred ....Mr. W. W. J.

Any pupil detected in catching flies or throwing spit-balls at the Dominie during the solemnities will be punished. The making of mud pies during school hours is strictly prohibited. Pop-guns and potato-quills are barred. No pupil will be allowed to "go out," unless he shall state what he wants to go out for.

I have seen many theatrical exhibitions, but none that equalled the above. If any of your sea-going friends imagine it is barren of fun, let them get themselves up in boys' costume and try it on the quarter-deck some dull night when other amusements are worn out—or in the way of private party performances in town. The hint is worth a good deal of money. We had a spelling, a reading and a geography class, but their performances were too execrable for complimentary mention. The spelling class spelt cow with a K, and the other two classes were not behind it much in ignorance.

When the Pacific voyage drew to a close, a large delegation of the passengers were sent, with a spokesman, to thank Captain Caverly, with all due ceremony but very heartily, for his watchful care of the comfort and well-being of the people on board, and likewise to thank his officers, through him, for their unfailing politeness, patience, and accommodating spirit toward the passengers (when they did not get a cent more for it than if they had never gone beyond the strict line of their official duties to do kindnesses and favors to the strangers within their ship). Was not that a neater and a more graceful thing to do than it would have been to publish one of those tiresome, stupid newspaper cards, signed by unknown people, and filled with cheap flattery of Captain and officers for "efficiency and attention to duty"? We owe no officers a deluge of compliments for being efficient and minding their business—they are paid in cash for all that and we expect it of them; but distinguished urbanity and gentlemanly conduct are rare and precious things on land and sea, and are not to be had for mere wages or estimated by any standard of dollars and cents, and these it is a pleasure to compliment; only these can make a long sea voyage cheerful and comfortable; and these were the subject of our well-meant and well-received speech-making on board the P.M.S.S. *Montana* at the time I have mentioned.[1]

When he returned home, Mark Twain set out to write a second book. He decided on a prequel to *The Innocents Abroad*, which he called *Roughing It*. In the middle of that book, apropos of nothing, the humorist spun a fantastic yarn about a storm on the ocean, and included a send-up of maritime poetry, set on a canal boat. Some critics have concluded that "The Aged Pilot Man" specifically lampoons "The Rime of the Ancient Mariner" (1798) by Samuel Taylor Coleridge (1772–1834), and that may be so. But the piece seems more like a shotgun blast fired at the whole storied genre of sea poetry than a sniper's bullet targeting only Coleridge's famous epic.

*   *   *

From *Roughing It*, Chapter 51

The Aged Pilot Man

On the Erie Canal, it was,
    All on a summer's day,
I sailed forth with my parents
    Far away to Albany.

From out the clouds at noon that day
    There came a dreadful storm,
That piled the billows high about,
    And filled us with alarm.

A man came rushing from a house,
    Saying, "Snub up[2] your boat I pray,
Snub up your boat, snub up, alas,
    Snub up while yet you may."

Our captain cast one glance astern,
    Then forward glancéd he,
And said, "My wife and little ones
    I never more shall see."

Said Dollinger the pilot man,
    In noble words, but few, —
"Fear not, but lean on Dollinger,
    And he will fetch you through."

The boat drove on, the frightened mules
    Tore through the rain and wind,
And bravely still, in danger's post,
    The whip-boy strode behind.

"Come 'board, come 'board," the captain cried,
    "Nor tempt so wild a storm;"
But still the raging mules advanced,
    And still the boy strode on.

Then said the captain to us all,
    "Alas, 'tis plain to me,
The greater danger is not there,
    But here upon the sea.

"So let us strive, while life remains,
    To save all souls on board,
And then if die at last we must,
    Let . . . I *cannot* speak the word!"

Said Dollinger the pilot man,
    Tow'ring above the crew,
"Fear not, but trust in Dollinger,
    And he will fetch you through."

"Low bridge! low bridge!" all heads went down,
    The laboring bark sped on;
A mill we passed, we passed a church,
    Hamlets, and fields of corn;
And all the world came out to see,
    And chased along the shore

Crying, "Alas, alas, the sheeted rain,
    The wind, the tempest's roar!

Alas, the gallant ship and crew,
    Can *nothing* help them more?"

And from our deck sad eyes looked out
    Across the stormy scene:
The tossing wake of billows aft,
    The bending forests green,

The chickens sheltered under carts
    In lee of barn the cows,
The skurrying swine with straw in mouth,
    The wild spray from our bows!

    "She balances!
    She wavers!
Now let her go about!
If she misses stays and broaches to,
We're all" — (then with a shout,)
    "Huray! huray!
    Avast! belay!
    Take in more sail!
    Lord, what a gale!
Ho, boy, haul taut on the hind mule's tail!

"Ho! lighten ship! ho! man the pump!
    Ho, hostler, heave the lead!

"And count ye all, both great and small,
    As numbered with the dead!
For the mariner for forty year,
    On Erie, boy and man,
I never yet saw such a storm,
    Or one 't with it began!"

So overboard a keg of nails
    And anvils three we threw,
Likewise four bales of gunny-sacks
    Two hundred pounds of glue,

Two sacks of corn, four ditto wheat,
    A box of books, a cow,
A violin, Lord Byron's works,
    A rip-saw and a sow.

A curve! a curve! the dangers grow!
    "Larboard—stabbord—s-t-e-a-d-y!—so!—
Hard-a-port, Do!—hellum-a-lee!
Haw the head mule!—the aft one gee!
    Luff!—bring her to the wind!"

"A quarter-three!—'tis shoaling fast!
    Three feet large!—t-h-r-e-e feet!—
Three feet scant!" I cried in fright;
    "Oh, is there *no* retreat?"

Said Dollinger, the pilot man,
    As on the vessel flew,
"Fear not, but trust in Dollinger,
    And he will fetch you through."

A panic struck the bravest hearts,
    The boldest cheek turned pale;
For plain to all, this shoaling said
A leak had burst the ditch's bed!
And, straight as bolt from crossbow sped,
Our ship swept on, with shoaling lead,
    Before the fearful gale!
"Sever the tow-line! Cripple the mules!"
    Too late! There comes a shock!

      * * * * * *

Another length, and the fated craft
    Would have swum in the saving lock!

Then gathered together the shipwrecked crew
    And took one last embrace,
While sorrowful tears from despairing eyes
    Ran down each hopeless face;

And some did think of their little ones
    Whom they never more might see,
And others of waiting wives at home,
    And mothers that grieved would be.

But of all the children of misery there
    On that poor sinking frame,
But one spake words of hope and faith,
    And I worshipped as they came:
Said Dollinger the pilot man, —
    (O brave heart, strong and true!) —
"Fear not, but trust in Dollinger,
    For he will fetch you through."

Lo! Scarce the words have passed his lips
    The dauntless prophet say'th,
When every soul about him seeth
    A wonder crown his faith!

For straight a farmer brought a plank, —
    (Mysteriously inspired) —
And laying it unto the ship,
    In silent awe retired.
Then every sufferer stood amazed
    That pilot man before;
A moment stood. Then wondering turned,
    And speechless walked ashore.[3]

Voyages to Europe on Passenger Liners

*S*amuel Clemens fell in love with London, having been drawn there for the first time in August 1872 in order to protect his copyright for *Roughing It* (he hadn't made a penny in international royalties for *Innocents Abroad*). The city and its literary glitterati seduced him. He contracted his newfound Anglophilia in the midst of the devastating grief of losing the first child that Livy had given birth to, regrettably prematurely, a sickly little boy they had named Langdon. He died of diphtheria when he was only nineteen months old. A combination of factors, then, pushed and pulled Clemens—distraction therapy for his emotional pain, the allure of London, an escape from his Stateside troubles, and the demands of various business concerns—to cross and recross the Atlantic in the ensuing years. By his own estimate, Clemens made the trans-Atlantic trip forty times!

When he decided to go to England in 1872, his only previous experience on the stormy North Atlantic had been aboard the antiquated *Quaker City*, five years before. This time, he booked passage with the leading company in the seagoing passenger transportation industry, the Cunard Line. On board the *Scotia*, he enjoyed a far more agreeable crossing, this time from New York to Liverpool. The RMS *Scotia* (Fig. 2) was Mark Twain's first "Cunarder." After a week on board, he wrote the following letter to "Livy."

* * *

Letter from RMS *Scotia*

Off Queenstown, Ireland,
Aug. 29/72.
Livy darling, I have little or nothing to write, except that I love you & think of you night & day, & wonder where you are, & what you are

FIGURE 2. Mark Twain's first voyage on a trans-Atlantic "passenger
liner"—as opposed to the *Quaker City*, which had been chartered for
its trip to the Mediterranean by the passengers—and his first time on a
Cunard Line ship was aboard "the last great ocean-going paddle-wheel
steamer—the *Scotia*," as the reverse of this card reads. "She was the
most magnificent ocean steamer of her time."
Will's Cigarettes, "Celebrated Ships, No. 27: RMS *Scotia*," W. D. & H. O. Wills,
Bristol and London, issued by the Imperial Tobacco Co. of Great Britain and Ireland,
Ltd. (1911). Courtesy of the Roorda/Doyle Collection.

doing, & how the Muggins comes on, & whether she ever speaks of me
—& whether mother is cheerful & happy. I hope & trust & pray that
you are all well & enjoying yourselves—but I can't say that I have been
enjoying myself, greatly, lost in a vast ship where our 40 or 50 passengers
flit about in the great dim distances like vagrant spirits. But latterly our
small clique have had a somewhat better time of it, though if one is absent
there can be no whist.

I have given the purser a ten-dollar telegram of 3 words to send to you
from Queenstown, & also my journal in 2 envelopes.

Saml.[1]

Mark Twain kept a journal of his travels in England in 1872, in which he wrote
this description of the Brighton Aquarium. Bracketed insertions are Twain's later
additions.

* * *

From Mark Twain's Journals

Tom Hood & I went down to Brighton (50 miles — 1½ hours) one of the favorite better-class watering places (made popular by Geo. 4 when Prince Regent,) — though in these days Scarborough is the boss place. Watering place. We went with Mr. Lee as his guests & Edmund Routledge preceded us. . . .

 The aquarium is a very large & handsome brick & stone structure whose top is on a level with the sea-front street of Brighton, & consequently one goes down a considerable flight of stairs to enter it. You first find yourself in a (roomy) hall ([Pompeiian] style of architecture) whose roof is supported by graceful columns whose capitals are carved into various kinds of fishes. On one side this opens into another roomy apartment where very complete & excellent breakfasts & dinners are served to all who desire them. On the other side you pass out into a spacious hall & on either side of you are long, tall walls of plate-glass through which one looks into roomy, comfortable chambers (or drawing rooms[)] filled with limpid water, floored with clean sand & enclosed (on three sides) with rugged walls of rock that counterfeit the picturesque caves of the sea — & then the inhabitants! Charming outlandish fishes that soar hither & thither as if in the transparent air, & fascinate one with their graceful forms & dainty colors; monster soldier-crabs & lobsters that go straddling about the sands & making the visitor's flesh crawl; hermit crabs traveling around in borrowed shells; ugly skates, that lie flat on the bottom & remind one of nothing within the possibilities of nature unless it be of a slice off some kind of a devil; still uglier [cuttle-fish] that remind one of an entire devil; prawns, in shoals & schools; fishes that have little slender legs, & walk on them; other fishes that are white when they lie asleep on the bottom, but turn red when they rise up & swim; specimens of a queer fish that takes the roe in his mouth when his wife is delivered of it, & carries it about with him, never allowing her [to] touch it — & circumstances have led to the belief that he washes down his dinner with one or two or a few dozen raw when nobody is looking, for the eggs seem to lose bulk under his protection; beautiful sea-anemones (some white, some pink & some purple) growing like the most natural of flowers, upon jutting headlands of the submerged rocks, & waiting for a chance to suck in & devour any small game that may wander above their treacherous blossoms; and, chief of the show, imposing sea turtles, big enough to carry passengers, go drifting airily about among [the] picturesque caverns of the glass-fronted ocean palace that contains a hundred & ten thousand gallons of water.

It is a wonderful place, the Brighton aquarium, & was a majestic curiosity to me, for I had never seen anything but our little toy affairs before, with half a dozen [goldfish] & a forlorn mud turtle.[2]

Samuel Clemens accumulated a wide repertoire of salty stories to tell and write about during his half-century at sea — tempests of Shakespearian intensity, a grim visitation from cholera, two weeks being becalmed — but none of those true-life adventures was as dramatic as his November 1872 voyage on the Cunard Line *Batavia* from Liverpool to New York, with John Elsey Mouland, the archetypal Cunard Line captain, in command. Captain Mouland guided the *Batavia* through a howling gale, and members of his crew rescued the crew of a sinking sailboat, under perilous circumstances. Mark Twain wrote this letter describing the events:

*   *   *

Letter from SS *Batavia*

On Board Cunard Steamer Batavia,
At Sea, November 20, 1872.
To the Royal Humane Society: —
Gentlemen, — The *Batavia* sailed from Liverpool on Tuesday, November 12. On Sunday night a strong west wind began to blow, not long after midnight it increased to a gale. By four o'clock the sea was running very high; at half-past seven our starboard bulwarks were stove in & the water entered the main saloon; at a later hour the gangway on the port side came in with a crash & the sea followed, flooding many of the staterooms on that side. At the same time a sea crossed the roof of the vessel & carried away one of our boats, splintering it to pieces & taking one of the davits with it. At half-past nine the glass was down to 28.35, & the gale was blowing with a severity which the officers say is not experienced oftener

than once in five or ten years. The storm continued during the day & all night, & also all day yesterday, but with moderated violence.

At 4 P.M. a dismasted vessel was sighted. A furious squall had just broken upon us & the sea was running mountains high, to use the popular expression. Nevertheless Captain Mouland immediately bore up for the wreck (which was making signals of distress), ordered out a life-boat & called for volunteers. To a landsman it seemed like deliberate suicide to go out in such a storm. But our third & fourth officers & eight men answered to the call with a promptness that compelled a cheer. Two of the men lost heart at the last moment, but the others stood fast & were started on their generous enterprise with another cheer. They carried a long line with them, several life buoys, & a lighted lantern, for the atmosphere was murky with the storm, & sunset was not far off.

The wreck, a barque, was in a pitiable condition. Her mainmast was naked, her mizen-mast & bowsprit were gone, & her foremast was but a stump, wreathed & cumbered with a ruin of sails & cordage from the fallen fore-top & fore-top gallant masts & yards. We could see nine men clinging to the main rigging. The stern of the vessel was gone & the sea made a clean breach over her, pouring in a cataract out of the broken stern & spouting through the parted planks of her bows.

Our boat pulled 300 yards & approached the wreck on the lee side. Then it had a hard fight, for the waves & the wind beat it constantly back. I do not know when anything has alternately so stirred me through & through & then disheartened me, as it did to see the boat every little while get almost close enough & then be hurled three lengths away again by a prodigious wave. And the darkness settling down all the time. But at last they got the line & buoy aboard, & after that we could make out nothing more. But presently we discovered the boat approaching us, & found she had saved every soul,—nine men. They had had to drag those men, one at a time, through the sea to the life-boat with the line & buoy— for of course they did not dare to touch the plunging vessel with the boat. The peril increased now, for every time the boat got close to our lee our ship rolled over on her & hid her from sight. But our people managed to haul the party aboard one at a time without losing a man, though I said they would lose every single one of them—I am therefore but a poor success as a prophet. As the fury of the squall had not diminished, & as

the sea was so heavy it was feared we might lose some men if we tried to
hoist the life-boat aboard, so she was turned adrift by the captain's order,
poor thing, after helping in such a gallant deed. But we have plenty more
boats, & very few passengers.

To speak by the log, & be accurate, Captain Mouland gave the order
to change our ship's course & bear down toward the wreck at 4.15 P.M.; at
5.15 our ship was under way again with those nine poor devils on board.
That is to say, this admirable thing was done in a tremendous sea & in the
face of a hurricane, in sixty minutes by the watch,—& if your honorable
society should be moved to give to Captain Mouland & his boat's crew
that reward which a sailor prizes & covets above all other distinctions,
the Royal Humane Society's medal, the parties whose names are signed
to this paper will feel as grateful as if they themselves were the recipients
of this great honor. Those who know him say that Captain Mouland has
risked his life many times to rescue shipwrecked men—in the days when
he occupied a subordinate position—& we hopefully trust that the seed
sown then is about to ripen to its harvest now.

The wrecked barque was the *Charles Ward*, Captain Bell, bound
from Quebec to Scotland with lumber.[3] The vessel went over on her
beam-ends at 9 o'clock Monday morning, & eleven men were washed
overboard & lost. Captain Bell & eight men remained, & these our boat
saved. They had been in the main rigging some thirty-one hours, without food or water, & were so frozen & exhausted that when we got them
aboard they could hardly speak, & the minds of several of them were
wandering. The wreck was out of the ordinary track of vessels, & was
1500 miles from land. She was in the centre of the Atlantic. Our life-boat
crew of volunteers consisted of the following: D. Gillies, third officer;
H. Kyle, fourth d[itt]o.; Nicholas Foley, quartermaster; Henry Foley,
d[itt]o.; Nathaniel Clark, d[itt]o.; Thomas Henry, seaman; John Park,
d[itt]o.; Richard Brennan, d[itt]o.

The officers tell me that those two, the Foley brothers, may be regarded as sort of permanent volunteers—they stand always ready for any
splendid deed of daring.

John Park is a sturdy young sailor, but young as he is I overheard him
say, "Well, that's the third time I've been out on that kind of an expedition." And then he added, with a kindly faith in his species that did him

no discredit, "But it's all right; I'll be in a close place like that myself, some day, & then somebody will do as much for me, I reckon."

When our lifeboat first started away on her mission it was such a gallant sight when she pinnacled herself on the fleecy crest of the first giant wave that our party of passengers, grouped together on deck, with one impulse broke out into cheer upon cheer. Officer Gillies said afterwards that about that time the thought of his wife & children had come upon him & his heart was sinking a bit, but the cheers were strong brandy & water to him & his heart never "went back on him" any more. We would have cheered their heads off only it interrupted the orders so much. Really & truly, these men while on their enterprise were safe at no time except when in the open sea between the vessels; all the time that they were near either the wreck or our own ship their lives were in great peril.

If I have been of any service toward rescuing these nine ship-wrecked human beings by standing around the deck in a furious storm, without any umbrella, keeping an eye on things & seeing that they were done right, & yelling whenever a cheer seemed to be the important thing, I am glad, & I am satisfied. I ask no reward. I would do it again under the same circumstances. But what I do plead for, & earnestly & sincerely, is that the Royal Humane Society will remember our captain & our life-boat crew; &, in so remembering them, increase the high honor & esteem in which the society is held all over the civilized world.

In this appeal our passengers all join with hearty sincerity, & in testimony thereof will sign their names. Begging that you will pardon me, a stranger, for addressing your honored society with such confidence & such absence of ceremony, & trusting that my motive may redeem my manner,

I am, gentlemen,
Your ob't servant,
Mark Twain (Samuel L. Clemens),
Hartford, Conn.

We the undersigned, passengers by the steamer *Batavia*, eye-witnesses of the action described by Mr. Clemens, are glad of this opportunity of expressing our admiration of the gallantry displayed by the volunteers of the lifeboat, & the cool judgment & skill of Captain Mouland in directing the affair, & we feel sure that never has a case more deserving of honorable recognition been brought before the notice of the Royal Humane Society.[4]

Mark Twain's letter to the *Boston Advertiser*, published November 26, the day after the *Batavia* arrived in Boston, immediately gained steam—that of printing presses reproducing it, mostly under the headline "Perils of the Sea," in other newspapers: the *New York Times*, *Boston Evening Transcript*, *Hartford Courant*, *Cleveland Leader*, *London Times*, and *London Morning Post*.

For a period of time after that eventful voyage, Sam and Livy Clemens kept up a personal friendship with Captain Mouland, as illustrated in the following letters.

*   *   *

Letters to Captain Mouland

To John E. Mouland

Hartford, Dec. 3.

Dear Captain:

You must run down next voyage & see us, if you can. Telegraph me what hour you will arrive & I'll go to the station & fetch you home. . . .

My wife is anxious that you should be put in command of the biggest Cunarder afloat, & then she thinks sea-sickness will deal less harshly by her. I hope, also, that you'll have a particularly big ship next May, for I am afraid my wife is going to have a hard time with sea-sickness. . . .

Hartford, Jan. 22.

My Dear Capt—

I am just as glad you got the gold medal, "old man," as if I'd got it myself—I am thoroughly glad. And I am glad the officers & men were so handsomely treated by the Humane Society. . . .

Well, they couldn't have conferred the gold medal on a better man, anyway. But by George, when I think how Wood & the General & I did swell around that perilous upper deck & help give orders it makes me marvel at our own intrepidity!

I am to lecture in N. Y. the last day of this month & the first day or two of Feb. 4. And after that I'm going to peg away at my book & be ready to sail for England in May. My wife said, weeks ago, when we were reading about the immensity & the palatial splendors of some of the other ships, "Well, it is no matter, we will not sail with anybody but Capt. Mouland." So that thing is settled, & entirely to my satisfaction, too. Ah, & won't we cut tobacco & smoke pipes & have a general good time? I rather think so. . . .

Faithfully Yours,
Saml. L. Clemens.[5]

Scenes of the perilous high-seas rescue of the survivors of the *Charles Ward* must have been fresh in Mark Twain's memory in April 1873, when he penned a letter the *New York Tribune* on the subject of shipwrecks.

* * *

Letter to the *New York Tribune*

To the Editor of *The Tribune.*

Sir: When the *Mississippi* was burned at sea some time ago, nearly all her boats were smashed in the effort to cast them loose, or were swamped the instant they struck the water, I wrote you a private letter (which you published) suggesting that ships be provided with life-rafts instead of these almost useless boats. I did not expect that the Government would jump at the suggestion, & I was not disappointed. The Government had business on hand at the time which would benefit not only our nation but the whole world—I mean the project of paying Congressmen over again for work which they had already been paid to do; that is to say, the labor of receiving Crédit Mobilier donations & forgetting the circumstance. But that shining public benefit being accomplished, why cannot the Government listen to me now?

The *Atlantic* had eight boats, of course—all steamers have. Not one of the boats saved a human life. The great cumbersome things were shivered to atoms by the seas that swept over the stranded vessel. And suppose they had not been shivered, would the case have been better? Would not the frantic people have plunged pell-mell into each boat as it was launched & instantly swamped it? They always do. But a life-raft is a different thing. All the people you can put on it cannot swamp it. Nobody understands davit-falls but a sailor, & he don't when he is frightened; but any goose can heave a life-raft overboard, & then some wise man can throw him after it. The sort of life-raft I have in my mind is an American invention, consisting of three inflated horizontal rubber tubes, with a platform lashed on top. These rafts are of all sizes, from a little affair the size of your back door, to a raft 22 feet long & six or eight feet wide. As you remember, no doubt, two men crossed the Atlantic from New York to London, some years ago, on one of these rafts of the latter size. That raft would carry 120 men. Nine such rafts would have saved the *Atlantic*'s 1,000 souls, & these rafts (fully inflated & ready for use) would not have occupied as much room on her deck as four of her lubberly boats; hardly more than the room of three of her boats, indeed. Her boats were probably 30 feet long, seven feet deep, & seven or eight feet [wide].

You could furnish a ship with medium & full-sized rafts—an equal number of each—& pile them up in the space now occupied by four boats, & then you could expect to save all her people, not merely a dozen or two. They would sail away through a storm, sitting high & dry from two to four feet above the tops of the waves. In addition to the rafts, the ship could carry a boat or two, for promiscuous general service, & for the drowning of old fogies who like old established ways. You could attach a raft to a ship with a ten fathom line & heave it overboard on the lee side in the roughest sea (& it can't fall any way but right side up), & there it will lie & ride the waves like a duck till it receives its freight of food & passengers—& then you can cut the line & let her go. But if you launch a boat, it usually falls upside down; & if it don't, the people crowd in & swamp it. Boats have sometimes gone away safely with people & taken them to land, but such accidents are rare.

I am not giving you a mere landsman's views upon this raft business; they are the views of several old sea captains & mates whom I have talked with, & their voice gives them weight & value. Our Government has so many important things to attend to that we cannot reasonably expect it to bother with life-rafts, & we cannot reasonably expect the English Government to bother with them because this admirable contrivance is a Yankee invention, & our mother is not given to adopting our inventions until she has had time to hunt around among her documents & discover that the crude idea originated with herself in some bygone time—then she adopts it & builds a monument to the crude originator. England has our life-raft on exhibition in a museum over there (the raft that made the wonderful voyage), & heaps of people have gone in every day for several years & paid for the privilege of looking at it. Perhaps many a bereaved poor soul whose idols lie stark & dead under the waves that wash the beach of Nova Scotia may wish, as I do, that it had been on exhibition on board the betrayed *Atlantic*.

Mark Twain.[6]

When Clemens made arrangements to travel to Europe in May 1873, he reserved a cabin for two (plus their first child and a maid) aboard the *Batavia*; it would be his wife Livy's first time at sea. Captain Mouland charmed Mrs. Clemens (seasickness did not), as she wrote in a letter to her mother: "Capt. Mouland is just about perfection, he has done every thing that he possibly could to make us comfortable and to make things pleasant for us. . . . The table is very good indeed but we lack appetites some what. . . . We have had two or three very rough days, not stormy but the waves high so that the vessel rocks frightfully."[7]

When the time came for Sam and Livy to go home, the *Batavia* was the only way to cross, in Mrs. Clemens's admiring eyes. They left on October 29 from Liverpool, headed to New York, with the dashing Captain Mouland at the helm. Clemens reported the following in a letter to his friend John Brown.

* * *

Letter from SS *Batavia*

Cunard Steam Ship *Batavia*
Oct. 30.
Our dear friend the doctor:

We have plowed a long way over the sea, & there's twenty-two hundred miles of restless water between us, now, beside the railway stretch. And yet you are so present with us, so close to us that a span & a whisper would bridge the distance.

The first three days were stormy, & wife, child, maid & Mrs. & Miss Spaulding were all sea-sick 25 hours out of the 24, & I was sorry I ever started. However, it has been smooth, & balmy, & sunny & altogether lovely for a day or two now, & at night there is a broad luminous highway stretching over the sea to the moon, over which the spirits of the sea are traveling up & down all through the secret night & having a genuine good time, I make no doubt.

To-day they discovered a "collie" on board! I find (as per advertisement which I sent you) that they won't carry dogs in these ships at any price. This one has been concealed up to this time. Now his owner has to pay £10 or heave him. Fortunately the doggie is a performing doggie & the money will be paid. So after all it was just as well you didn't entrust your collie to us.

A poor little child died at midnight & was buried at dawn this morning—sheeted & shotted & sunk in the middle of the lonely ocean in water three thousand fathoms deep. Pity the poor mother.

With our love,

S. L. Clemens[8]

Mark Twain turned on his heel and returned to Liverpool within days, on November 10, but this time he opted for the *City of Chester* of the Inman Line (Fig. 3) for what was becoming the usual commute from New York to Liverpool.

As the *City of Chester* departed, he dashed off a letter to his wife, who was at home with their nineteen-month-old daughter, Olivia Susan, known as "Susy." Her father dubbed the child "the Modoc," a Native American tribe of northern California and Oregon, who escaped their reservation, lost the "Modoc War," and had to relocate to Oklahoma in 1873.

* * *

Letters from the *City of Chester*

9 A.M.

Livy darling, it is just a lovely ship, & this smoking room is perfection.

The *Batavia* left considerably ahead of us, but we overtook her in half an hour & swept by her as if she were standing still. She looks like a yawl beside this vast vessel. Capt. Mouland sent a very regretful letter, which smote me. Bless you, dear old darling, & good-by. Kiss mother & the Modoc.

Saml

FIGURE 3. After several laps back and forth across the stormy North Atlantic aboard "Cunarders," Mark Twain booked a berth on the Inman Line's *City of Chester*, which he found to be an immense improvement.

Inman Line, Inman & International Steamship Comp'y, Limited, list of Saloon Passengers (1889). Courtesy of the Roorda/Doyle Collection.

On Shipboard,
3 days out from N. Y.
Livy darling, you really don't know what a steamship is. The *Batavia* is
316 feet long. This ship is nearly 500. The great dining saloon is square,
stretches from side to side of the vessel; has 8 tables in it (each seating
only 14 people); is brightly lighted by long rows of side-ports [and] is elegantly "papered" with polished fancy wood. The two ends are just great
mirrors framed in fluted columns of polished dark wood; there is a piano
& elegant book cases; the ship does not rock & pitch,—so we do not
need racks on the table; there are no staterooms anywhere near,—so you
eat in peace & hear no nasty sounds of vomiting in your vicinity. When
we passed the *Batavia* she was wildly rolling & plunging, but our ship
was as steady as a prairie.

The smoking room is prettily upholstered & lighted with big windows, & has six marble-top card-tables in it.

My port[hole] is so large that I can lie in my berth (on a delicious
spring mattress) & read, as if out of doors.

At night I can read with perfect ease (& all night long,) for a swinging
lamp hangs above my head. I can lie there & pull a knob & a flood of
clean water gushes into my wash-bowl. At any hour of the whole night I
can turn over & touch an electrical bell & a steward comes in a moment.
My comb & tooth brush lie always on a smooth, level surface & the trifling motion of the ship never disturbs them. Wherever I place my shoes
or any other article, there they remain.

The ship & the smoking room & ladies' upper deck saloons are
warmed by steam.

Our first day's run (simply under steam) was over 350 miles.

The hallways are wide & light & comfortable. The stairways are of
elegant workmanship, & easy of ascent & descent. No danger of breaking
one's neck, & no need to take hold of the balusters. The ship is thoroughly well ordered, officered & served. The captain has commanded
steamers more than 20 years & never lost one.

The library is large & singularly well selected.

It is a charming ship. The time slides by in comfort & satisfaction &
I seem to enjoy every hour of it. I do so regret taking you in the *Batavia*,
for this captain would have been just as kind to you & would have put the

thousand resources of the ship at the service of yourself & the Modoc. Your journey would have been a hundred times pleasanter. . . .

Telegraphed you. Also wrote from N. Y., & also by the pilot.[9]

7th day out.

Livy darling, we have had a half-gale & a very tumultuous sea for 2 days & nights, & I found that this ship could roll, though nothing compared to the *Batavia*. The seas swept the ship several times & gushed through the saloon in volumes. Last night at dinner fifty dishes leaped clear off the table & fell in one common ruin. My dead-light did not fit closely, & so all night the seas came in—my floor got as much as a barrel of water, altogether. Now the port is well caulked with tallow & is all right. I have read all night during this weather.—Sleep would only tire me. Yesterday two or three people were hurt by being thrown down on the deck. A lurch ~~sent a~~ hurled a steerage passenger across the ship & against a boat. People heard the concussion a great distance. He wilted down limp & senseless.

But she is a much more comfortable ship than any Cunarder. . . .

Saml.[10]

Despite these unfavorable comments, Clemens was back aboard a Cunarder at the start of 1874, embarking on the *Parthia* on January 13 for the trip back to the United States, from Liverpool to Boston. More than three years would pass before his next ocean voyage.

8

Escapes and Excursions

Mark Twain composed his twin masterpieces *The Adventures of Tom Sawyer* and *The Adventures of Huckleberry Finn* during the mid-1870s, a relatively sedentary period in his life, when the Clemens clan spent their summers in Livy's hometown of Elmira, New York. They split their time between her family's stately house in town, where her mother resided, and the house on a hilltop where Livy's sister, Susan, and her husband, Theodore Crane, lived, in a happy little world apart named Quarry Hill Farm. Mark Twain wrote both *Tom* and *Huck* there. He did so in an octagonal gazebo that his considerate and perceptive sister-in-law decided he needed and had built for him in 1874, set apart on a spur of Quarry Hill. It was a sunny study with commanding views all around, something like the pilothouse of a steamboat or the bridge of a ship. Perhaps that has something to do with all the salty references contained in the books Twain wrote there, summer after fruitful summer. And the two works that tower above the others have their share of salt.

In *The Adventures of Tom Sawyer* (1876), when Huckleberry Finn and his friends form a "Gang," they elect Tom "first captain" and Joe Harper "second captain" of the Gang. After Becky Thatcher, the love of Tom's life, shuns him in the schoolyard, he and Joe decide to run away. Then they have to choose a career path.

* * *

From *The Adventures of Tom Sawyer*, Chapter 8

The Young Pirates

As the two boys walked sorrowing along, they made a new compact to stand by each other and be brothers and never separate till death relieved them of their troubles. Then they began to lay their plans. Joe was for being a hermit, and living on crusts in a remote cave, and dying, some time, of cold and want and grief; but after listening to Tom, he conceded that there were some conspicuous advantages about a life of crime, and so he consented to be a pirate.

Three miles below St. Petersburg, at a point where the Mississippi River was a trifle over a mile wide, there was a long, narrow, wooded island, with a shallow bar at the head of it, and this offered well as a rendezvous. It was not inhabited; it lay far over toward the further shore, abreast a dense and almost wholly unpeopled forest. So Jackson's Island was chosen. Who were to be the subjects of their piracies was a matter that did not occur to them. Then they hunted up Huckleberry Finn, and he joined them promptly, for all careers were one to him; he was indifferent. They presently separated to meet at a lonely spot on the river-bank two miles above the village at the favorite hour—which was midnight. There was a small log raft there which they meant to capture. Each would bring hooks and lines, and such provision as he could steal in the most dark and mysterious way—as became outlaws. And before the afternoon was done, they had all managed to enjoy the sweet glory of spreading the fact that pretty soon the town would "hear something." All who got this vague hint were cautioned to "be mum and wait."

About midnight Tom arrived with a boiled ham and a few trifles, and stopped in a dense undergrowth on a small bluff overlooking the meeting-place. It was starlight, and very still. The mighty river lay like an ocean at rest. Tom listened a moment, but no sound disturbed the quiet. Then he gave a low, distinct whistle. It was answered from under the bluff. Tom whistled twice more; these signals were answered in the same way. Then a guarded voice said:

"Who goes there?"

"Tom Sawyer, the Black Avenger of the Spanish Main. Name your names."

"Huck Finn the Red-Handed, and Joe Harper the Terror of the Seas." Tom had furnished these titles, from his favorite literature.

" 'Tis well. Give the countersign."

Two hoarse whispers delivered the same awful word simultaneously to the brooding night:

"BLOOD!"

Then Tom tumbled his ham over the bluff and let himself down after it, tearing both skin and clothes to some extent in the effort. There was an easy, comfortable path along the shore under the bluff, but it lacked the advantages of difficulty and danger so valued by a pirate.

The Terror of the Seas had brought a side of bacon, and had about worn himself out with getting it there. Finn the Red-Handed had stolen a skillet and a quantity of half-cured leaf tobacco, and had also brought a few corn-cobs to make pipes with. But none of the pirates smoked or "chewed" but himself. The Black Avenger of the Spanish Main said it would never do to start without some fire. That was a wise thought; matches were hardly known there in that day. They saw a fire smouldering upon a great raft a hundred yards above, and they went stealthily thither and helped themselves to a chunk. They made an imposing adventure of it, saying, "Hist!" every now and then, and suddenly halting with finger on lip; moving with hands on imaginary dagger-hilts; and giving orders in dismal whispers that if "the foe" stirred, to "let him have it to the hilt," because "dead men tell no tales." They knew well enough that the raftsmen were all down at the village laying in stores or having a spree, but still that was no excuse for their conducting this thing in an unpiratical way.

They shoved off, presently, Tom in command, Huck at the after oar and Joe at the forward. Tom stood amidships, gloomy-browed, and with folded arms, and gave his orders in a low, stern whisper:

"Luff, and bring her to the wind!"

"Aye-aye, sir!"

"Steady, steady-y-y-y!"

"Steady it is, sir!"

"Let her go off a point!"

"Point it is, sir!"

As the boys steadily and monotonously drove the raft toward midstream it was no doubt understood that these orders were given only for "style," and were not intended to mean anything in particular.

"What sail's she carrying?"

"Courses, tops'ls, and flying-jib, sir."

"Send the r'yals up! Lay out aloft, there, half a dozen of ye—foretopmaststuns'l! Lively, now!"

"Aye-aye, sir!"

"Shake out that maintogalans'l! Sheets and braces! Now my hearties!"

"Aye-aye, sir!"

"Hellum-a-lee—hard a port! Stand by to meet her when she comes! Port, port! Now, men! With a will! Stead-y-y-y!"

"Steady it is, sir!" . . .

The Black Avenger stood still with folded arms, "looking his last" upon the scene of his former joys and his later sufferings, and wishing "she"[1] could see him now, abroad on the wild sea, facing peril and death with dauntless heart, going to his doom with a grim smile on his lips.[2]

During his picaresque wanderings, Huckleberry Finn encounters two tellers of tall tales, "the king"—"the pore disappeared Dauphin, Looy the Seventeen"—and "the Duke of Bridgewater." After these charlatans meet, the king persists in calling the duke "Bilgewater," a reference to the foul-smelling liquid that accumulates in the deepest bowels of a ship. When they come across a "camp meeting," a back country religious revival convened by an itinerant member of the evangelical clergy, the king takes on a maritime persona to milk the faithful, gullible crowd.

* * *

From *The Adventures of Huckleberry Finn*, Chapter 20

The Duke of Bilgewater and the Dauphin King Looey
"Oh, come to the mourners' bench! come, black with sin! (Amen!) come, sick and sore! (Amen!) come, lame and halt and blind! (Amen!) come, pore and needy, sunk in shame! (A-A-Men!) come, all that's worn and soiled and suffering!—come with a broken spirit! come with a contrite heart! come in your rags and sin and dirt! the waters that cleanse is free, the door of heaven stands open—oh, enter in and be at rest!" (A-A-Men! Glory, Glory Hallelujah!)

And so on. You couldn't make out what the preacher said any more, on account of the shouting and crying. Folks got up everywheres in the crowd, and worked their way just by main strength to the mourners' bench, with the tears running down their faces; and when all the mourners had got up there to the front benches in a crowd, they sung and shouted and flung themselves down on the straw, just crazy and wild.

Well, the first I knowed the king got a-going, and you could hear him over everybody; and next he went a-charging up on to the platform, and the preacher he begged him to speak to the people, and he done it. He told them he was a pirate—been a pirate for thirty years out in the Indian Ocean—and his crew was thinned out considerable last spring in a fight, and he was home now to take out some fresh men, and thanks to goodness he'd been robbed last night and put ashore off of a steamboat without a cent, and he was glad of it; it was the blessedest thing that ever happened to him, because he was a changed man now, and happy for the first time in his life; and, poor as he was, he was going to start right off and work his way back to the Indian Ocean, and put in the rest of his life trying to turn the pirates into the true path; for he could do it better than anybody else, being acquainted with all pirate crews in that ocean; and though it would take him a long time to get there without money, he would get there anyway, and every time he convinced a pirate he would say to him, "Don't you thank me, don't you give me no credit; it all belongs to them dear people in Pokeville camp-meeting, natural brothers and benefactors of the race, and that dear preacher there, the truest friend a pirate ever had!"

And then he busted into tears, and so did everybody. Then somebody sings out, "Take up a collection for him, take up a collection!" Well, a half a dozen made a jump to do it, but somebody sings out, "Let him pass the hat around!" Then everybody said it, the preacher too.

So the king went all through the crowd with his hat swabbing his eyes, and blessing the people and praising them and thanking them for being so good to the poor pirates away off there; and every little while the prettiest kind of girls, with the tears running down their cheeks, would up and ask him would he let them kiss him for to remember him by; and he always done it; and some of them he hugged and kissed as many as five or six times—and he was invited to stay a week; and everybody wanted him to live in their houses, and said they'd think it was an honor; but he said as this was the last day of the camp-meeting he couldn't do no good, and besides he was in a sweat to get to the Indian Ocean right off and go to work on the pirates.

When we got back to the raft and he come to count up he found he had collected eighty-seven dollars and seventy-five cents. And then he had fetched away a three-gallon jug of whisky, too, that he found under a wagon when he was starting home through the woods. The king said, take it all around, it laid over any day he'd ever put in in the missionarying line. He said it warn't no use talking, heathens don't amount to shucks alongside of pirates to work a camp-meeting with.[3]

After being away from the sea for three years, Clemens decided to take a voyage to Bermuda. In a letter to his sister-in-law, Susan Crane, sent prior to his departure from New York on May 17, 1877, Clemens expressed his frame of mind at the time, with reference to Quarry Hill Farm, where his hilltop writing retreat overlooked Elmira, New York: "I am going on a sea voyage. . . . It is to get the devil out of my head so that I can start fresh at the farm early June."[4] He wrote about this sea voyage in the *Atlantic Monthly*.

* * *

From "Some Rambling Notes of an Idle Excursion"

Chapter 1

All the journeyings I had ever done had been purely in the way of business. The pleasant May weather suggested a novelty, namely, a trip for pure recreation, the bread-and-butter element left out. The Reverend said he would go, too; a good man, one of the best of men, although a clergyman. By eleven at night we were in New Haven and on board the New York boat. We bought our tickets, and then went wandering around here and there, in the solid comfort of being free and idle, and of putting distance between ourselves and the mails and telegraphs. . . .

The next day, in New York, was a hot one. Still we managed to get more or less entertainment out of it. Toward the middle of the afternoon we arrived on board the staunch steamship *Bermuda*, with bag and baggage, and hunted for a shady place. It was blazing summer weather, until we were half-way down the harbor. Then I buttoned my coat closely; half an hour later I put on a spring overcoat and buttoned that. As we passed the light-ship I added an ulster and tied a handkerchief around the collar to hold it snug to my neck. So rapidly had the summer gone and winter come again!

By nightfall we were far out at sea, with no land in sight. No telegrams could come here, no letters, no news. This was an uplifting thought. It was still more uplifting to reflect that the millions of harassed people on shore behind us were suffering just as usual.

The next day brought us into the midst of the Atlantic solitudes—out of smoke-colored sounding into fathomless deep blue; no ships visible anywhere over the wide ocean; no company but Mother Carey's chickens wheeling, darting, skimming the waves in the sun.[5]

There were some seafaring men among the passengers, and conversation drifted into matters concerning ships and sailors. One said that "true as the needle to the pole" was a bad figure, since the needle seldom pointed to the pole. He said a ship's compass was not faithful to any particular point, but was the most fickle and treacherous of the servants of man. It was forever changing. It changed every day in the year; consequently the amount of the daily variation had to be ciphered out and allowance made for it, else the mariner would go utterly astray. Another said there was a vast fortune waiting for the genius who should invent a compass that would not be affected by the local influences of an iron ship. He said there was only one creature more fickle than a wooden ship's compass, and that was the compass of an iron ship. Then came reference to the well known fact that an experienced mariner can look at the compass of a new iron vessel, thousands of miles from her birthplace, and tell which way her head was pointing when she was in process of building.

Now an ancient whale-ship master fell to talking about the sort of crews they used to have in his early days. Said he:

"Sometimes we'd have a batch of college students. Queer lot. Ignorant? Why, they didn't know the catheads from the main brace. But if you took them for fools you'd get bit, sure. They'd learn more in a month than another man would in a year. We had one, once, in the *Mary Ann*, that came aboard with gold spectacles on. And besides, he was rigged out from main truck to keelson in the nobbiest clothes that ever saw a fo'castle. He had a chestful, too: cloaks, and broadcloth coats, and velvet vests; everything swell, you know; and didn't the saltwater fix them out for him? I guess not! Well, going to sea, the mate told him to go aloft and help shake out the foreto'gallants'l. Up he shins to the foretop, with his spectacles on, and in a minute down he comes again, looking insulted. Says the mate, 'What did you come down for?' Says the chap, 'P'r'aps you didn't notice that there ain't any ladders above there.' You see we hadn't any shrouds above the foretop. The men bursted out in a laugh such as I guess you never heard the like of. Next night, which was dark and rainy, the mate ordered this chap to go aloft about something, and I'm dummed if he didn't start up with an umbrella and a lantern! But no matter; he made a mighty good sailor before the voyage was done, and we had to hunt up something else to laugh at. Years afterwards, when I had forgot all about him, I comes into Boston, mate of a ship, and was loafing around town with the second mate, and it so happened that we stepped into the Revere House, thinking maybe we would chance the salt-horse in that big dining-room for a flyer, as the boys say. Some fellows were talking just at our elbow, and one says, 'Yonder's the new governor of Massachusetts — at that table over there with the ladies.' We took a good look my mate and I, for we hadn't either of us ever seen a governor before. I looked and looked at that face and then all of a sudden it popped on me! But I didn't give any sign. Says I, 'Mate, I've a notion to go over and shake hands with him.' Says he, 'I think I see you doing it, Tom.' Says I, 'Mate I'm a-going to do it.' Says he, 'Oh, yes, I guess so. Maybe you don't want to bet you will, Tom?' Say I, 'I don't mind going a V on it, mate.' Says he 'Put it up.' 'Up she goes,' says I, planking the cash. This surprised him. But he covered it, and says pretty sarcastic, 'Hadn't you better take your grub with the governor and the ladies, Tom?' Says I, 'Upon second thoughts, I will.' Says he, 'Well Tom, you are a dum fool.' Says I, 'Maybe I am maybe I ain't; but the main question is, do you want to risk two and a half that I won't do it?' 'Make it a V,' says he. 'Done,' says I. I started, him a-giggling and slapping his hand on his thigh, he felt so good. I went over there and leaned my knuckles on the table a minute and looked the governor in the face, and says I, 'Mr. Gardner, don't you know me?' He stared, and I stared, and he stared. Then all of a sudden he sings out, 'Tom Bowling, by the holy poker! Ladies, it's old Tom Bowling, that you've heard me talk about — shipmate of mine in the *Mary Ann*.' He rose up and shook hands with me ever so hearty — I sort

of glanced around and took a realizing sense of my mate's saucer eyes
—and then says the governor, 'Plant yourself, Tom, plant yourself; you
can't cat your anchor again till you've had a feed with me and the ladies!' I
planted myself alongside the governor, and canted my eye around toward
my mate. Well, sir, his dead-lights were bugged out like tompions; and his
mouth stood that wide open that you could have laid a ham in it without
him noticing it."

There was great applause at the conclusion of the old captain's story;
then, after a moment's silence, a grave, pale young man said:

"Had you ever met the governor before?"

The old captain looked steadily at this inquirer awhile, and then got
up and walked aft without making any reply. One passenger after another
stole a furtive glance at the inquirer; but failed to make him out, and so
gave him up. It took some little work to get the talk-machinery to running smoothly again after this derangement; but at length a conversation sprang up about that important and jealously guarded instrument, a
ship's timekeeper, its exceeding delicate accuracy, and the wreck and de-
struction that have sometimes resulted from its varying a few seemingly
trifling moments from the true time; then, in due course, my comrade,
the Reverend, got off on a yarn, with a fair wind and everything drawing.
It was a true story, too—about Captain Rounceville's shipwreck—true in
every detail. It was to this effect:

Captain Rounceville's vessel was lost in mid-Atlantic, and likewise his
wife and his two little children. Captain Rounceville and seven seamen
escaped with life, but with little else. A small, rudely constructed raft was
to be their home for eight days. They had neither provisions nor water.
They had scarcely any clothing; no one had a coat but the captain. This
coat was changing hands all the time, for the weather was very cold. Whenever a man became exhausted with the cold, they put the coat on him and
laid him down between two shipmates until the garment and their bodies
had warmed life into him again. Among the sailors was a Portuguese who
knew no English. He seemed to have no thought of his own calamity, but
was concerned only about the captain's bitter loss of wife and children.
By day he would look his dumb compassion in the captain's face; and by
night, in the darkness and the driving spray and rain, he would seek out
the captain and try to comfort him with caressing pats on the shoulder.

One day, when hunger and thirst were making their sure inroads upon the men's strength and spirits, a floating barrel was seen at a distance. It seemed a great find, for doubtless it contained food of some sort. A brave fellow swam to it, and after long and exhausting effort got it to the raft. It was eagerly opened. It was a barrel of magnesia! On the fifth day an onion was spied. A sailor swam off and got it. Although perishing with hunger, he brought it in its integrity and put it into the captain's hand. The history of the sea teaches that among starving, shipwrecked men selfishness is rare, and a wonder-compelling magnanimity the rule. The onion was equally divided into eight parts, and eaten with deep thanksgivings. On the eighth day a distant ship was sighted. Attempts were made to hoist an oar, with Captain Rounceville's coat on it for a signal. There were many failures, for the men were but skeletons now, and strengthless. At last success was achieved, but the signal brought no help. The ship faded out of sight and left despair behind her. By and by another ship appeared, and passed so near that the castaways, every eye eloquent with gratitude, made ready to welcome the boat that would be sent to save them. But this ship also drove on, and left these men staring their unutterable surprise and dismay into each other's ashen faces. Late in the day, still another ship came up out of the distance, but the men noted with a pang that her course was one which would not bring her nearer. Their remnant of life was nearly spent; their lips and tongues were swollen, parched, cracked with eight days' thirst; their bodies starved; and here was their last chance gliding relentlessly from them; they would not be alive when the next sun rose. For a day or two past the men had lost their voices, but now Captain Rounceville whispered, "Let us pray." The Portuguese patted him on the shoulder in sign of deep approval. All knelt at the base of the oar that was waving the signal-coat aloft, and bowed their heads. The sea was tossing; the sun rested, a red, rayless disk, on the sea-line in the west. When the men presently raised their heads they would have roared a hallelujah if they had had a voice—the ship's sails lay wrinkled and flapping against her masts—she was going about! Here was rescue at last, and in the very last instant of time that was left for it. No, not rescue yet —only the imminent prospect of it. The red disk sank under the sea, and darkness blotted out the ship. By and by came a pleasant sound—oars moving in a boat's rowlocks. Nearer it came, and nearer—within thirty steps, but nothing visible. Then a deep voice: "Hol-lo!" The castaways could not answer; their swollen tongues refused voice. The boat skirted round and round the raft, started away—the agony of it!—returned, rested the oars, close at hand, listening, no doubt. The deep voice again: "Hol-lo! Where are ye, shipmates?" Captain Rounceville whispered to his men, saying: "Whisper your best, boys! now—all at once!" So they sent out an eightfold whisper in hoarse concert: "Here!," There was life in it if it succeeded; death if it failed. After that supreme moment Captain Rounceville was conscious of nothing until he came to himself on board the saving ship. Said the Reverend, concluding:

"There was one little moment of time in which that raft could be visible from that ship, and only one. If that one little fleeting moment had passed unfruitful, those men's doom was sealed. As close as that does God shave events foreordained from the beginning of the world. When the sun reached the water's edge that day, the captain of that ship was sitting on deck reading his prayer-book. The book fell; he stooped to pick it up, and happened to glance at the sun. In that instant that far-off raft appeared for a second against the red disk, its needlelike oar and diminutive signal cut sharp and black against the bright surface, and in the next instant was thrust away into the dusk again. But that ship, that captain, and that pregnant instant had had their work appointed for them in the dawn of time and could not fail of the performance. The chronometer of God never errs!"

There was deep, thoughtful silence for some moments. Then the grave, pale young man said:

"What is the chronometer of God?"

Chapter 2

At dinner, six o'clock, the same people assembled whom we had talked with on deck and seen at luncheon and breakfast this second day out, and at dinner the evening before. That is to say, three journeying shipmasters, a Boston merchant, and a returning Bermudian who had been absent from his Bermuda thirteen years; these sat on the starboard side. On the port side sat the Reverend in the seat of honor; the pale young man next to him; I next; next to me an aged Bermudian, returning to his sunny islands after an absence of twenty-seven years. Of course, our captain was at the head of the table, the purser at the foot of it. A small company, but small companies are pleasantest.

No racks upon the table; the sky cloudless, the sun brilliant, the blue sea scarcely ruffled; then what had become of the four married couples, the three bachelors, and the active and obliging doctor from the rural districts of Pennsylvania?—for all these were on deck when we sailed down New York harbor. This is the explanation. I quote from my note-book:

Thursday, 3.30 P.M. Under way, passing the Battery. The large party, of four married couples, three bachelors, and a cheery, exhilarating doctor from the wilds of Pennsylvania, are evidently traveling together. All but the doctor grouped in camp-chairs on deck.

Passing principal fort. The doctor is one of those people who has an infallible preventive of seasickness; is flitting from friend to friend administering it and saying, "Don't you be afraid; I know this medicine; absolutely infallible; prepared under my own supervision." Takes a dose himself, intrepidly.

4.15 P.M. Two of those ladies have struck their colors, notwithstanding the "infallible." They have gone below. The other two begin to show distress.

5 P.M. Exit one husband and one bachelor. These still had their infallible in cargo when they started, but arrived at the companion-way without it.

5.10. Lady No. 3, two bachelors, and one married man have gone below with their own opinion of the infallible.

5.20. Passing Quarantine Hulk. The infallible has done the business for all the party except the Scotchman's wife and the author of that formidable remedy.

Nearing the Light-Ship. Exit the Scotchman's wife, head drooped on stewardess's shoulder.

Entering the open sea. Exit doctor!

The rout seems permanent; hence the smallness of the company at table since the voyage began. Our captain is a grave, handsome Hercules of thirty-five, with a brown hand of such majestic size that one cannot eat for admiring it and wondering if a single kid or calf could furnish material for gloving it. . . .

Twice since we left port our engines have stopped for a couple of minutes at a time. Now they stop again. Says the pale young man, meditatively, "There!—that engineer is sitting down to rest again."

Grave stare from the captain, whose mighty jaws cease to work, and whose harpooned potato stops in midair on its way to his open, paralyzed mouth. Presently he says in measured tones, "Is it your idea that the engineer of this ship propels her by a crank turned by his own hands?"

The pale young man studies over this a moment, then lifts up his guileless eyes, and says, "Don't he?"

Thus gently falls the death-blow to further conversation, and the dinner drags to its close in a reflective silence, disturbed by no sounds but the murmurous wash of the sea and the subdued clash of teeth.

After a smoke and a promenade on deck, where is no motion to discompose our steps, we think of a game of whist. We ask the brisk and capable stewardess from Ireland if there are any cards in the ship.

"Bless your soul, dear, indeed there is. Not a whole pack, true for ye, but not enough missing to signify."

However, I happened by accident to bethink me of a new pack in a morocco case, in my trunk, which I had placed there by mistake, thinking it to be a flask of something. So a party of us conquered the tedium of the evening with a few games and were ready for bed at six bells, mariner's time, the signal for putting out the lights.

There was much chat in the smoking-cabin on the upper deck after luncheon to-day, mostly whaler yarns from those old sea-captains. Captain Tom Bowling was garrulous. He had that garrulous attention to minor detail which is born of secluded farm life or life at sea on long voyages, where there is little to do and time no object. He would sail along till he was right in the most exciting part of a yarn, and then say, "Well, as I was saying, the rudder was fouled, ship driving before the gale, head-on, straight for the iceberg, all hands holding their breath, turned to stone, top-hamper giving 'way, sails blown to ribbons, first one stick going, then another, boom! smash! crash! duck your head and stand from under! when up comes Johnny Rogers, capstan-bar in hand, eyes a-blazing, hair a-flying . . . no, 'twa'n't Johnny Rogers . . . lemme see . . . seems to me Johnny Rogers wa'n't along that voyage; he was along one voyage, I know that mighty well, but somehow it seems to me that he signed the articles for this voyage, but—but—whether he come along or not, or got left, or something happened—"

And so on and so on till the excitement all cooled down and nobody cared whether the ship struck the iceberg or not.

In the course of his talk he rambled into a criticism upon New England degrees of merit in ship building. Said he, "You get a vessel built away down Maine-way; Bath, for instance; what's the result? First thing you do, you want to heave her down for repairs—that's the result! Well, sir, she hain't been hove down a week till you can heave a dog through her seams. You send that vessel to sea, and what's the result? She wets her oakum the first trip! Leave it to any man if 'tain't so. Well, you let our folks build you a vessel—down New Bedford-way. What's the result? Well, sir, you might take that ship and heave her down, and keep her hove down six months, and she'll never shed a tear!"

Everybody, landsmen and all, recognized the descriptive neatness of that figure, and applauded, which greatly pleased the old man. A moment later, the meek eyes of the pale young fellow heretofore mentioned came up slowly, rested upon the old man's face a moment, and the meek mouth began to open.

"Shet your head!" shouted the old mariner.

It was a rather startling surprise to everybody, but it was effective in the matter of its purpose. So the conversation flowed on instead of perishing.

There was some talk about the perils of the sea, and a landsman delivered himself of the customary nonsense about the poor mariner wandering in far oceans, tempest-tossed, pursued by dangers, every storm-blast and thunderbolt in the home skies moving the friends by snug firesides to compassion for that poor mariner, and prayers for his succor. Captain Bowling put up with this for a while, and then burst out with a new view of the matter.

"Come, belay there! I have read this kind of rot all my life in poetry and tales and such-like rubbage. Pity for the poor mariner! sympathy for the poor mariner! All right enough, but not in the way the poetry puts it. Pity for the mariner's wife! all right again, but not in the way the poetry puts it. Look-a here! whose life's the safest in the whole world? The poor mariner's. You look at the statistics, you'll see. So don't you fool away any sympathy on the poor mariner's dangers and privations and sufferings. Leave that to the poetry muffs. Now you look at the other side a minute. Here is Captain Brace, forty years old, been at sea thirty. On his way now to take command of his ship and sail south from Bermuda. Next week he'll be under way; easy times; comfortable quarters; passengers, sociable company; just enough to do to keep his mind healthy and not tire him; king over his ship, boss of everything and everybody; thirty years' safety to learn him that his profession ain't a dangerous one. Now you look back at his home. His wife's a feeble woman; she's a stranger in New York; shut up in blazing hot or freezing cold lodgings, according to the season; don't know anybody hardly; no company but her lonesomeness and her thoughts; husband gone six months at a time. She has borne eight children; five of them she has buried without her husband ever setting eyes on them. She watched them all the long nights till they died—he comfortable on the sea; she followed them to the grave, she heard the clods fall that broke her heart—he comfortable on the sea; she mourned at home, weeks and weeks, missing them every day and every hour—he cheerful at sea, knowing nothing about it. Now look at it a minute—turn it over in your mind and size it: five children born, she among strangers, and him not by to hearten her; buried, and him not by to comfort her; think of that! Sympathy for the poor mariner's perils is rot; give it to his wife's hard lines, where it belongs! Poetry makes out that all the wife worries about is the dangers her husband's running. She's got substantialer things to worry over, I tell you. Poetry's always pitying the poor mariner on account of his perils at sea; better a blamed sight pity him for the nights he can't sleep for thinking of how he had to leave his wife in her very birth pains, lonesome and friendless, in the thick of disease and trouble and death. If there's one thing that can make me madder than another, it's this sappy, damned maritime poetry!"

Captain Brace was a patient, gentle, seldom speaking man, with a pathetic something in his bronzed face that had been a mystery up to this time, but stood interpreted now since we had heard his story. He had voyaged eighteen times to the Mediterranean, seven times to India, once to the arctic pole in a discovery-ship, and "between times" had visited all the remote seas and ocean corners of the globe. But he said that twelve years ago, on account of his family, he "settled down," and ever since then had ceased to roam. And what do you suppose was this simple-hearted, lifelong wanderer's idea of settling down and ceasing to roam? Why, the making of two five-month voyages a year between Surinam and Boston for sugar and molasses!

Among other talk to-day, it came out that whale-ships carry no doctor. The captain adds the doctorship to his own duties. He not only gives medicines, but sets broken limbs after notions of his own, or saws them off and sears the stump when amputation seems best. The captain is provided with a medicine-chest, with the medicines numbered instead of named. A book of directions goes with this. It describes diseases and symptoms, and says, "Give a teaspoonful of No. 9 once an hour," or "Give ten grains of No. 12 every half-hour," etc. One of our sea-captains came across a skipper in the North Pacific who was in a state of great surprise and perplexity. Said he:

"There's something rotten about this medicine-chest business. One of my men was sick—nothing much the matter. I looked in the book: it said give him a teaspoonful of No. 15. I went to the medicine-chest, and I see I was out of No. 15. I judged I'd got to get up a combination somehow that would fill the bill; so I hove into the fellow half a teaspoonful of No. 8 and half a teaspoonful of No. 7, and I'll be hanged if it didn't kill him in fifteen minutes! There's something about this medicine-chest system that's too many for me!" . . . [6]

At eight o'clock on the third morning out from New York, land was sighted. Away across the sunny waves one saw a faint dark stripe stretched along under the horizon—or pretended to see it, for the credit of his eyesight. Even the Reverend said he saw it, a thing which was manifestly not so. But I never have seen any one who was morally strong enough to confess that he could not see land when others claimed that they could.

By and by the Bermuda Islands were easily visible. The principal one lay upon the water in the distance, a long, dull-colored body; scalloped with slight hills and valleys. We could not go straight at it, but had to travel all the way around it, sixteen miles from shore, because it is fenced with an invisible coral reef. At last we sighted buoys, bobbing here and there, and then we glided into a narrow channel among them, "raised the reef," and came upon shoaling blue water that soon further shoaled into pale green, with a surface scarcely rippled. Now came the resurrection hour; the berths gave up their dead. Who are these pale specters in plug-hats and silken flounces that file up the companionway in melancholy procession and step upon the deck? These are they which took the infallible preventive of seasickness in New York harbor and then disappeared and were forgotten. Also there came two or three faces not seen before until this moment. One's impulse is to ask, "Where did you come aboard?"[7]

Mark Twain included very little about the voyages that bracketed the sixteen months in Europe he recounted in *A Tramp Abroad* (1880). He confined to a single sentence his comments about going from New York to Hamburg in April 1878: "Toward the middle of April we sailed in the *Holsatia*, Captain Brandt, and had a very pleasant trip, indeed."[8] But the handful of entries he recorded in his notebooks tell a different story, some of it in the German language he was assiduously learning—and learning to despise!

*   *   *

From Mark Twain's Notebook

An exceedingly steady ship in an ordinary sea is the *Holsatia*—rolls very little. . . .

17th April a most remarkable day—frequent hail, sleet, snow & wind-squalls, with dark lowering ~~sk~~ *Himmel, und mit hölle Sonnenschein zwischen. Sehr hohe See-wellen, mit blenden grün in dem zerbrochenen Spitze.* [Heavens, and with rare sunshine in between. Very high waves, with dazzling green in the broken crest.][9] . . .

Meist-rückwärts Kammer—shriek-Stimme Kinder [Rear-most room—scream-voiced boy], the ceaseless metallic clatter of that old cracked kettle of a piano, & thunder ~~& thump~~ & pounding of the screw, with an occasional avalanche of crockery as the ship lurches—this is the afternoon hell in this ship, daily.

> But the piano is the *special* hell—how it racks one's head!
> Until it stops—then you think the scream-voiced boy is it.
> There goes the b's crying baby!
> Now a guffaw of beastly laughter—

Now the little Spanish boy is hurled headlong down into our gangway by a lurch of the ship, & fetches up against the bulkhead with a heavy bang & a pile of books & rubbish tumbles down.

(20th Apr.)

3 days of heavy sea, now. . . .

22d Apl—It breaks our hearts, this sunny magnificent morning, to sail along the lovely shores of England & can't go ashore.

Inviting.

Have some people dissatisfied because Heaven is an absolute monarchy, with many viceroys, when they expected a leatherleaded Republic with the damnation of unrestricted suffrage.

It is a marvel that never loses its surprise by repetition, this aiming a ship at a mark 3000 miles away & hitting the bull's-eye in a fog—as we did. When the fog fell on us the Capt. said we ought to be at such & such spot (it had been 18 hours since an observation was had) with the Scilly islands bearing so-&-so & bout so many miles away. Hove the lead & got 48 fathoms—looked on the chart & sure enough this depth of water showed that we were right where Capt. said we were.

Another idea. For ages man probably did not know why God carpeted the ocean-bottom with sand in one place, shells in another, & so on.— But we see, now; the kind of bottom the lead brings up shows where a ship is when the soundings don't—& also it *confirms* the soundings.

Lying story-books which make boys fall in love with the sea. Capt. Brandt's experience . . . & a million other instances show 2 things (Dana's & that of the young Canadian of the Astor expedition[10])—: that a common sailor's life is often a hell; & that there are probably more brutes in command of little ships than in any other occupation in life.[11]

When Clemens titled chapter 27 of *A Tramp Abroad* "I Spare an Awful Bore," it foreshadowed the prattle about ships inevitably encountered when traveling; boring small talk on ships was a bit of a theme for Twain. This passage is from the beginning of his sixteenth-month journey in Europe.

* * *

From *A Tramp Abroad*, Chapter 27

I Spare an Awful Bore

I was interrupted by a young and care-free voice:

"You're an American, I think—so'm I."

He was about eighteen, or possibly nineteen; slender and of medium height; open, frank, happy face; a restless but independent eye; a snub nose, which had the air of drawing back with a decent reserve from the silky new-born mustache below it until it should be introduced; a loosely hung jaw, calculated to work easily in the sockets. He wore a low-crowned, narrow-brimmed straw hat, with a broad blue ribbon around it which had a white anchor embroidered on it in front; nobby short-tailed coat, pantaloons, vest, all trim and neat and up with the fashion; red-striped stockings, very low-quarter patent-leather shoes, tied with black ribbon; blue ribbon around his neck, wide-open collar; tiny diamond studs; wrinkleless kids; projecting cuffs, fastened with large oxidized silver sleeve-buttons, bearing the device of a dog's face—English pug. He carried a slim cane, surmounted with an English pug's head with red glass eyes. Under his arm he carried a German grammar—Otto's. His hair was short, straight, and smooth, and presently when he turned his head a moment, I saw that it was nicely parted behind. He took a cigarette out of a dainty box, stuck it into a meerschaum holder which he carried in a morocco case, and reached for my cigar. While he was lighting, I said:

"Yes—I am an American."

"I knew it—I can always tell them. What ship did you come over in?"

"*Holsatia.*"

"We came in the *Batavia*—Cunard, you know. What kind of passage did you have?"

"Tolerably rough."

"So did we. Captain said he'd hardly ever seen it rougher. Where are you from?"

"New England."

"So'm I. I'm from New Bloomfield. Anybody with you?"

"Yes—a friend."

"Our whole family's along. It's awful slow, going around alone—don't you think so?"

"Rather slow."

"Ever been over here before?"

"Yes."

"I haven't. My first trip. But we've been all around—Paris and everywhere. I'm to enter Harvard next year. Studying German all the time, now. Can't enter till I know German. I know considerable French—I get along pretty well in Paris, or anywhere where they speak French. What hotel are you stopping at?"

"Schweitzerhof."

"No! is that so? I never see you in the reception-room. I go to the reception-room a good deal of the time, because there's so many Americans there. I make lots of acquaintances. I know an American as soon as I see him—and so I speak to him and make his acquaintance. I like to be always making acquaintances—don't you?"

"Lord, yes!"

"You see it breaks up a trip like this, first rate. I never get bored on a trip like this, if I can make acquaintances and have somebody to talk to. But I think a trip like this would be an awful bore, if a body couldn't find anybody to get acquainted with and talk to on a trip like this. I'm fond of talking, ain't you?"

"Passionately."

"Have you felt bored, on this trip?"

"Not all the time, part of it."

"That's it!—you see you ought to go around and get acquainted, and talk. That's my way. That's the way I always do—I just go 'round, 'round, 'round and talk, talk, talk—I never get bored. You been up the Rigi yet?"

"No."

"Going?"

"I think so."

"What hotel you going to stop at?"

"I don't know. Is there more than one?"

"Three. You stop at the Schreiber—you'll find it full of Americans. What ship did you say you came over in?"

"*City of Antwerp.*"

"German, I guess. You going to Geneva?"

"Yes."

"What hotel you going to stop at?"

"Hôtel de l'Ecu de Génève."

"Don't you do it! No Americans there! You stop at one of those big hotels over the bridge—they're packed full of Americans."

"But I want to practice my Arabic."

"Good gracious, do you speak Arabic?"

"Yes—well enough to get along."

"Why, hang it, you won't get along in Geneva—they don't speak Arabic, they speak French. What hotel are you stopping at here?"

"Hotel Pension-Beaurivage."

"Sho, you ought to stop at the Schweitzerhof. Didn't you know the Schweitzerhof was the best hotel in Switzerland?—look at your Baedeker."

"Yes, I know—but I had an idea there warn't any Americans there."

"No Americans! Why, bless your soul, it's just alive with them! I'm in the great reception-room most all the time. I make lots of acquaintances there. Not as many as I did at first, because now only the new ones stop in there—the others go right along through. Where are you from?"

"Arkansaw."

"Is that so? I'm from New England—New Bloomfield's my town when I'm at home. I'm having a mighty good time today, ain't you?"

"Divine."

"That's what I call it. I like this knocking around, loose and easy, and making acquaintances and talking. I know an American, soon as I see him; so I go and speak to him and make his acquaintance. I ain't ever bored, on a trip like this, if I can make new acquaintances and talk. I'm awful fond of talking when I can get hold of the right kind of a person, ain't you?"

"I prefer it to any other dissipation."

"That's my notion, too. Now some people like to take a book and sit down and read, and read, and read, or moon around yawping at the lake or these mountains and things, but that ain't my way; no, sir, if they like it, let 'em do it, I don't object; but as for me, talking's what I like. You been up the Rigi?"

"Yes."

"What hotel did you stop at?"

"Schreiber."

"That's the place!—I stopped there too, full of Americans, wasn't it? It always is—always is. That's what they say. Everybody says that. What ship did you come over in?"

"*Ville de Paris.*"

"French, I reckon. What kind of a passage did . . . excuse me a minute, there's some Americans I haven't seen before."

And away he went. He went uninjured, too—I had the murderous impulse to harpoon him in the back with my alpenstock, but as I raised the weapon the disposition left me; I found I hadn't the heart to kill him, he was such a joyous, innocent, good-natured numbskull. . . .

The steamer's benches were ranged back to back across the deck. My back hair was mingling innocently with the back hair of a couple of ladies. Presently they were addressed by some one and I overheard this conversation:

"You are Americans, I think? So'm I."

"Yes—we are Americans."

"I knew it—I can always tell them. What ship did you come over in?"

"*City of Chester.*"

"Oh, yes—Inman line. We came in the *Batavia*—Cunard, you know. What kind of a passage did you have?"

"Pretty fair."

"That was luck. We had it awful rough. Captain said he'd hardly seen it rougher. Where are you from?"

"New Jersey."

"So'm I. No—I didn't mean that; I'm from New England. New Bloomfield's my place. These your children?—belong to both of you?"

"Only to one of us; they are mine; my friend is not married."

"Single, I reckon? So'm I. Are you two ladies traveling alone?"

"No—my husband is with us."

"Our whole family's along. It's awful slow, going around alone—don't you think so?"

"I suppose it must be."

"Hi, there's Mount Pilatus coming in sight again. Named after Pontius Pilate, you know, that shot the apple off of William Tell's head. Guide-book tells all about it, they say. I didn't read it—an American told me. I don't read when I'm knocking around like this, having a good time. Did you ever see the chapel where William Tell used to preach?"

"I did not know he ever preached there."

"Oh, yes, he did. That American told me so. He don't ever shut up his guide-book. He knows more about this lake than the fishes in it. Besides, they call it 'Tell's Chapel'—you know that yourself. You ever been over here before?"

"Yes."

"I haven't. It's my first trip. But we've been all around—Paris and everywhere. I'm to enter Harvard next year. Studying German all the time now. Can't enter till I know German. This book's Otto's grammar. It's a mighty good book to get the *ich habe gehabt haben*'s out of. But I don't really study when I'm knocking around this way. If the notion takes me, I just run over my little old *ich habe gehabt, du hast gehabt, er hat gehabt, wir haben gehabt, ihr haben gehabt, sie haben gehabt*—kind of 'Now-I-lay-me-down-to-sleep' fashion, you know, and after that, maybe I don't buckle to it for three days. It's awful undermining to the intellect, German is; you want to take it in small doses, or first you know your brains all run together, and you feel them sloshing around in your head same as so much drawn butter. But French is different; French ain't anything. I ain't any more afraid of French than a tramp's afraid of pie; I can rattle off my little *j'ai, tu as, il a*, and the rest of it, just as easy as a-b-c. I get along pretty well in Paris, or anywhere where they speak French. What hotel are you stopping at?"

"The Schweitzerhof."

"No! is that so? I never see you in the big reception-room. I go in there a good deal of the time, because there's so many Americans there. I make lots of acquaintances. You been up the Rigi yet?"

"No."

"Going?"

"We think of it."

"What hotel you going to stop at?"

"I don't know."

"Well, then you stop at the Schreiber—it's full of Americans. What ship did you come over in?"

"*City of Chester.*"

"Oh, yes, I remember I asked you that before. But I always ask everybody what ship they came over in, and so sometimes I forget and ask again. You going to Geneva?"

"Yes."

"What hotel you going to stop at?"

"We expect to stop in a pension."

"I don't hardly believe you'll like that; there's very few Americans in the pensions. What hotel are you stopping at here?"

"The Schweitzerhof."

"Oh, yes. I asked you that before, too. But I always ask everybody what hotel they're stopping at, and so I've got my head all mixed up with hotels. But it makes talk, and I love to talk. It refreshes me up so—don't it you—on a trip like this?"

"Yes—sometimes."

"Well, it does me, too. As long as I'm talking I never feel bored—ain't that the way with you?"

"Yes—generally. But there are exceptions to the rule."

"Oh, of course. I don't care to talk to everybody, myself. If a person starts in to jabber-jabber-jabber about scenery, and history, and pictures, and all sorts of tiresome things, I get the fan-tods mighty soon. I say 'Well, I must be going now—hope I'll see you again'—and then I take a walk. Where you from?"

"New Jersey."

"Why, bother it all, I asked you that before, too. Have you seen the Lion of Lucerne?"

"Not yet."

"Nor I, either. But the man who told me about Mount Pilatus says it's one of the things to see. It's twenty-eight feet long. It don't seem reasonable, but he said so, anyway. He saw it yesterday; said it was dying, then, so I reckon it's dead by this time. But that ain't any matter, of course they'll stuff it. Did you say the children are yours—or hers?"

"Mine."

"Oh, so you did. Are you going up the . . . no, I asked you that. What ship . . . no, I asked you that, too. What hotel are you . . . no, you told me that. Let me see . . . um. . . . Oh, what kind of voy . . . no, we've been over

that ground, too. Um . . . um . . . well, I believe that is all. *Bonjour*—I am
very glad to have made your acquaintance, ladies. *Guten tag.*"[12]

After his adventures on foot in Europe, Mark Twain said almost nothing about his
trip home at sea, returning from Liverpool aboard the Cunard Line's *Gallia* in late
August of 1879. Again, he devoted just one sentence to the voyage, on the last page
of the book: "We crossed to England, and then made the homeward passage in the
Cunarder *Gallia*, a very fine ship."[13] And again, his notebook provides illustrative
details.

* * *

From Mark Twain's Notebook

Aug. 31—At sea in the *Gallia*, approaching New York (left Liverpool
23rd)—about 9 PM brilliant moon, a calm sea, & a magnificent lunar
rainbow—complete arch, the colors part of the time as brilliant as if it
were noonday—some said not *quite* as brilliant, softened with a degree
of vagueness, but to me it was not different from a daylight rainbow. One
cannot see this wonder twice in his life. . . .

The dead passenger lies in life-boat No. 6, port side abaft the smoking
room (the people don't know it) & the hilarious passengers sing & laugh
& joke under him & the melting ice drips on them. Grisly.

Sailor in the Xtrees had apoplectic fit but comrades saved him when
about to fall to the deck yesterday.[14]

9

About All Kinds of Ships

Samuel Clemens returned to the ocean again in June 1891, going with his family from New York to Le Havre aboard *La Gascogne*, of the Compagnie Générale Transatlantique, better known as the French Line. In the coming years, he would shuttle back and forth on Atlantic crossings repeatedly, becoming well versed with the cutting-edge passenger liners of the day. On this voyage of reintroduction, he took his accustomed notes of shipboard culture, which on this occasion included a group of bicyclists among the passengers.

* * *

From Mark Twain's Notebook

[June 2?] Twenty young wheelmen paying a specific sum apiece, in charge of a personal conductor who wheels them all over Europe and relieves them of all care and expense.

With such seas as this they could practice on these long decks if they chose.

One man says they do practice, two hours after midnight and spin along silently like ghosts.

The strenuous insistent muffled burr or buzz of the propeller flange, like the humming bird's buzz—lulling and not unpleasant.

June 8. Certainly the sunniest and most beautiful day the Atlantic ever saw. But little sea—though what there is would be seriously felt on a smaller vessel. This one has no motion.

The phosphorescent waves at night are very intense on the black surface.

Life preservers: Square blocks of cork—Nicholson pavement—over my head, supported on slats.

I have often yearned to know how you get them down and how you use them, and I think it a mark of perfection of my native procrastination that I continually put it off. Are there ten in our 300 who have done differently?

Divans all around a great square salon, occupied by silent folk in the squeamish stage. A piano in there—hated by the above.

Contrasts between the menu here and that of the old Cunarder, with the candles out at eleven, without notice.

June 11, 1891. The loneliness of the ship at 4 A.M. Saw just one person, for an instant, flit thru the gray of yesterday's dawn. Very rough—winds singing—first wet deck. Electrics seem to burn dim. Smoking sty stunk unendurably.[1]

In March 1892, the Hamburg-America Line steamer *Lahn* took Clemens back to New York, then the following month he returned to Hamburg on the same ship. He booked another passage on Hamburg-America's eponymous route in June 1892, this time with the *Havel*, which impressed him more than any ship in his life (Fig. 4). That voyage brought forth a written reflection on his long experience at sea, an over-looked essay that Mark Twain first published in 1893.

* * *

From *The Million-Pound Bank Note*

ABOUT ALL KINDS OF SHIPS
The Modern Steamer and the Obsolete Steamer
We are victims of one common superstition—the superstition that we realize the changes that are daily taking place in the world because we read about them and what they are. I should not have supposed that the modern ship could be a surprise to me, but it is. It seems to be as much of a surprise to me as it could have been if I had never read anything about it. I walk about this great vessel, the *Havel*, as she plows her way through the Atlantic, and every detail that comes under my eye brings up the miniature counterpart of it as it existed in the little ships I crossed the ocean in, fourteen, seventeen, eighteen, and twenty years ago.

FIGURE 4. The comfort and efficiency of the modern steamships of the
turn of the twentieth century deeply impressed Mark Twain. He extolled
the vessels of the Hamburg-America Line, especially the *Havel*, which inspired
him to write "About All Kinds of Ships" in 1892, and the Atlantic Transport
Line, such as the *Minnehaha*, pictured here, which took him from England
to New York in October 1900.

Tuck's Postcards, Celebrated Liners—"Atlantic Transport," Raphael Tuck and Sons,
Art Publishers to their Majesties the King and Queen, "Oilette" postcard 9126,
SS *Minnehaha* (1908). Courtesy of the Roorda/Doyle Collection.

In the *Havel* one can be in several respects more comfortable than he
can be in the best hotels on the continent of Europe. For instance, she has
several bath rooms, and they are as convenient and as nicely equipped as
the bath rooms in a fine private house in America; whereas in the hotels
of the continent one bath room is considered sufficient, and it is generally
shabby and located in some out of the way corner of the house; moreover,
you need to give notice so long beforehand that you get over wanting a
bath by the time you get it. In the hotels there are a good many different
kinds of noises, and they spoil sleep; in my room in the ship I hear no
sounds. In the hotels they usually shut off the electric light at midnight;
in the ship one may burn it in one's room all night.

In the steamer *Batavia*, twenty years ago, one candle, set in the bulkhead between two state-rooms, was there to light both rooms, but did

not light either of them. It was extinguished at 11 at night, and so were all the saloon lamps except one or two, which were left burning to help the passenger see how to break his neck trying to get around in the dark. The passengers sat at table on long benches made of the hardest kind of wood; in the *Havel* one sits on a swivel chair with a cushioned back to it. In those old times the dinner bill of fare was always the same: a pint of some simple, homely soup or other, boiled codfish and potatoes, slab of boiled beef, stewed prunes for dessert—on Sundays "dog in a blanket," on Thursdays "plum duff." In the modern ship the menu is choice and elaborate, and is changed daily. In the old times dinner was a sad occasion; in our day a concealed orchestra enlivens it with charming music. In the old days the decks were always wet, in our day they are usually dry, for the promenade-deck is roofed over, and the sea seldom comes aboard. In a moderately disturbed sea, in the old days, a landsman could hardly keep his legs, but in such a sea in our day, the decks are level as a table. In the old days the inside of a ship was the plainest and barrenest thing, and the most modern is a marvel of rich and costly decoration and sumptuous appointment, and is equipped with every comfort and convenience that money can buy. The old ships had no place of assembly but the dining-room, the new ones have several spacious and beautiful drawing rooms. The old ships offered the passenger no choice to smoke except in the place that was called the "fiddle." It was a repulsive den made of rough boards (full of cracks) and its office was to protect the main hatch. It was grimy and dirty; there were no seats; the only light was a lamp of the rancid-oil-and-rag kind; the place was very cold, and never dry, for the seas broke in through the cracks every little while and drenched the cavern thoroughly. In the modern ship there are three or four large smoking-rooms, and they have card tables and cushioned sofas, and are heated by steam and lighted by electricity. There are few European hotels with such smoking-rooms.

The former ships were built of wood, and had two or three water-tight compartments in the hold with doors in them which were often left open, particularly when the ship was going to hit a rock. The modern leviathan is built of steel, and the water-tight bulkheads have no doors in them; they divide the ship into nine or ten water-tight compartments and endow her with as many lives as a cat. Their complete efficiency was established by the happy results following the memorable accident to the *City of Paris* a year or two ago.[2]

One curious thing which is at once noticeable in the great modern ship is the absence of the hubbub, clatter, rush of feet, roaring of orders. That is all gone by. The elaborate maneuvers necessary in working the vessel into her dock are conducted without sound; one sees nothing of the processes, hears no commands. A Sabbath stillness and solemnity reign, in place of the turmoil and racket of the earlier days. The modern ship has a spacious bridge fenced chin high with sailcloth and floored with wooden gratings; and this bridge, with its fenced fore-and-aft annexes, could accommodate a seated audience of a hundred and fifty men. There are three steering equipments, each competent if the other should break. From the bridge the ship is steered, and also handled. The handling is not done by shout or whistle, but by signaling with patent automatic gongs. There are three tell-tales, with plainly lettered dials—for steering, handling the engines, and for communicating orders to the invisible mates who are conducting the landing of the ship or casting off. The officer who is astern is out of sight and too far away to hear trumpet calls; but the gongs near him tell him to haul in, pay out, make fast, let go, and so on; he hears, but the passengers do not, and so the ship seems to land herself without human help.

This great bridge is thirty or forty feet above the water, but the sea climbs up there sometimes; so there is another bridge twelve or fifteen feet higher still, for use in these emergencies. The force of water is a strange thing. It slips between one's fingers like air, but upon occasion it acts like a solid body and will bend a thin iron rod. In the *Havel* it has splintered a heavy oaken rail into broom-straws instead of merely breaking it in two as would have been the seemingly natural thing for it to do. At the time of the awful Johnstown disaster, according to the testimony of several witnesses, rocks were carried some distance on the surface of the stupendous torrent; and at St. Helena, many years ago, a vast sea-wave carried a battery of cannon forty feet up a steep slope and deposited the guns there in a row.[3] But the water has done a still stranger thing, and it is one which is credibly vouched for. A marlinspike is an implement about a foot long which tapers from its butt to the other extremity and ends in a sharp point. It is made of iron and is heavy. A wave came aboard a ship in a storm and raged aft, breast high, carrying a marlinspike point-first with it, and with such lightning-like swiftness and force as to drive it three or four inches into a sailor's body and kill him.

In all ways the ocean greyhound of to-day is imposing and impressive to one who carries in his head no ship-pictures of a recent date. In bulk she comes near to rivaling the Ark; yet this monstrous mass of steel is driven five hundred miles through the waves in twenty-four hours. I remember the brag run of a steamer which I traveled in once on the Pacific —it was two hundred and nine miles in twenty-fours; a year or so later I was a passenger in the excursion-tub *Quaker City*, and on one occasion in a level and glassy sea, it was claimed that she reeled off two hundred and eleven miles between noon and noon, but it was probably a campaign lie. That little steamer had seventy passengers, and a crew of forty men, and seemed a good deal of a bee-hive. But in this present ship we are living in a sort of solitude, these soft summer days, with sometimes a hundred passengers scattered about the spacious distances, and sometimes nobody in sight at all; yet, hidden in the vessel's bulk, there are (including crew,) near eleven hundred people.

The stealthiest lines in the literature of the sea are these:

"*Britannia* needs no bulwark, no towers along the steep—
Her march is o'er the mountain wave, her home is on the deep!"

There it is. In those old times the little ships climbed over the waves and wallowed down into the trough on the other side; the giant ship of our day does not climb over the waves, but crushes her way through them. Her formidable weight and mass and impetus give her mastery over any but extraordinary storm-waves.

The ingenuity of man! I mean in this passing generation. To-day I found in the chart-room a frame of removable wooden slats on the wall, and on the slats was painted uninforming information like this:

Trim Tank...........................Empty
Double-Bottom No. 1...........Full
Double-Bottom No. 2 ....Full
Double-Bottom No. 3 ....Full
Double-Bottom No. 4 ....Full

While I was trying to think out what kind of a game this might be and how a stranger might best go to work to beat it, a sailor came in and pulled out the "Empty" end of the first slat and put it back with its reverse side to the front, marked "Full." He made some other change, I did not notice what. The slat-frame was soon explained. Its function was to indicate how the ballast in the ship was distributed. The striking thing was, that the ballast was water. I did not know that a ship had ever been ballasted with water. I merely read, some time or other, that such an experiment was to be tried. But that is the modern way: between experimental trial of a new thing and its adoption, there is no need to waste time, if the trial proves its value.

On the wall, near the slat-frame, there was an outline drawing of the ship, and this betrayed the fact that the vessel has twenty-two considerable lakes of water in her. These lakes are in her bottom; they are imprisoned between real bottom and false bottom. They are separated from each other, thwartships, by water-tight bulkheads, and separated down the middle by a bulkhead running from the bow four-fifths of the way to the stern. It is a chain of lakes four hundred feet long and five to seven feet deep. Fourteen of the lakes contain fresh water brought from the shore, and the aggregate weight of it is four hundred tons. The rest of the lakes contain salt water—six hundred and eighteen tons. Upwards of a thousand tons of water, altogether.

Think how handy this ballast is. The ship leaves port with the lakes all full. As she lightens forward through consumption of coal, she loses trim—her head rises, her stern sinks down. Then they spill one of the sternward lakes into the sea, and the trim is restored. This can be repeated right along as occasion may require. Also, a lake at one end of the ship can be moved to the other end by pipes and steam pumps. When the sailor changed the slat-frame to-day, he was posting a transference of that kind. The sea had been increasing, and the vessel's head needed more weighting, to keep from rising on the waves instead of plowing through them; therefore, twenty-five tons of water had been transferred to the bow from a lake situated well toward the stern.

A water compartment is kept either full or empty. The body of water must be compact, so that it cannot slosh around. A shifting ballast would not do, of course. The modern ship is full of beautiful ingenuities, but it

seems to me that this one is the king. I would rather be the originator of
that idea than of any of the others. Perhaps the trim of a ship was never perfectly ordered and preserved until now. A vessel out of trim will not steer,
her speed is maimed, she strains and labors in the seas. Poor creature,
for six thousand years she has had no comfort until these latest days. For
six thousand years she swam through the best and cheapest ballast in the
world, the only perfect ballast, but she couldn't tell her master and he had
not the wit to find it out for himself. It is odd to reflect that there is nearly
as much water inside this ship as there is outside, yet there is no danger.

Noah's Ark

The progress made in the great art of ship-building since Noah's time
is quite noticeable. Also, the looseness of the navigation laws in the time
of Noah is in quite striking contrast with the strictness of the navigation
laws in our time. It would not be possible for Noah to do in our day what
he was permitted to do in his own. Experience has taught us the necessity
of being more particular, more conservative, more careful of human life.
Noah would not be allowed to sail from Bremen in our day. The inspec-
tors would come and examine the Ark, and make all sorts of objections. A
person who knows Germany can imagine the scene and the conversation
without difficulty and without missing detail. The inspector would be
in careful military uniform; he would be respectful, dignified, kindly, the
perfect gentleman, but steady as the north star to the last requirement of
his duty. He would make Noah tell him where he was born, and how old
he was, and what religious sect he belonged to, and the amount of his income, and the grade and position he claimed socially, and the name and
style of his occupation, and how many wives and children he had, and
how many servants, and the name, sex and age of the whole of them; and
if he hadn't a passport he would be courteously required to get one right
away. Then he would take up the matter of the Ark:

"What is her length?"
"Six hundred feet."
"Depth?"
"Sixty-five."
"Beam?"
"Fifty or sixty."

"Built of—"

"Wood."

"What kind?"

"Shittim and gopher."

"Interior and exterior decorations?"

"Pitched within and without."

"Passengers?"

"Eight."

"Sex?"

"Half male, the other female."

"Ages?"

"From a hundred years up."

"Up to where?"

"Six hundred."

"Ah—going to Chicago; a good idea, too. Surgeon's name?"

"We have no surgeon."

"Must provide a surgeon. Also an undertaker—particularly the undertaker. These people must not be left without the necessities of life at their age. Crew?"

"The same eight."

"The same eight?"

"The same eight."

"And half of them women?"

"Yes, sir."

"Have they ever served as seamen?"

"No, sir."

"Have the men?"

"No, sir."

"Where were you reared?"

"On a farm—all of us."

"This vessel requires a crew of eight hundred men, she not being a steamer. You must provide them. She must provide them. She must have four mates and nine cooks. Who is captain?"

"I am, sir."

"You must get a captain. Also a chambermaid. Also sick nurses for the old people. Who designed this vessel?"

"I did, sir."

"Is it your first attempt?"

"Yes, sir."

"I partly suspected it. Cargo?"

"Animals."

"Kind?"

"All kinds."

"Wild or tame?"

"Mainly wild."

"Foreign or domestic?"

"Mainly foreign."

"Principal wild ones?"

"Megatherium, elephant, rhinoceros, lion, tiger, wolf, snakes — all the wild things of all climes — two of each."

"Securely caged?"

"No, not caged."

"They must have iron cages. Who feeds and waters the menagerie?"

"We do."

"The old people?"

"Yes, sir."

"It is dangerous — for both. The animals must be cared for by a competent force. How many animals are there?"

"Big ones, seven thousand; big and little together, ninety-eight thousand."

"You must provide twelve hundred keepers. How is the vessel lighted?"

"By two windows."

"Where are they?"

"Up under the eaves."

"Two windows for a tunnel six hundred feet long and sixty five feet deep? You must put in the electric light — a few arc lights and fifteen hundred incandescents. What do you do in case of leaks? How many pumps have you?"

"None, sir."

"You must provide pumps. How do you get water for the passengers and the animals?"

"We let down the buckets from the windows."

"It is inadequate. What is your motive power?"

"What is my which?"

"Motive power. What power do you use in the driving ship?"

"None."

"You must provide sails or steam. What is the nature of your steering apparatus?"

"We haven't any."

"Haven't you a rudder?"

"No, sir."

"How do you steer the vessel?"

"We don't."

"You must provide a rudder, and properly equip it. How many anchors have you?"

"None."

"You must provide six. One is not permitted to sail a vessel like this without that protection. How many life boats have you?"

"None, sir."

"Provide twenty-five. How many life preservers?"

"None."

"You will provide two thousand. How long are you expecting your voyage to last?"

"Eleven or twelve months."

"Eleven or twelve months. Pretty slow—but you will be in time for the Exposition. What is your ship sheathed with—copper?"

"Her hull is bare—not sheathed at all."

"Dear man, the wood-boring creatures of the sea would riddle her like a sieve and send her to the bottom in three months. She *cannot* be allowed to go away, in this condition; she must be sheathed. Just a word more: Have you reflected that Chicago is an inland city and not reachable with a vessel like this?"

"Shecargo? What is Shecargo? I am not going to Shecargo."

"Indeed? Then may I ask what the animals are for?"

"Just to breed others from."

"Others? Is it possible that you haven't enough?"

"For the present needs of civilization, yes; but the rest are going to be drowned in a flood, and these are to renew the supply."

"A flood?"

"Yes, sir."

"Are you sure of that?"

"Perfectly sure. It is going to rain for forty days and forty nights."

"Give yourself no concern about that, dear sir, it often does that here."

"Not this kind of rain. This is going to cover the mountain tops, and the earth will pass from sight."

"Privately—but of course not officially—I am sorry you revealed this, for it compels me to withdraw the option I gave you to sails or steam. I must require you to use steam. Your ship cannot carry the hundredth part of an eleven-months' water-supply for the animals. You will have condensed water."

"But I tell you I am going to dip water from outside with buckets."

"It will not answer. Before the flood reaches the mountain tops the fresh waters will have joined the salt seas, and it will be all salt. You must put in steam and condense your water. I will now bid you good-day, sir. Did I understand you to say that this was your very first attempt at ship building?"

"My very first, sir, I give you the honest truth. I built this Ark without having ever had the slightest training or experience or instruction in marine architecture."

"It is remarkable work, sir, a most remarkable work. I consider that it contains more features that are new—absolutely new and unhackneyed —than are to be found in any other vessel that swims the seas."

"This compliment does me infinite honor, dear sir, infinite; and I shall cherish the memory of it while life shall last. Sir, I offer my duty, and most grateful thanks. Adieu!"

No, the inspector would be limitlessly courteous to Noah, and would make him feel that he was among friends, but he wouldn't let him go to sea with that Ark.

Columbus's Craft

Between Noah's time and the time of Columbus, naval architecture underwent some changes, and from being unspeakably bad was improved to a point which may be described as less unspeakably bad. I have read somewhere, some time or other, that one of Columbus's ships was a ninety-ton vessel. By comparing that ship with the ocean greyhounds of our time one is able to get down to a comprehension of how small that Spanish bark was, and how little fitted she would be to run opposition in the Atlantic passenger trade to-day. It would take seventy-four of her to match the tonnage of the *Havel* and carry the *Havel*'s trip. If I remember rightly, it took her ten weeks to make the passage. With our ideas this would now be considered an objectionable gait. She probably had a captain, a mate, and a crew consisting of four seamen and a boy. The crew of a modern greyhound numbers two hundred and fifty persons.

Columbus's ship being small and very old, we know that we may draw from these two facts several absolute certainties in the way of minor details which history has left unrecorded. For instance: being small, we know that she rolled and pitched and tumbled, in any ordinary sea, and stood on her head or her tail, or lay down with her ear in the water when storm-seas ran high; also, that she was used to having billows plunge aboard and wash her decks from stem to stern; also, that the storm-racks were on the table all the way over, and that nevertheless a man's soup was oftener landed in his lap than in his stomach; also, that the dining-saloon was about ten feet by seven, dark, airless, and suffocating with oil-stench; also, that there was only about one state-room—the size of a grave—with a tier of two or three berths in it of the dimensions and comfortableness of coffins, and that when the light was out, the darkness in there was so thick and real that you could bite into it and chew it like gum; also, that the only promenade was on the lofty poop-deck astern (for the ship was shaped like a high-quarter shoe)—a streak sixteen feet long by three feet wide, all the rest of the vessel being littered with ropes and flooded by the seas.

We know all these things to be true, from the mere fact that we know the vessel was small. As the vessel was old, certain other truths follow, as matters of course. For instance: she was full of rats; she was full of cockroaches; the heavy seas made her seams open and shut like your fingers, and she leaked like a basket; where leakage is, there also, of necessity, is bilgewater; and where bilgewater is, only the dead can enjoy life. This is on account of the smell. In the presence of bilgewater, Limburger cheese becomes odorless and ashamed.

From these absolutely sure data we can competently picture the daily

life of the great discoverer. In the early morning he paid his devotions
at the shrine of the Virgin. At eight bells he appeared on the poop-deck
promenade. If the weather was chilly he came up clad from plumed hel-
met to spurred heel in magnificent plate armor inlaid with arabesques of
gold, having previously warmed it at the galley fire. If the weather was
warm, he came up in the ordinary sailor toggery of the time: great slouch
hat of blue velvet with a flowing brush of snowy ostrich plumes, fastened
on with a flashing cluster of diamonds and emeralds; gold-embroidered
doublet of green velvet with slashed sleeves exposing under-sleeves of
crimson satin; deep collar and cuff-ruffles of rich limp lace; trunk hose of
pink velvet, with big knee-knots of brocaded yellow ribbon; pearl-tinted
silk stockings, clocked and daintily embroidered; lemon-colored buskins
of unborn kid, funnel-topped, and drooping low to expose the pretty
stockings; deep gauntlets of finest white heretic skin, from the factory of
the Holy Inquisition, formerly part of the person of a lady of rank; rapier
with sheath crusted with jewels, and hanging from a broad baldric upholstered with rubies and sapphires.

He walked the promenade thoughtfully, he noted the aspects of the
sky and the course of the wind; he kept an eye out for drifting vegetation
and other signs of land; he jawed the man at the wheel for pastime; he got
out an imitation egg and kept himself in practice on his old trick of making it stand on its end; now and then he hove a life-line below and fished
up a sailor who was drowning on the quarter-deck; the rest of his watch
he gaped and yawned and stretched and said he wouldn't make the trip
again to discover six Americas. For that was the kind of natural human
person Columbus was when not posing for posterity.

At noon he took the sun and ascertained that the good ship had made
three hundred yards in twenty-four hours, and this enabled him to win
the pool. Anybody can win the pool when nobody but himself has the
privilege of straightening out the ship's run and getting it right.

The Admiral has breakfast alone, in state: bacon, beans, and gin; at
noon he dines alone in state: bacon, beans, and gin; at six he sups alone in
state: bacon, beans, and gin; at eleven P.M. he takes a night-relish, alone,
in state: bacon, beans, and gin. At none of these orgies is there any music;
the ship-orchestra is modern. After his final meal he returned thanks for

his many blessings, a little over-rating their value, perhaps, and then he laid off his silken splendors or his gilded hardware, and turned in, in his little coffin-bunk, and blew out his flickering stencher and began to refresh his lungs with inverted sighs freighted with the rich odors of rancid oil and bilgewater. The sighs returned as snores, and then the rats and cockroaches swarmed out in brigades and divisions and army corps and had a circus all over him. Such was the daily life of a great discoverer in his marine basket during several historic weeks; and the difference between his ship and his comforts and ours is visible almost at a glance.

When he returned, the King of Spain, marveling, said—as history records:

"This ship seems to be leaky. Did she leak badly?"

"You shall judge for yourself, sire. I pumped the Atlantic ocean through her sixteen times on the passage."

This is General Horace Porter's account. Other authorities say fifteen.

It can be shown that the differences between that ship and the one I am writing these historical contributions in are in several respects remarkable. Take the matter of decoration, for instance. I have been looking around again, yesterday and today, and have noted several details which I conceive to have been absent from Columbus's ship, or at least slurred over and not elaborated and perfected. I observe state-room doors three inches thick, of solid oak polished. I note companionway vestibules with walls, doors and ceilings paneled in polished hard woods, some light, some dark, all dainty and delicate joiner-work, and yet every joint compact and tight; with beautiful pictures inserted, composed of blue tiles—some of the pictures containing as many as sixty tiles—and the joinings of those tiles perfect. These are daring experiments. One would have said that the first time the ship went straining and laboring through a storm-tumbled sea those tiles would gape apart and drop out. That they have not done so is evidence that the joiner's art has advanced a good deal since the days when ships were so shackly that when a giant sea gave them a wrench the doors came unbolted. I find the walls of the dining-saloon upholstered with mellow pictures wrought in tapestry, and the ceiling aglow with pictures done in oil. In other places of assembly I find great panels filled with embossed Spanish leather, the figures rich with gild-ing and bronze. Everywhere I find sumptuous masses of color—color, color, color—color all about, color of every shade and tint and variety; and as a result, the ship is bright and cheery to the eye, and this cheeriness invades one's spirit and contents it. To fully appreciate the force and spiritual value of this radiant and opulent dream of color, one must stand outside at night in the pitch dark and the rain, and look through a port, and observe it in the lavish splendor of the electric lights. The old-time ships were dull, plain, graceless, gloomy, and horribly depressing. They compelled the blues; one could not escape the blues in them. The modern idea is right: to surround the passenger with conveniences, luxuries, and abundance of inspiring color. As a result, the ship is the pleasantest place one can be in, except, perhaps, one's home.

A Vanished Sentiment

One thing is gone, to return no more forever—the romance of the sea. Soft sentimentality about the sea has retired from the activities of this life, and is but a memory of the past, already remote and much faded. But within the recollection of men still living, it was in the breast of every individual; and the further any individual lived from salt water the more of it he kept in stock. It was as pervasive, as universal, as the atmosphere itself. The mere mention of the sea, the romantic sea, would make any company of people sentimental and mawkish at once. The great majority of the songs that were sung by the people of the back settlements had the melancholy wanderer for subject and his mouthings about the sea for refrain. Picnic parties paddling down a creek in a canoe when the twilight shadows were gathering, always sang:

> Homeward bound, homeward bound
> From a foreign shore;

and this was also a favorite in the West with the passengers on sternwheel steamboats. There was another—

> My boat is by the shore
> And my bark is on the sea,
> But before I go, Tom Moore,
> Here's a double health to thee.

And this one, also—

> O, pilot, 'tis a fearful night,
> There's danger on the deep.

And this—

> A life on the ocean wave
> And home on the rolling deep,
> Where the scattered waters rave
> And the winds their revels keep!

And this—

> A wet sheet and a flowing sea,
> And a wind that follows fair.

And this—

> My foot is on my gallant deck,
> Once more the rover is free!

And the "Larboard Watch"—the person referred to below is at the masthead, or somewhere up there—

> O, who can tell what joy he feels,
> As o'er the foam his vessel reels,
> And his tired eyelids slumb'ring fall,
> He rouses at the welcome call
> Of "Larboard watch—ahoy!"

Yes, and there was forever and always some jackass-voiced person braying out—

> Rocked in the cradle of the deep,
> I lay me down in peace to sleep!

Other favorites had these suggestive titles: "The Storm at Sea;" "The Bird at Sea;" "The Sailor Boy's Dream;" "The Captive Pirate's Lament;" "We are far from Home on the Stormy Main"—and so on, and so on, the list is endless. Everybody on a farm lived chiefly amid the dangers of the deep on those days, in fancy.

But all that is gone, now. Not a vestige of it is left. The iron-clad, with her unsentimental aspect and frigid attention to business, banished romance from the war marine, and the unsentimental streamer has banished it from the commercial marine. The dangers and uncertainties which made sea life romantic have disappeared and carried the poetic element along with them. In our day the passengers never sing sea-songs on board a ship, and the band never plays them. Pathetic songs about the wanderer in strange lands far from home, once so popular and contributing such fire and color to the imagination by reason of the rarity of that kind of wanderer, have lost their charm and fallen silent, because everybody is a wanderer in the far lands now, and the interest in that detail is dead. Nobody is worried about the wanderer; there are no perils of the sea for him, there are no uncertainties. He is safer in the ship than he would probably be at home, for there he is always liable to have to attend some friend's funeral and stand over the grave in the sleet, bareheaded—and that means pneumonia for him, if he gets his deserts; and the uncertainties of his voyage are reduced to whether he will arrive on the other side on the appointed afternoon, or have to wait till morning.

The first ship I was ever in was a sailing vessel. She was twenty-eight days going from San Francisco to the Sandwich Islands. But the main reason for this particularly slow passage was, that she got becalmed and lay in one spot fourteen days in the centre of the Pacific two thousand miles from land. I hear no sea-songs in this present vessel, but I heard the entire layout in that one. There were a dozen young people—they are pretty old now, I reckon—and they used to group themselves on the stern, in the starlight or the moonlight, every evening, and sing sea-songs till after midnight, in that hot, silent, motionless calm. They had no sense of humor, and they always sang "Homeward Bound," without reflecting that that was practically ridiculous, since they were standing still and not proceeding in any direction at all; and they often followed that song with "Are we almost there, are we almost there, said the dying girl as she drew near home?"

It was a very pleasant company of young people, and I wonder where they are now. Gone, oh, none knows whither; and the bloom and grace and beauty of their youth, where is that? Among them was a liar; all tried to reform him, but none could do it. And so, gradually, he was left to himself, none of us would associate with him. Many a time since, I have seen in fancy that forsaken figure, leaning forlorn against the taffrail, and have reflected that perhaps if we had tried harder, and been more patient, we might have won him from his fault and persuaded him to relinquish it. But it is hard to tell; with him the vice was extreme, and was probably incurable. I like to think—and indeed I do think—that I did the best that in me lay to lead him to higher and better ways.

There was a singular circumstance. The ship lay becalmed that entire fortnight in exactly the same spot. Then a handsome breeze came fanning over the sea, and we spread our white wings for flight. But the vessel did not budge. The sails bellied out, the gale strained at the ropes, but the vessel moved not a hair's breadth from her place. The captain was surprised. It was some hours before we found out what the cause of the detention was. It was barnacles. They collect very fast in that part of the Pacific. They had fastened themselves to the ship's bottom; then others fastened themselves to the first bunch, others to these, and so on, down and down and down, and the last bunch had glued the column hard and fast to the bottom of the sea, which is five miles deep at that point. So the ship was simply become the handle of a walking cane five miles long —yes, and no more moveable by wind and sail than a continent is. It was regarded by every one as remarkable.

Well, the next week—however, Sandy Hook is in sight.[4]

Returning to the United States in early spring 1893, Mark Twain made the following notes aboard the *Kaiser Wilhelm II* of the Hamburg-America Line. The captain's surname, Störmer, foreshadowed an inclement passage.

* * *

From Mark Twain's Notebook

Tuesday, March 28. The usual brilliant sunshine, the usual soft summer weather. Sea polished and nearly flat—almost a dead calm. We have never had a sea that disturbed the dishes on the table to speak of.

Wednesday, March 29. Nice ball on deck, with colored electric lights.

I opened with Capt. Störmer—waltzed with overcoat. Danced a Virginia reel, with Longfellow for a partner.

Good Friday, March 31. Exceedingly rough—a deal of rain. A very sturdy ship, but of course this sort of thing makes her roll heavily—as it would any ship.

April 1. A wild wind and a wild sea yesterday afternoon. Several falls but nobody hurt. Went to bed at eight and slept till 8. Still a heavy sea this morning.[5]

His return passage to Europe on the same ship, May 13-25, 1893, was uneventful in the extreme, as this entry indicates:

Wednesday, May 24. Sailing along the Balearic Islands, this forenoon. Due at Genoa tomorrow night. A perfectly smooth voyage, but unspeakably tedious. I am older by ten years than I was when I left New York. The fact is, the voyage is *too* smooth.[6]

After so many quiet voyages, Clemens may have missed the raucous old days of trans-Atlantic travel. In his novel *The American Claimant* (1892), one of Mark Twain's most popular characters, Colonel Mulberry Sellers, invents something to evoke that era.

* * *

From *The American Claimant*, Chapter 17

"It's my grand adaptation of the phonograph to the marine service. You store up profanity in it for use at sea. You know that sailors don't fly around worth a cent unless you swear at them—so the mate that can do the best job of swearing is the most valuable man. In great emergencies his talent saves the ship. But a ship is a large thing, and he can't be everywhere at once; so there have been times when one mate has lost a ship which could have been saved if they had had a hundred. Prodigious storms, you know. Well, a ship can't afford a hundred mates; but she can afford a hundred Cursing Phonographs, and distribute them all over the vessel—and there, you see, she's armed at every point. Imag-

ine a big storm, and a hundred of my machines all cursing away at once
—splendid spectacle, splendid!—you couldn't hear yourself think. Ship
goes through that storm perfectly serene—she's just as safe as she'd be
on shore."

"It's a wonderful idea. How do you prepare the thing?"

"Load it—simply load it."

"How?"

"Why you just stand over it and swear into it."

"That loads it, does it?"

"Yes—because every word it collars, it *keeps*—keeps it forever. Never
wears out. Any time you turn the crank, out it'll come. In times of great
peril, you can reverse it, and it'll swear backwards. *That* makes a sailor
hump himself!"

"Oh, I see. Who loads them?—the mate?"

"Yes, if he chooses. Or I'll furnish them already loaded. I can hire an
expert for $75 a month who will load a hundred and fifty phonographs
in 150 hours, and do it *easy*. And an expert can furnish a stronger article,
of course, than the mere average uncultivated mate could. Then you see,
all the ships of the world will buy them ready loaded—for I shall have
them loaded in any language a customer wants. Hawkins, it will work
the grandest moral reform of the 19th century. Five years from now, *all*
the swearing will be done by machinery—you won't ever hear a profane word come from human lips on a ship. Millions of dollars have been
spent by the churches, in the effort to abolish profanity in the commercial
marine. Think of it—my name will live forever in the affections of good
men as the man, who, solitary and alone, accomplished this noble and
elevating reform."[7]

Equatorial Circumnavigation

For much of his life, Mark Twain earned most of his income not from writing, but on the lecture circuit, because the royalties he received from his published work did not cover his lavish expenses. Although he had become an international celebrity, his fame failed to make his fortune. When his financial situation, never secure, grew desperate in the 1890s, the author relocated to Europe.

The Clemens family's financial exile in Europe reduced their expenses, but income was needed to repay the patriarch's debts. To begin to do that, Mark Twain embarked upon an ambitious lecture tour around the world. His fourteen-month circuit presaged the international concert tours of star performers that proliferated in the late twentieth century and generated an ongoing global industry. *Following the Equator* (1897) is his account of that late-career circumnavigation by steamship, in the company of his wife, Livy, and daughter Clara. This chapter presents an array of passages from it.

* * *

To Australia, from *Following the Equator*

[From Chapter 1]
The starting point of this lecturing-trip around the world was Paris, where we had been living a year or two.

We sailed for America, and there made certain preparations. This took but little time. Two members of my family elected to go with me. Also a carbuncle. The dictionary says a carbuncle is a kind of jewel. Humor is out of place in a dictionary.

We started westward from New York in midsummer, with Major Pond to manage the platform-business as far as the Pacific. It was warm work, all the way, and the last fortnight of it was suffocatingly smoky, for in Oregon and British Columbia the forest fires were raging. We had an added week of smoke at the seaboard, where we were obliged to wait awhile for our ship. She had been getting herself ashore in the smoke, and she had to be docked and repaired.

We sailed at last; and so ended a snail-paced march across the continent, which had lasted forty days.

We moved westward about mid-afternoon over a rippled and sparkling summer sea; an enticing sea, a clean and cool sea, and apparently a welcome sea to all on board; it certainly was to me, after the distressful dustings and smokings and swelterings of the past weeks. The voyage would furnish a three-weeks holiday, with hardly a break in it.

We had the whole Pacific ocean in front of us, with nothing to do but do nothing and be comfortable. The city of Victoria was twinkling dim in the deep heart of her smoke-cloud, and getting ready to vanish; and now we closed the field-glasses and sat down on our steamer chairs contented and at peace. But they went to wreck and ruin under us and brought us to shame before all the passengers. They had been furnished by the largest furniture-dealing house in Victoria, and were worth a couple of farthings a dozen, though they had cost us the price of honest chairs. In the Pacific and Indian Oceans one must still bring his own deck-chair on board or go without, just as in the old forgotten Atlantic times—those Dark Ages of sea travel.[1]

Ours was a reasonably comfortable ship, with the customary seagoing fare—plenty of good food furnished by the Deity and cooked by the devil. The discipline observable on board was perhaps as good as it is anywhere in the Pacific and Indian Oceans. The ship was not very well arranged for tropical service; but that is nothing, for this is the rule for ships which ply in the tropics. She had an over-supply of cockroaches, but this is also the rule with ships doing business in the summer seas—at least such as have been long in service.

Our young captain was a very handsome man, tall and perfectly formed, the very figure to show up a smart uniform's finest effects. He was a man of the best intentions, and was polite and courteous even to courtliness. There was a soft grace and finish about his manners which made whatever place he happened to be in seem for the moment a drawing-room. He avoided the smoking-room. He had no vices. He did not

smoke or chew tobacco or take snuff; he did not swear, or use slang, or
rude, or coarse, or indelicate language, or make puns, or tell anecdotes,
or laugh intemperately, or raise his voice above the moderate pitch en-
joined by the canons of good form. When he gave an order, his manner
modified it into a request. After dinner he and his officers joined the ladies and gentlemen in the ladies' saloon, and shared in the singing and
piano playing, and helped turn the music. He had a sweet and sympathetic tenor voice, and used it with taste and effect. After the music he
played whist there, always with the same partner and opponents, until
the ladies' bedtime. The electric lights burned there as late as the ladies
and their friends might desire, but they were not allowed to burn in the
smoking-room after eleven. There were many laws on the ship's statute
book, of course; but so far as I could see, this and one other were the
only ones that were rigidly enforced. The captain explained that he enforced this one because his own cabin adjoined the smoking-room, and
the smell of tobacco smoke made him sick. I did not see how our smoke
could reach him, for the smoking-room and his cabin were on the upper
deck, targets for all the winds that blew; and besides there was no crack
of communication between them, no opening of any sort in the solid in-
tervening bulkhead. Still, to a delicate stomach even imaginary smoke
can convey damage.

The captain, with his gentle nature, his polish, his sweetness, his
moral and verbal purity, seemed pathetically out of place in his rude and
autocratic vocation. It seemed another instance of the irony of fate.

He was going home under a cloud. The passengers knew about his
trouble, and were sorry for him. Approaching Vancouver through a narrow and difficult passage densely befogged with smoke from the forest
fires, he had had the ill-luck to lose his bearings and get his ship on the
rocks. A matter like this would rank merely as an error with you and me;
it ranks as a crime with the directors of steamship companies. The captain had been tried by the Admiralty Court at Vancouver, and its verdict
had acquitted him of blame. But that was insufficient comfort. A sterner
court would examine the case in Sydney—the Court of Directors, the
lords of a company in whose ships the captain had served as mate a number of years. This was his first voyage as captain.

The officers of our ship were hearty and companionable young men, and they entered into the general amusements and helped the passengers pass the time. Voyages in the Pacific and Indian Oceans are but pleasure excursions for all hands.[2]

[From Chapter 2]
About four days out from Victoria we plunged into hot weather, and all the male passengers put on white linen clothes. One or two days later we crossed the 25th parallel of north latitude, and then, by order, the officers of the ship laid away their blue uniforms and came out in white linen ones. All the ladies were in white by this time. This prevalence of snowy costumes gave the promenade deck an invitingly cool and cheerful and picnicky aspect.[3]

[From Chapter 3]
We had a sunset of a very fine sort. The vast plain of the sea was marked off in bands of sharply-contrasted colors: great stretches of dark blue, others of purple, others of polished bronze; the billowy mountains showed all sorts of dainty browns and greens, blues and purples and blacks, and the rounded velvety backs of certain of them made one want to stroke them, as one would the sleek back of a cat. The long, sloping promontory projecting into the sea at the west turned dim and leaden and spectral, then became suffused with pink—dissolved itself in a pink dream, so to speak, it seemed so airy and unreal. Presently the cloud-rack was flooded with fiery splendors, and these were copied on the surface of the sea, and it made one drunk with delight to look upon it.[4]

[From Chapter 4]
Sailed from Honolulu. From diary:
    Sept. 2. Flocks of flying fish—slim, shapely, graceful, and intensely white. With the sun on them they look like a flight of silver fruit-knives. They are able to fly a hundred yards.
    Sept. 3. In 9° 50′ north latitude, at breakfast. Approaching the equator on a long slant. Those of us who have never seen the equator are a good deal excited. I think I would rather see it than any other thing in the world. We entered the "doldrums" last night—variable winds, bursts of rain, intervals of calm, with chopping seas and a wobbly and drunken

motion to the ship—a condition of things findable in other regions sometimes, but present in the doldrums always. The globe-girdling belt called the doldrums is 20 degrees wide, and the thread called the equator lies along the middle of it.

Sept. 4. Total eclipse of the moon last night. At 7.30 it began to go off. At total—or about that—it was like a rich rosy cloud with a tumbled surface framed in the circle and projecting from it—a bulge of strawberry-ice, so to speak. At half-eclipse the moon was like a gilded acorn in its cup.

Sept. 5. Closing in on the equator this noon. A sailor explained to a young girl that the ship's speed is poor because we are climbing up the bulge toward the center of the globe; but that when we should once get over, at the equator, and start "down-hill," we should fly. When she asked him the other day what the fore-yard was, he said it was the front yard, the open area in the front end of the ship. That man has a good deal of learning stored up, and the girl is likely to get it all.

Afternoon. Crossed the equator. In the distance it looked like a blue ribbon stretched across the ocean. Several passengers kodak'd it. We had no fool ceremonies, no fantastics, no horseplay. All that sort of thing has gone out. In old times a sailor, dressed as Neptune, used to come in over the bows, with his suite, and lather up and shave everybody who was crossing the equator for the first time, and then cleanse these unfortunates by swinging them from the yard-arm and ducking them three times in the sea. This was considered funny. Nobody knows why. No, that is not true. We do know why. Such a thing could never be funny on land; no part of the old-time grotesque performances gotten up on shipboard to celebrate the passage of the line could ever be funny on shore—they would seem dreary and witless to shore people. But the shore people would change their minds about it at sea, on a long voyage. On such a voyage, with its eternal monotonies, people's intellects deteriorate; the owners of the intellects soon reach a point where they almost seem to prefer childish things to things of a maturer degree. One is often surprised at the juvenilities which grown people indulge in at sea, and the interest they take in them, and the consuming enjoyment they get out of them. This is on long voyages only. The mind gradually becomes inert, dull, blunted; it loses its accustomed interest in intellectual things; nothing but horse-play can rouse it, nothing but wild and foolish grotesque-

FIGURE 5. Twain and some of his shipmates paused while playing
shuffleboard to pose for this photograph aboard the steamship *Minneapolis*
in June 1907, when he was en route to England to accept an honorary degree
from Oxford University. The shuffleboard diagram chalked on the deck in
the foreground is like the one Twain included in *Following the Equator*.
Courtesy of the Mark Twain Project, Bancroft Library, University of California–Berkeley

ries can entertain it. On short voyages it makes no such exposure of itself;
it hasn't time to slump down to this sorrowful level.

The short-voyage passenger gets his chief physical exercise out of
"horse-billiards"—shovel-board [Fig. 5]. It is a good game. We play it
in this ship. A quartermaster chalks off a diagram like this—on the deck.

The player uses a cue that is like a broom-handle with a quarter-moon
of wood fastened to the end of it. With this he shoves wooden disks the
size of a saucer—he gives the disk a vigorous shove and sends it fifteen
or twenty feet along the deck and lands it in one of the squares if he can.
If it stays there till the inning is played out, it will count as many points
in the game as the figure in the square it has stopped in represents. The
adversary plays to knock that disk out and leave his own in its place—
particularly if it rests upon the 9 or 10 or some other of the high numbers;
but if it rests in the "10-off" he backs it up—lands his disk behind it a foot

or two, to make it difficult for its owner to knock it out of that damaging place and improve his record. When the inning is played out it may be found that each adversary has placed his four disks where they count; it may be found that some of them are touching chalk lines and not counting; and very often it will be found that there has been a general wreckage, and that not a disk has been left within the diagram. Anyway, the result is recorded, whatever it is, and the game goes on. The game is 100 points, and it takes from twenty minutes to forty to play it, according to luck and the condition of the sea. It is an exciting game, and the crowd of spectators furnish abundance of applause for fortunate shots and plenty of laughter for the other kind. It is a game of skill, but at the same time the uneasy motion of the ship is constantly interfering with skill; this makes it a chancy game, and the element of luck comes largely in.

We had a couple of grand tournaments, to determine who should be "Champion of the Pacific"; they included among the participants nearly all the passengers, of both sexes, and the officers of the ship, and they afforded many days of stupendous interest and excitement, and murderous exercise—for horse-billiards is a physically violent game. . . .

To return to the ship.

The average human being is a perverse creature; and when he isn't that, he is a practical joker. The result to the other person concerned is about the same: that is, he is made to suffer. The washing down of the decks begins at a very early hour in all ships; in but few ships are any measures taken to protect the passengers, either by waking or warning them, or by sending a steward to close their ports. And so the deck-washers have their opportunity, and they use it. They send a bucket of water slashing along the side of the ship and into the ports, drenching the passenger's clothes, and often the passenger himself. This good old custom prevailed in this ship, and under unusually favorable circumstances, for in the blazing tropical regions a removable zinc thing like a sugar-shovel projects from the port to catch the wind and bring it in; this thing catches the wash-water and brings it in, too—and in flooding abundance. Mrs. I., an invalid, had to sleep on the locker-sofa under her port, and every time she over-slept and thus failed to take care of herself, the deck-washers drowned her out.

And the painters, what a good time they had! This ship would be going into dock for a month in Sydney for repairs; but no matter, painting was going on all the time somewhere or other. The ladies' dresses were constantly getting ruined, nevertheless protests and supplications went for nothing. Sometimes a lady, taking an afternoon nap on deck near a ventilator or some other thing that didn't need painting, would wake up by and by and find that the humorous painter had been noiselessly daubing that thing and had splattered her white gown all over with little greasy yellow spots.

The blame for this untimely painting did not lie with the ship's officers, but with custom. As far back as Noah's time it became law that ships must be constantly painted and fussed at when at sea; custom grew out of the law, and at sea custom knows no death; this custom will continue until the sea goes dry.

Sept. 8. — Sunday. We are moving so nearly south that we cross only about two meridians of longitude a day. This morning we were in longitude 178 west from Greenwich, and 57 degrees west from San Francisco. To-morrow we shall be "close to the center of the globe"—the 180th degree of west longitude and 180th degree of east longitude.

And then we must drop out a day—lose a day out of our lives, a day never to be found again. We shall all die one day earlier than from the beginning of time we were foreordained to die. We shall be a day behindhand all through eternity. We shall always be saying to the other angels, "Fine day today," and they will be always retorting, "But it isn't to-day, it's to-morrow." We shall be in a state of confusion all the time and shall never know what true happiness is.

Next day. Sure enough, it has happened. Yesterday it was September 8, Sunday; to-day, per the bulletin-board at the head of the companion way, it is September 10, Tuesday. There is something uncanny about it. And uncomfortable. In fact, nearly unthinkable, and wholly unrealizable, when one comes to consider it. While we were crossing the 180th meridian it was Sunday in the stern of the ship where my family were, and Tuesday in the bow where I was. They were there eating the half of a fresh apple on the 8th, and I was at the same time eating the other half of it on the 10th—and I could notice how stale it was, already. The family were the same age that they were when I had left them five minutes before, but I was a day older now than I was then. The day they were living in stretched behind them half way round the globe, across the Pacific Ocean and America and Europe; the day I was living in stretched in front of me around the other half to meet it. They were stupendous days for bulk and stretch; apparently much larger days than we had ever been in before. All previous days had been but shrunk-up little things by comparison. The difference in temperature between the two days was very marked, their day being hotter than mine because it was closer to the equator.

Along about the moment that we were crossing the Great Meridian a child was born in the steerage, and now there is no way to tell which day it was born on. The nurse thinks it was Sunday, the surgeon thinks it was Tuesday. The child will never know its own birthday. It will always be choosing first one and then the other, and will never be able to make up its mind permanently. This will breed vacillation and uncertainty in its opinions about religion, and politics, and business, and sweethearts, and everything, and will undermine its principles, and rot them away, and make the poor thing characterless, and its success in life impossible. Every one in the ship says so. And this is not all—in fact, not the worst. For there is an enormously rich brewer in the ship who said as much as ten days ago, that if the child was born on his birthday he would give it ten thousand dollars to start its little life with. His birthday was Monday, the 9th of September.

If the ships all moved in the one direction—westward, I mean—the world would suffer a prodigious loss in in the matter of valuable time, through the dumping overboard on the Great Meridian of such multitudes of days by ships' crews and passengers. But fortunately the ships do not all sail west; half of them sail east. So there is no real loss. These latter pick up all the discarded days and add them to the world's stock again; and about as good as new, too; for of course the salt water preserves them.[5]

[From Chapter 5]

We are moving steadily southward—getting further and further down under the projecting paunch of the globe. Yesterday evening we saw the Big Dipper and the north star sink below the horizon and disappear from our world. No, not "we," but they. They saw it—somebody saw it—and told me about it. But it is no matter, I was not caring for those things, I am tired of them, any way. I think they are well enough, but one doesn't want them always hanging around. My interest was all in the Southern Cross. I had heard about it all my life, and it was but natural that I should be burning to see it. No other constellation makes so much talk. I had nothing against the Big Dipper—and naturally couldn't have anything against it, since it is a citizen of our own sky, and the property of the United States—but I did want it to move out of the way and give this foreigner a chance. Judging by the size of the talk which the Southern Cross had made, I supposed it would need a sky all to itself.

But that was a mistake. We saw the Cross to-night, and it is not large. Not large, and not strikingly bright. But it was low down toward the horizon, and it may improve when it gets up higher in the sky. It is ingeniously named, for it looks just as a cross would look if it looked like something else. But that description does not describe; it is too vague, too general, too indefinite. It does after a fashion suggest a cross—a cross that is out of repair—or out of drawing; not correctly shaped. It is long, with a short cross-bar, and the cross-bar is canted out of the straight line.

It consists of four large stars and one little one. The little one is out of line and further damages the shape. It should have been placed at the intersection of the stem and the cross-bar. If you do not draw an imaginary line from star to star it does not suggest a cross—nor anything in particular.

One must ignore the little star, and leave it out of the combination—it confuses everything. If you leave it out, then you can make out of the four stars a sort of cross—out of true; or a sort of kite—out of true; or a sort of coffin—out of true.

Constellations have always been troublesome things to name. If you give one of them a fanciful name, it will always refuse to live up to it; it will always persist in not resembling the thing it has been named for. Ultimately, to satisfy the public, the fanciful name has to be discarded for a common-sense one, a manifestly descriptive one. The Great Bear remained the Great Bear—and unrecognizable as such—for thousands of years; and people complained about it all the time, and quite properly; but as soon as it became the property of the United States, Congress changed it to the Big Dipper, and now everybody is satisfied, and there is no more talk about riots. I would not change the Southern Cross to the Southern Coffin, I would change it to the Southern Kite; for up there in the general emptiness is the proper home of a kite, but not for coffins and crosses and dippers. In a little while, now—I cannot tell exactly how long it will be—the globe will belong to the English-speaking race; and of course the skies also. Then the constellations will be re-organized, and polished up, and re-named—the most of them "Victoria," I reckon, but this one will sail thereafter as the Southern Kite, or go out of business.[6]

[From Chapter 7]

From Diary: For a day or two we have been plowing among an invisible vast wilderness of "islands," catching now and then a shadowy glimpse of a member of it. There does seem to be a prodigious lot of islands this year; the map of this region is freckled and fly-specked all over with them. Their number would seem to be uncountable. We are moving among the Fijis now—224 islands and islets in the group. In front of us, to the west, the wilderness stretches toward Australia, then curves upward to New Guinea, and still up and up to Japan; behind us, to the east, the wilderness stretches sixty degrees across the wastes of the Pacific; south of us is New Zealand. Somewhere or other among these myriads Samoa is concealed, and not discoverable on the map. Still, if you wish to go there, you will have no trouble about finding it if you follow the directions given by Robert Louis Stevenson to Dr. Conan Doyle and to Mr. J. M. Barrie. "You go to America, cross the continent to San Francisco, and then it's the second turning to the left." To get the full flavor of the joke one must take a glance at the map.

Wednesday, September 11. Yesterday we passed close to an island or so, and recognized the published Fiji characteristics: a broad belt of clean white coral sand around the island; back of it a graceful fringe of leaning palms, with native huts nestling cosily among the shrubbery at their bases; back of these a stretch of level land clothed in tropic vegetation; back of that, rugged and picturesque mountains. A detail of the immediate foreground: a mouldering ship perched high up on a reef-bench. This completes the composition, and makes the picture artistically perfect.

In the afternoon we sighted Suva, the capital of the group, and

threaded our way into the secluded little harbor—a placid basin of bril-
liant blue and green water tucked snugly in among the sheltering hills.
A few ships rode at anchor in it—one of them a sailing vessel flying the
American flag; and they said she came from Duluth! There's a journey!
Duluth is several thousand miles from the sea, and yet she is entitled
to the proud name of Mistress of the Commercial Marine of the United
States of America. There is only one free, independent, unsubsidized
American ship sailing the foreign seas, and Duluth owns it. All by itself
that ship is the American fleet. All by itself it causes the American name
and power to be respected in the far regions of the globe. All by itself it
certifies to the world that the most populous civilized nation in the earth
has a just pride in her stupendous stretch of sea-front, and is determined
to assert and maintain her rightful place as one of the Great Maritime
Powers of the Planet. All by itself it is making foreign eyes familiar with
a Flag which they have not seen before for forty years, outside of the
museum. For what Duluth has done, in building, equipping, and main-
taining at her sole expense the American Foreign Commercial Fleet, and
in thus rescuing the American name from shame and lifting it high for the
homage of the nations, we owe her a debt of gratitude which our hearts
shall confess with quickened beats whenever her name is named hence-
forth. Many national toasts will die in the lapse of time, but while the flag
flies and the Republic survives, they who live under their shelter will still
drink this one, standing and uncovered: Health and prosperity to Thee,
O Duluth, American Queen of the Alien Seas!

Row-boats began to flock from the shore; their crews were the first
natives we had seen. These men carried no overplus of clothing, and
this was wise, for the weather was hot. Handsome, great dusky men they
were, muscular, clean-limbed, and with faces full of character and intelligence. It would be hard to find their superiors anywhere among the dark
races, I should think.[7]

[From Chapter 8]
Indeed, the Island Wilderness is the very home of romance and dreams
and mystery. The loneliness, the solemnity, the beauty, and the deep
repose of this wilderness have a charm which is all their own for the
bruised spirit of men who have fought and failed in the struggle for life

in the great world; and for men who have been hunted out of the great
world for crime; and for other men who love an easy and indolent existence; and for others who love a roving free life, and stir and change and
adventure; and for yet others who love an easy and comfortable career
of trading and money-getting, mixed with plenty of loose matrimony by
purchase, divorce without trial or expense, and limitless spreeing thrown
in to make life ideally perfect.

We sailed again, refreshed.[8]

[From Chapter 9]
Sept. 15—Night. Close to Australia now, Sydney 50 miles distant.

That note recalls an experience. The passengers were sent for, to come
up in the bow and see a fine sight. It was very dark. One could not follow
with the eye the surface of the sea more than fifty yards in any direction
—it dimmed away and became lost to sight at about that distance from
us. But if you patiently gazed into the darkness a little while, there was a
sure reward for you. Presently, a quarter of a mile away you would see a
blinding splash or explosion of light on the water—a flash so sudden and
so astonishingly brilliant that it would make you catch your breath; then
that blotch of light would instantly extend itself and take the corkscrew
shape and imposing length of the fabled sea-serpent, with every curve
of its body and the "break" spreading away from its head, and the wake
following behind its tail clothed in a fierce splendor of living fire. And
my, but it was coming at a lightning gait! Almost before you could think,
this monster of light, fifty feet long, would go flaming and storming by,
and suddenly disappear. And out in the distance whence he came you
would see another flash; and another and another and another, and see
them turn into sea-serpents on the instant; and once sixteen flashed up at
the same time and came tearing towards us, a swarm of wiggling curves,
a moving conflagration, a vision of bewildering beauty, a spectacle of fire
and energy whose equal the most of those people will not see again until
after they are dead.

It was porpoises—porpoises aglow with phosphorescent light. They
presently collected in a wild and magnificent jumble under the bows, and
there they played for an hour, leaping and frollicking and carrying on,
turning summersaults in front of the stem or across it and never getting

hit, never making a miscalculation, though the stem missed them only about an inch, as a rule. They were porpoises of the ordinary length — eight or ten feet — but every twist of their bodies sent a long procession of united and glowing curves astern. That fiery jumble was an enchanting thing to look at, and we stayed out the performance; one cannot have such a show as that twice in a lifetime. The porpoise is the kitten of the sea; he never has a serious thought, he cares for nothing but fun and play. But I think I never saw him at his winsomest until that night. It was near a center of civilization, and he could have been drinking.

By and by, when we had approached to somewhere within thirty miles of Sydney Heads the great electric light that is posted on one of those lofty ramparts began to show, and in time the little spark grew to a great sun and pierced the firmament of darkness with a far-reaching sword of light.

Sydney Harbor is shut in behind a precipice that extends some miles like a wall, and exhibits no break to the ignorant stranger. It has a break in the middle, but it makes so little show that even Captain Cook sailed by it without seeing it. Near by that break is a false break which resembles it, and which used to make trouble for the mariner at night, in the early days before the place was lighted. It caused the memorable disaster to the *Duncan Dunbar*, one of the most pathetic tragedies in the history of that pitiless ruffian, the sea. The ship was a sailing vessel; a fine and favorite passenger packet, commanded by a popular captain of high reputation. She was due from England, and Sydney was waiting, and counting the hours; counting the hours, and making ready to give her a heart-stirring welcome; for she was bringing back a great company of mothers and daughters, the long-missed light and bloom of life of Sydney homes; daughters that had been years absent at school, and mothers that had been with them all that time watching over them. Of all the world only India and Australasia have by custom freighted ships and fleets with their hearts, and know the tremendous meaning of that phrase; only they know what the waiting is like when this freightage is entrusted to the fickle winds, not steam, and what the joy is like when the ship that is returning this treasure comes safe to port and the long dread is over.

On board the *Duncan Dunbar*, flying toward Sydney Heads in the waning afternoon, the happy home-comers made busy preparation, for it was not doubted that they would be in the arms of their friends before the day was done; they put away their sea-going clothes and put on clothes meeter for the meeting, their richest and their loveliest, these poor brides of the grave. But the wind lost force, or there was a miscalculation, and before the Heads were sighted the darkness came on. It was said that ordinarily the captain would have made a safe offing and waited for the morning; but this was no ordinary occasion; all about him were appealing faces, faces pathetic with disappointment. So his sympathy moved him to try the dangerous passage in the dark. He had entered the Heads seventeen times, and believed he knew the ground. So he steered straight for the false opening, mistaking it for the true one. He did not find out that he was wrong until it was too late. There was no saving the ship. The great seas swept her in and crushed her to splinters and rubbish upon the rock tushes at the base of the precipice. Not one of all that fair and gracious company was ever seen again alive. The tale is told to every stranger that passes the spot, and it will continue to be told to all that come, for generations; but it will never grow old, custom cannot stale it, the heart-break that is in it can never perish out of it.

There were two hundred persons in the ship, and but one survived the disaster. He was a sailor. A huge sea flung him up the face of the precipice and stretched him on a narrow shelf of rock midway between the top and the bottom, and there he lay all night. At any other time he would have lain there for the rest of his life, without chance of discovery; but the next morning the ghastly news swept through Sydney that the *Duncan Dunbar* had gone down in sight of home, and straightway the walls of the Heads were black with mourners; and one of these, stretching himself out over the precipice to spy out what might be seen below, discovered this miraculously preserved relic of the wreck. Ropes were brought and the nearly impossible feat of rescuing the man was accomplished. He was a person with a practical turn of mind, and he hired a hall in Sydney and exhibited himself at sixpence a head till he exhausted the output of the gold fields for that year.

We entered and cast anchor, and in the morning went oh-ing and ah-ing in admiration up through the crooks and turns of the spacious and beautiful harbor—a harbor which is the darling of Sydney and the wonder of the world. It is not surprising that the people are proud of it, nor that they put their enthusiasm into eloquent words. A returning citizen asked me what I thought of it, and I testified with a cordiality which I judged would be up to the market rate. I said it was beautiful—superbly beautiful. Then by a natural impulse I gave God the praise. The citizen did not seem altogether satisfied. He said:

"It is beautiful, of course it's beautiful—the Harbor; but that isn't all of it, it's only half of it; Sydney's the other half, and it takes both of them together to ring the supremacy-bell. God made the Harbor, and that's all right; but Satan made Sydney."[9]

* * *

To New Zealand,
from *Following the Equator*

[From Chapter 31]
Sailed last night in the *Flora*, from Lyttelton.

So we did. I remember it yet. The people who sailed in the *Flora* that night may forget some other things if they live a good while, but they will not live long enough to forget that. The *Flora* is about the equivalent of a cattle-scow; but when the Union Company find it inconvenient to keep a contract and lucrative to break it, they smuggle her into passenger service, and "keep the change."

They give no notice of their projected depredation; you innocently buy tickets for the advertised passenger boat, and when you get down to Lyttelton at midnight, you find that they have substituted the scow. They have plenty of good boats, but no competition—and that is the trouble. It is too late now to make other arrangements if you have engagements ahead.

It is a powerful company, it has a monopoly, and everybody is afraid of it—including the government's representative, who stands at the end of the stage-plank to tally the passengers and see that no boat receives a greater number than the law allows her to carry. This conveniently-blind representative saw the scow receive a number which was far in excess of its privilege, and winked a politic wink and said nothing. The passengers bore with meekness the cheat which had been put upon them, and made no complaint.

It was like being at home in America, where abused passengers act in just the same way. A few days before, the Union Company had discharged a captain for getting a boat into danger, and had advertised this act as evidence of its vigilance in looking after the safety of the passengers —for thugging a captain costs the company nothing, but when opportunity offered to send this dangerously overcrowded tub to sea and save a little trouble and a tidy penny by it, it forgot to worry about the passengers' safety.

The first officer told me that the *Flora* was privileged to carry 125 passengers. She must have had all of 230 on board. All the cabins were full, all the cattle-stalls in the main stable were full, the spaces at the heads of companionways were full, every inch of floor and table in the swill-room was packed with sleeping men and remained so until the place was required for breakfast, all the chairs and benches on the hurricane deck were occupied, and still there were people who had to walk about all night!

If the *Flora* had gone down that night, half of the people on board would have been wholly without means of escape.

The owners of that boat were not technically guilty of conspiracy to commit murder, but they were morally guilty of it.

I had a cattle-stall in the main stable—a cavern fitted up with a long double file of two-storied bunks, the files separated by a calico partition —twenty men and boys on one side of it, twenty women and girls on the other. The place was as dark as the soul of the Union Company, and smelt like a kennel. When the vessel got out into the heavy seas and began to pitch and wallow, the cavern prisoners became immediately sea-sick, and then the peculiar results that ensued laid all my previous experiences of the kind well away in the shade. And the wails, the groans, the cries, the shrieks, the strange ejaculations—it was wonderful.

The women and children and some of the men and boys spent the night in that place, for they were too ill to leave it; but the rest of us got up, by and by, and finished the night on the hurricane-deck.

That boat was the foulest I was ever in; and the smell of the breakfast saloon when we threaded our way among the layers of steaming passengers stretched upon its floor and its tables was incomparable for efficiency.

A good many of us got ashore at the first way-port to seek another ship. After a wait of three hours we got good rooms in the *Mahinapua*, a wee little bridal-parlor of a boat — only 205 tons burthen; clean and comfortable; good service; good beds; good table, and no crowding. The seas danced her about like a duck, but she was safe and capable.

Next morning early she went through the French Pass — a narrow gateway of rock, between bold headlands — so narrow, in fact, that it seemed no wider than a street. The current tore through there like a mill-race, and the boat darted through like a telegram. The passage was made in half a minute; then we were in a wide place where noble vast eddies swept grandly round and round in shoal water, and I wondered what they would do with the little boat. They did as they pleased with her. They picked her up and flung her around like nothing and landed her gently on the solid, smooth bottom of sand — so gently, indeed, that we barely felt her touch it, barely felt her quiver when she came to a standstill. The water was as clear as glass, the sand on the bottom was vividly distinct, and the fishes seemed to be swimming about in nothing. Fishing lines were brought out, but before we could bait the hooks the boat was off and away again.[10]

[From Chapter 34]
November 27. To-day we reached Gisborne, and anchored in a big bay; there was a heavy sea on, so we remained on board.

We were a mile from shore; a little steam-tug put out from the land; she was an object of thrilling interest; she would climb to the summit of a billow, reel drunkenly there a moment, dim and gray in the driving storm of spindrift, then make a plunge like a diver and remain out of sight until one had given her up, then up she would dart again, on a steep slant toward the sky, shedding Niagaras of water from her forecastle — and this she kept up, all the way out to us. She brought twenty-five passengers in her stomach — men and women — mainly a traveling dramatic company. In sight on deck were the crew, in sou'westers, yellow waterproof canvas suits, and boots to the thigh. The deck was never quiet for a moment, and seldom nearer level than a ladder, and noble were the seas which leapt aboard and went flooding aft. We rove a long line to the yard-arm, hung a most primitive basket-chair to it and swung it out into the spacious air

of heaven, and there it swayed, pendulum-fashion, waiting for its chance
—then down it shot, skillfully aimed, and was grabbed by the two men
on the forecastle. A young fellow belonging to our crew was in the chair,
to be a protection to the lady-comers. At once a couple of ladies appeared
from below, took seats in his lap, we hoisted them into the sky, waited a
moment till the roll of the ship brought them in, overhead, then we lowered suddenly away, and seized the chair as it struck the deck. We took
the twenty-five aboard, and delivered twenty-five into the tug—among
them several aged ladies, and one blind one—and all without accident. It
was a fine piece of work.

Ours is a nice ship, roomy, comfortable, well-ordered, and satisfactory.
Now and then we step on a rat in a hotel, but we have had no rats on shipboard lately; unless, perhaps, in the *Flora*; we had more serious things to
think of there, and did not notice. I have noticed that it is only in ships
and hotels which still employ the odious Chinese gong, that you find rats.
The reason would seem to be, that as a rat cannot tell the time of day by
a clock, he won't stay where he cannot find out when dinner is ready.[11]

[From Chapter 36]
Friday, December 13. Sailed, at 3 p. m., in the *Mararoa*. Summer seas and
a good ship—life has nothing better.

Monday. Three days of paradise. Warm and sunny and smooth; the
sea a luminous Mediterranean blue. . . . One lolls in a long chair all day
under deck-awnings, and reads and smokes, in measureless content. One
does not read prose at such a time, but poetry.[12]

*   *   *

The Indian Ocean,
from *Following the Equator*

[From Chapter 37]
Monday, December 23, 1895. Sailed from Sydney for Ceylon in the
P. & O. steamer *Oceana*. A Lascar crew mans this ship—the first I have
seen. White cotton petticoat and pants; barefoot; red shawl for belt; straw
cap, brimless, on head, with red scarf wound around it; complexion a

rich dark brown; short straight black hair; whiskers fine and silky; lustrous and intensely black. Mild, good faces; willing and obedient people; capable, too; but are said to go into hopeless panics when there is danger. They are from Bombay and the coast thereabouts. . . . Left some of the trunks in Sydney, to be shipped to South Africa by a vessel advertised to sail three months hence. The proverb says: "Separate not yourself from your baggage." This *Oceana* is a stately big ship, luxuriously appointed. She has spacious promenade decks. Large rooms; a surpassingly comfortable ship. The officers' library is well selected; a ship's library is not usually that. . . . For meals, the bugle call, man-of-war fashion; a pleasant change from the terrible gong. . . . Three big cats—very friendly loafers; they wander all over the ship; the white one follows the chief steward around like a dog. There is also a basket of kittens. One of these cats goes ashore, in port, in England, Australia, and India, to see how his various families are getting along, and is seen no more till the ship is ready to sail. No one knows how he finds out the sailing date, but no doubt he comes down to the dock every day and takes a look, and when he sees baggage and passengers flocking in, recognizes that it is time to get aboard. This is what the sailors believe. . . . The Chief Engineer has been in the China and India trade thirty-three years, and has had but three Christmases at home in that time. . . .

January 4, 1896. Christmas in Melbourne, New Year's Day in Adelaide, and saw most of the friends again in both places. . . . Lying here at anchor all day—Albany (King George's Sound), Western Australia. It is a perfectly landlocked harbor, or roadstead—spacious to look at, but not deep water. Desolate-looking rocks and scarred hills. Plenty of ships arriving now, rushing to the new gold-fields. The papers are full of wonderful tales of the sort always to be heard in connection with new gold diggings. A sample: a youth staked out a claim and tried to sell half for £5; no takers; he stuck to it fourteen days, starving, then struck it rich and sold out for £10,000. . . . About sunset, strong breeze blowing, got up the anchor. We were in a small deep puddle, with a narrow channel leading out of it, minutely buoyed, to the sea.

I stayed on deck to see how we were going to manage it with such a big ship and such a strong wind. On the bridge our giant captain, in uniform; at his side a little pilot in elaborately gold-laced uniform; on the forecastle a white mate and quartermaster or two, and a brilliant crowd of Lascars standing by for business. Our stern was pointing straight at the head of the channel; so we must turn entirely around in the puddle—and the wind blowing as described. It was done, and beautifully. It was done by help of a jib. We stirred up much mud, but did not touch the bottom. We turned right around in our tracks—a seeming impossibility. We had several casts of quarter-less 5, and one cast of half 4—27 feet; we were drawing 26 astern. By the time we were entirely around and pointed, the first buoy was not more than a hundred yards in front of us. It was a fine piece of work, and I was the only passenger that saw it. However, the others got their dinner; the P. & O. Company got mine. . . . More cats developed. Smythe says it is a British law that they must be carried; and he instanced a case of a ship not allowed to sail till she sent for a couple. The bill came, too: "Debtor, to 2 cats, 20 shillings." . . .

A vulture on board; bald, red, queer-shaped head, featherless red places here and there on his body, intense great black eyes set in featherless rims of inflamed flesh; dissipated look; a business-like style, a selfish, conscienceless, murderous aspect—the very look of a professional assassin, and yet a bird which does no murder. What was the use of getting him up in that tragic style for so innocent a trade as his? For this one isn't the sort that wars upon the living, his diet is offal—and the more out of date it is the better he likes it. Nature should give him a suit of rusty black; then he would be all right, for he would look like an undertaker and would harmonize with his business; whereas the way he is now he is horribly out of true.

January 5. At 9 this morning we passed Cape Leeuwin (lioness) and ceased from our long due-west course along the southern shore of Australia. Turning this extreme southwestern corner, we now take a long straight slant nearly N.W., without a break, for Ceylon. As we speed northward it will grow hotter very fast—but it isn't chilly, now. . . .

January 13. Unspeakably hot. The equator is arriving again. We are within eight degrees of it. Ceylon present. Dear me, it is beautiful! . . .

In this palatial ship the passengers dress for dinner. The ladies' toilettes make a fine display of color, and this is in keeping with the elegance of the vessel's furnishings and the flooding brilliancies of the electric light. On the stormy Atlantic one never sees a man in evening dress, except at the rarest intervals; and then there is only one, not two; and he shows up but once on the voyage—the night before the ship makes port—the night when they have the "concert" and do the amateur wailings and recitations. He is the tenor, as a rule. . . . There has been a deal of cricket-playing on board; it seems a queer game for a ship, but they enclose the promenade deck with nettings and keep the ball from flying overboard, and the sport goes very well, and is properly violent and exciting. . . . We must part from this vessel here.[13]

[From Chapter 38]
Evening—14th. Sailed in the *Rosetta.* This is a poor old ship, and ought to be insured and sunk. As in the *Oceana,* just so here: everybody dresses for dinner; they make it a sort of pious duty. These fine and formal costumes are a rather conspicuous contrast to the poverty and shabbiness of the surroundings. . . . If you want a slice of a lime at four o'clock tea, you must sign an order on the bar. Limes cost 14 cents a barrel.[14]

[From Chapter 62]
We sailed from Calcutta toward the end of March; stopped a day at Madras; two or three days in Ceylon; then sailed westward on a long flight for Mauritius. From my diary:

April 7. We are far abroad upon the smooth waters of the Indian Ocean, now; it is shady and pleasant and peaceful under the vast spread of the awnings, and life is perfect again—ideal.

The difference between a river and the sea is, that the river looks fluid, the sea solid—usually looks as if you could step out and walk on it.

The captain has this peculiarity—he cannot tell the truth in a plausible way. In this he is the very opposite of the austere Scot who sits midway of the table; he cannot tell a lie in an implausible way. When the captain finishes a statement the passengers glance at each other privately, as who should say, "Do you believe that?" When the Scot finishes one, the look says, "How strange and interesting." The whole secret is in the manner and method of the two men. The captain is a little shy and diffident, and he states the simplest fact as if he were a little afraid of it, while the Scot delivers himself of the most abandoned lie with such an air of stern veracity that one is forced to believe it although one knows it isn't so. For instance, the Scot told about a pet flying-fish he once owned, that lived in a little fountain in his conservatory, and supported itself by catching birds and frogs and rats in the neighboring fields. It was plain that no one at the table doubted this statement. . . .

Lots of pets on board—birds and things. In these far countries the white people do seem to run remarkably to pets. Our host in Cawnpore had a fine collection of birds—the finest we saw in a private house in India. And in Colombo, Dr. Murray's great compound and commodious bungalow were well populated with domesticated company from the woods: frisky little squirrels; a Ceylon mina walking sociably about the house; a small green parrot that whistled a single urgent note of call without motion of its beak; also chuckled; a monkey in a cage on the back veranda, and some more out in the trees; also a number of beautiful macaws in the trees; and various and sundry birds and animals of breeds not known to me. But no cat. Yet a cat would have liked that place.

April 10. The sea is a Mediterranean blue; and I believe that that is about the divinest color known to nature.

It is strange and fine—Nature's lavish generosities to her creatures. At least to all of them except man. For those that fly she has provided a home that is nobly spacious—a home which is forty miles deep and envelops the whole globe, and has not an obstruction in it. For those that swim she has provided a more than imperial domain—a domain which is miles deep and covers four-fifths of the globe. But as for man, she has cut him off with the mere odds and ends of the creation. She has given him the thin skin, the meagre skin which is stretched over the remaining one-fifth —the naked bones stick up through it in most places. On the one-half of this domain he can raise snow, ice, sand, rocks, and nothing else. So the valuable part of his inheritance really consists of but a single fifth of the family estate; and out of it he has to grub hard to get enough to keep him alive and provide kings and soldiers and powder to extend the blessings of civilization with. Yet man, in his simplicity and complacency and inability to cipher, thinks Nature regards him as the important member of the family—in fact, her favorite. Surely, it must occur to even his dull head, sometimes, that she has a curious way of showing it.

Afternoon. The captain has been telling how, in one of his Arctic voyages, it was so cold that the mate's shadow froze fast to the deck and had to be ripped loose by main strength. And even then he got only about two-thirds of it back. Nobody said anything, and the captain went away; I think he is becoming disheartened. . . .

Customs in tropic seas. At 5 in the morning they pipe to wash down the decks, and at once the ladies who are sleeping there turn out and they and their beds go below. Then one after another the men come up from the bath in their pyjamas, and walk the decks an hour or two with bare legs and bare feet. Coffee and fruit served. The ship cat and her kitten now appear and get about their toilets; next the barber comes and flays us on the breezy deck. Breakfast at 9.30, and the day begins. I do not know how a day could be more reposeful: no motion; a level blue sea; nothing in sight from horizon to horizon; the speed of the ship furnishes a cooling breeze; there is no mail to read and answer; no newspapers to excite you; no telegrams to fret you or fright you—the world is far, far away; it has ceased to exist for you—seemed a fading dream, along in the first days; has dissolved to an unreality now; it is gone from your mind with all its businesses and ambitions, its prosperities and disasters, its exultations and despairs, its joys and griefs and cares and worries. They are no concern of yours any more; they have gone out of your life; they are a storm which has passed and left a deep calm behind. The people group themselves about the decks in their snowy white linen, and read, smoke, sew, play cards, talk, nap, and so on. In other ships the passengers are always ciphering about when they are going to arrive; out in these seas it is rare, very rare, to hear that subject broached. In other ships there is always an eager rush to the bulletin board at noon to find out what the "run" has been; in these seas the bulletin seems to attract no interest; I have seen no one visit it; in thirteen days I have visited it only once. Then I happened to notice the figures of the day's run. On that day there happened to be talk, at dinner, about the speed of modern ships. I was the only passenger present who knew this ship's gait. Necessarily, the Atlantic custom of betting on the ship's run is not a custom here—nobody ever mentions it.

I myself am wholly indifferent as to when we are going to "get in"; if any one else feels interested in the matter he has not indicated it in my hearing. If I had my way we should never get in at all. This sort of sea life is charged with an indestructible charm. There is no weariness, no fatigue, no worry, no responsibility, no work, no depression of spirits.

There is nothing like this serenity, this comfort, this peace, this deep contentment, to be found anywhere on land. If I had my way I would sail on for ever and never go to live on the solid ground again.

One of Kipling's ballads has delivered the aspect and sentiment of this bewitching sea correctly:

> "The Injian Ocean sets an' smiles
> So sof', so bright, so bloomin' blue;
> There aren't a wave for miles an' miles
> Excep' the jiggle from the screw."

April 14th. — It turns out that the astronomical apprentice worked off a section of the Milky Way on me for the Magellan Clouds. A man of more experience in the business showed one of them to me last night. It was small and faint and delicate, and looked like the ghost of a bunch of white smoke left floating in the sky by an exploded bombshell.[15]

* * *

Completing the Circle,
from _Following the Equator_

[From Chapter 64]

The _Arundel Castle_ is the finest boat I have seen in these seas. She is thoroughly modern, and that statement covers a great deal of ground. She has the usual defect, the common defect, the universal defect, the defect that has never been missing from any ship that ever sailed — she has imperfect beds. Many ships have good beds, but no ship has very good ones. In the matter of beds all ships have been badly edited, ignorantly edited, from the beginning. The selection of the beds is given to some hearty, strong-backed, self-made man, when it ought to be given to a frail woman accustomed from girlhood to backaches and insomnia. Nothing is so rare, on either side of the ocean, as a perfect bed; nothing is so difficult to make. Some of the hotels on both sides provide it, but no ship ever does or ever did. In Noah's Ark the beds were simply scandalous. Noah set the fashion, and it will endure in one degree of modification or another till the next flood.

8 A.M. Passing Isle de Bourbon. Broken-up sky-line of volcanic mountains in the middle. Surely it would not cost much to repair them, and it seems inexcusable neglect to leave them as they are.

It seems stupid to send tired men to Europe to rest. It is no proper rest for the mind to clatter from town to town in the dust and cinders, and examine galleries and architecture, and be always meeting people and lunching and teaing and dining, and receiving worrying cables and letters. And a sea voyage on the Atlantic is of no use—voyage too short, sea too rough. The peaceful Indian and Pacific Oceans and the long stretches of time are the healing thing.

May 2, A.M. A fair, great ship in sight, almost the first we have seen in these weeks of lonely voyaging. We are now in the Mozambique Channel, between Madagascar and South Africa, sailing straight west for Delagoa Bay.

Last night, the burly chief engineer, middle-aged, was standing telling a spirited seafaring tale, and had reached the most exciting place, where a man overboard was washing swiftly astern on the great seas, and uplifting despairing cries, everybody racing aft in a frenzy of excitement and fading hope, when the band, which had been silent a moment, began impressively its closing piece, the English national anthem. As simply as if he was unconscious of what he was doing, he stopped his story, uncovered, laid his laced cap against his breast, and slightly bent his grizzled head. The few bars finished, he put on his cap and took up his tale again as naturally as if that interjection of music had been a part of it. There was something touching and fine about it, and it was moving to reflect that he was one of a myriad, scattered over every part of the globe, who by turn was doing as he was doing every hour of the twenty-four—those awake doing it while the others slept—those impressive bars forever floating up out of the various climes, never silent and never lacking reverent listeners.

All that I remember about Madagascar is that Thackeray's little Billie went up to the top of the mast and there knelt him upon his knee, saying, "I see

Jerusalem and Madagascar,
And North and South Amerikee."

May 3. Sunday. Fifteen or twenty Africaners who will end their voyage to-day and strike for their several homes from Delagoa Bay to-morrow, sat up singing on the after-deck in the moonlight till 3 A.M. Good fun and wholesome. And the songs were clean songs, and some of them were hallowed by tender associations. Finally, in a pause, a man asked, "Have you heard about the fellow that kept a diary crossing the Atlantic?" It was a discord, a wet blanket. The men were not in the mood for humorous dirt. The songs had carried them to their homes, and in spirit they sat by those far hearthstones, and saw faces and heard voices other than those that were about them. And so this disposition to drag in an old indecent anecdote got no welcome; nobody answered. The poor man hadn't wit enough to see that he had blundered, but asked his question again. Again there was no response. It was embarrassing for him. In his confusion he chose the wrong course, did the wrong thing—began the anecdote. Began it in a deep and hostile stillness, where had been such life and stir and warm comradeship before. He delivered himself of the brief details of the diary's first day, and did it with some confidence and a fair degree of eagerness. It fell flat. There was an awkward pause. The two rows of men sat like statues. There was no movement, no sound. He had to go on; there was no other way, at least none that an animal of his caliber could think of. At the close of each day's diary the same dismal silence followed. When at last he finished his tale and sprung the indelicate surprise which is wont to fetch a crash of laughter, not a ripple of sound resulted. It was as if the tale had been told to dead men. After what seemed a long, long time, somebody sighed, somebody else stirred in his seat; presently, the men dropped into a low murmur of confidential talk, each with his neighbor, and the incident was closed. There were indications that that man was fond of his anecdote; that it was his pet, his standby, his shot that never missed, his reputation-maker. But he will never tell it again. No doubt he will think of it sometimes, for that cannot well be helped; and then he will see a picture, and always the same picture—the double rank of dead men; the vacant deck stretching away in dimming perspective beyond them, the wide desert of smooth sea all abroad; the rim of the moon spying from behind a rag of black cloud; the remote top of the mizzenmast shearing a zigzag path through the fields of stars in the deeps of space; and this soft picture will remind him of the time that he sat in the midst of it and told his poor little tale and felt so lonesome when he got through.

Fifty Indians and Chinamen asleep in a big tent in the waist of the ship forward; they lie side by side with no space between; the former wrapped up, head and all, as in the Indian streets, the Chinamen uncovered; the lamp and things for opium smoking in the center. . . .

Monday, May 4. Steaming slowly in the stupendous Delagoa Bay, its dim arms stretching far away and disappearing on both sides. It could furnish plenty of room for all the ships in the world, but it is shoal. The lead has given us 3½ fathoms several times and we are drawing that, lacking 6 inches.

A bold headland—precipitous wall, 150 feet high, very strong, red color, stretching a mile or so. A man said it was Portuguese blood—battle fought here with the natives last year. I think this doubtful. Pretty cluster of houses on the tableland above the red and rolling stretches of grass and groups of trees, like England.[16]

[From the Conclusion]
We sailed on the 15th of July in the *Norman*, a beautiful ship, perfectly appointed. The voyage to England occupied a short fortnight, without a stop except at Madeira. A good and restful voyage for tired people, and there were several of us. I seemed to have been lecturing a thousand years, though it was only a twelvemonth, and a considerable number of the others were Reformers who were fagged out with their five months of seclusion in the Pretoria prison.

Our trip around the earth ended at the Southampton pier, where we embarked thirteen months before. It seemed a fine and large thing to have accomplished—the circumnavigation of this great globe in that little time, and I was privately proud of it. For a moment. Then came one of those vanity-snubbing astronomical reports from the Observatory-people, whereby it appeared that another great body of light had lately flamed up in the remotenesses of space which was traveling at a gait which would enable it to do all that I had done in a minute and a half. Human pride is not worth while; there is always something lying in wait to take the wind out of it.[17]

What Mark Twain opted not to mention in his conclusion was the devastating news the family received as they were completing their voyage on August 16, 1873. The first-born of the three Clemens girls, "Susy," the one most like her father, had fallen ill back in Connecticut. Her malady proved to be typhus. She died two days later.

Mark Twain's Iconic Sea Captain

aptain Edgar "Ned" Wakeman (1818–1875) provided the model for several of Mark Twain's characters: Captain Ned Blakely, Captain "Hurricane" Jones, Captain Saltmarsh, and a figure named Stormfield—Captain and Admiral—that Twain worked on for forty years. Stormfield was the name he gave his mansion in Redding, Connecticut, because he built part of it with the money he made selling a story featuring the voluble captain. When he was in his advanced years, Clemens would slip and conflate the real Captain Wakeman with the fictional Captain Stormfield, saying "Wakefield" with reference to both.

Born in Connecticut in 1818, Edgar Wakeman rounded Cape Horn to reach San Francisco at the height of the gold rush, and became a legend in California. Captain "Ned" Wakeman was probably a bigger celebrity in San Francisco than "Mark Twain" was when they first met in December 1866 aboard the *America*, en route to Nicaragua. Sam Clemens, the former riverman, recently introduced to blue water, cottoned quickly to the endearingly blustery old salt. That charismatic figure must have seemed to the writer to be a personification—a mash-up—of the literary captains of his youth. His vividly positive first impressions of Wakeman found reinforcement when their paths crossed again two years later in Panama. Mark Twain first inserted Wakeman into his writings soon after meeting him, calling him "Captain Waxman" in his letters to the *Alta California*. But when Twain returned to California the following year, he called him by his real name in his published correspondence, beginning with this letter of September 6, 1868:

* * *

From the *Alta California* Letters

September 6, 1868

We found Panama in the same place. It has not changed perceptibly. They had no revolution while we were there. I do not know why, but it is true that there had not been a revolution for as much as two weeks. The very same President was at the head of the Government that was at the head of it a fortnight before. It was very curious. I suppose they have hanged him before this, however. While I was standing in the bar of the Grand Hotel talking with a citizen about Admiral Shubry (who is one of the most enterprising Americans on the Isthmus, and has had a steamer built in New York at a cost of $100,000 for the purpose of bringing live stock down from his ranch for the steamers), I heard a familiar voice holding forth in this wise:

"Monkeys! don't tell me nothing about monkeys, sir! I know all about 'em! Didn't I take the *Mary Ann* through the Monkey Islands? — snakes as big as a ship's mainmast, sir! — and monkeys! — God bless my soul, sir, just at daylight she fetched up at a dead stand-still, sir! — what do you suppose it was, sir? It was monkeys! Millions of 'em, sir! — banked up as high as the cat-heads, sir! — trying to swim across the channel, sir, and crammed it full! I took my glass to see thirteen mile of monkeys, two mile wide and sixty fathom deep, sir! — counted, ninety-seven million of 'em, and the mate set 'em down, sir — kept tally till his pencils was all used up and his arm was paralyzed, sir! Don't tell me nothing about monkeys, sir — because I've been there — I know all about 'em, sir!"

It is hardly possible, but still there may be people who are so ignorant as not to know that this voice belonged to Captain Ned Wakeman, of the steamship *America*. Cheerful as ever, as big-hearted as ever, as splendid an old salt as walks the deck of any ship — this is Wakeman. But he is failing under that Panama sun. They have had him lying up for months in charge of a spare ship, and it has been pretty severe on him. They ought to let him go to sea a while, now, and recuperate. He says the sun gets so hot in Panama, sometimes, it is as much as a man can do to tell the truth.[1]

In chapter 50 of *Roughing It*, Mark Twain resumed using an alias for Wakeman, but this tale of frontier justice at sea—or on the "guano islands" of the Chincha archipelago, to be more exact—is a true story. The narrative makes a powerful statement for civil rights.

* * *

From *Roughing It*, Chapter 50

These murder and jury statistics remind me of a certain very extraordinary trial and execution of twenty years ago; it is a scrap of history familiar to all old Californians, and worthy to be known by other peoples of the earth that love simple, straightforward justice unencumbered with nonsense. I would apologize for this digression but for the fact that the information I am about to offer is apology enough in itself. And since I digress constantly anyhow, perhaps it is as well to eschew apologies altogether and thus prevent their growing irksome.

Capt. Ned Blakely—that name will answer as well as any other fictitious one (for he was still with the living at last accounts, and may not desire to be famous)—sailed ships out of the harbor of San Francisco for many years. He was a stalwart, warm-hearted, eagle-eyed veteran, who had been a sailor nearly fifty years—a sailor from early boyhood. He was a rough, honest creature, full of pluck, and just as full of hard-headed simplicity, too. He hated trifling conventionalities—"business" was the word, with him. He had all a sailor's vindictiveness against the quips and quirks of the law, and steadfastly believed that the first and last aim and object of the law and lawyers was to defeat justice.

He sailed for the Chincha Islands in command of a guano ship. He had a fine crew, but his negro mate was his pet—on him he had for years lavished his admiration and esteem. It was Capt. Ned's first voyage to the Chinchas, but his fame had gone before him—the fame of being a man who would fight at the dropping of a handkerchief, when imposed upon, and would stand no nonsense. It was a fame well earned. Arrived in the islands, he found that the staple of conversation was the exploits of one Bill Noakes, a bully, the mate of a trading ship. This man had created a small reign of terror there. At nine o'clock at night, Capt. Ned, all alone, was pacing his deck in the starlight. A form ascended the side, and approached him. Capt. Ned said:

"Who goes there?"

"I'm Bill Noakes, the best man in the islands."

"What do you want aboard this ship?"

"I've heard of Capt. Ned Blakely, and one of us is a better man than 'tother — I'll know which, before I go ashore."

"You've come to the right shop — I'm your man. I'll learn you to come aboard this ship without an invite."

He seized Noakes, backed him against the mainmast, pounded his face to a pulp, and then threw him overboard.

Noakes was not convinced. He returned the next night, got the pulp renewed, and went overboard head first, as before. He was satisfied.

A week after this, while Noakes was carousing with a sailor crowd on shore, at noonday, Capt. Ned's colored mate came along, and Noakes tried to pick a quarrel with him. The negro evaded the trap, and tried to get away. Noakes followed him up; the negro began to run; Noakes fired on him with a revolver and killed him. Half a dozen sea-captains witnessed the whole affair. Noakes retreated to the small after-cabin of his ship, with two other bullies, and gave out that death would be the portion of any man that intruded there. There was no attempt made to follow the villains; there was no disposition to do it, and indeed very little thought of such an enterprise. There were no courts and no officers; there was no government; the islands belonged to Peru, and Peru was far away; she had no official representative on the ground; and neither had any other nation.

However, Capt. Ned was not perplexing his head about such things. They concerned him not. He was boiling with rage and furious for justice. At nine o'clock at night he loaded a double-barreled gun with slugs, fished out a pair of handcuffs, got a ship's lantern, summoned his quartermaster, and went ashore. He said:

"Do you see that ship there at the dock?"

"Ay-ay, sir."

"It's the *Venus*."

"Ay-ay, sir."

"You — you know *me*."

"Ay-ay, sir."

"Very well, then. Take the lantern. Carry it just under your chin. I'll walk behind you and rest this gun-barrel on your shoulder, p'inting forward—so. Keep your lantern well up so's I can see things ahead of you good. I'm going to march in on Noakes—and take him—and jug the other chaps. If you flinch—well, you know *me*."

"Ay-ay, sir."

In this order they filed aboard softly, arrived at Noakes's den, the quartermaster pushed the door open, and the lantern revealed the three desperadoes sitting on the floor. Capt. Ned said:

"I'm Ned Blakely. I've got you under fire. Don't you move without orders—any of you. You two kneel down in the corner; faces to the wall —now. Bill Noakes, put these handcuffs on; now come up close. Quartermaster, fasten 'em. All right. Don't stir, sir. Quartermaster, put the key in the outside of the door. Now, men, I'm going to lock you two in; and if you try to burst through this door—well, you've heard of me. Bill Noakes, fall in ahead, and march. All set. Quartermaster, lock the door."[2]

Here's how Clemens encapsulated the conclusion in his autobiography:

* * *

From the *Autobiography of Mark Twain*

I have told how [Wakeman] brought the murderer of his colored mate to trial in the Chincha Islands before the assembled captains of the ships in port, and how when sentence had been passed he drew the line there. He had intended to capture and execute the murderer all by himself, but had been persuaded by the captains to let them try him with the due formalities, and under the forms of law. He had yielded that much, though most reluctantly, but when the captains proposed to do the executing also, that was too much for Wakeman, and he struck. He hanged the man himself. He put the noose around the murderer's neck, threw the bight[3] of the line over the limb of a tree, and made his last moments a misery to him by reading him nearly into premature death with random and irrelevant chapters from the Bible.[4]

The following evocation of Wakeman as "Hurricane Jones" comes from "Some Rambling Notes of an Idle Excursion." The dinner table discussion recounted in it took place on Mark Twain's voyage from Hamilton, Bermuda, to New York, May 24 to 27, 1877, as shown by the entry in the author's notebook titled "Old Wakeman's stories about Isaac and Dan'l."[5] Wakeman told these same tales himself in his autobiography, published in 1878.[6]

* * *

From "Some Rambling Notes of an Idle Excursion"

There was a good deal of pleasant gossip about old Captain "Hurricane" Jones, of the Pacific Ocean—peace to his ashes! Two or three of us present had known him; I particularly well, for I had made four sea-voyages with him. He was a very remarkable man. He was born in a ship; he picked up what little education he had among his shipmates; he began life in the forecastle, and climbed grade by grade to the captaincy. More than fifty years of his sixty-five were spent at sea. He had sailed all oceans, seen all lands, and borrowed a tint from all climates. When a man has been fifty years at sea he necessarily knows nothing of men, nothing of the world but its surface, nothing of the world's thought, nothing of the world's learning but its A B C, and that blurred and distorted by the unfocused lenses of an untrained mind. Such a man is only a gray and bearded child. That is what old Hurricane Jones was—simply an innocent, lovable old infant. When his spirit was in repose he was as sweet and gentle as a girl; when his wrath was up he was a hurricane that made his nickname seem tamely descriptive. He was formidable in a fight, for he was of powerful build and dauntless courage. He was frescoed from head to heel with pictures and mottoes tattooed in red and blue India ink. I was with him one voyage when he got his last vacant space tattooed; this vacant space was around his left ankle. During three days he stumped about the ship with his ankle bare and swollen, and this legend gleaming red and angry out from a clouding of India ink: "Virtue is its own R'd." (There was a lack of room.) He was deeply and sincerely pious, and swore like a fishwoman. He considered swearing blameless, because sailors would not understand an order unillumined by it. He was a profound biblical scholar—that is, he thought he was. He believed everything in the Bible, but he had his own methods of arriving at his beliefs. He was of the "advanced" school of thinkers, and applied natural laws to the interpretation of all miracles, somewhat on the plan of the people who make the six days of creation six geological epochs, and so forth. Without being aware of it, he was a rather severe satire on modern scientific religionists. Such a man as I have been describing is rabidly fond of disquisition and argument; one knows that without being told it.

One trip the captain had a clergyman on board, but did not know he was a clergyman, since the passenger-list did not betray the fact. He took a great liking to this Reverend Mr. Peters, and talked with him a great deal; told him yarns, gave him toothsome scraps of personal history, and wove a glittering streak of profanity through his garrulous fabric that was refreshing to a spirit weary of the dull neutralities of undecorated speech. One day the captain said, "Peters, do you ever read the Bible?"

"Well—yes."

"I judge it ain't often, by the way you say it. Now, you tackle it in dead earnest once, and you'll find it'll pay. Don't you get discouraged, but hang right on. First, you won't understand it; but by and by things will begin to clear up, and then you wouldn't lay it down to eat."

"Yes, I have heard that said."

"And it's so, too. There ain't a book that begins with it. It lays over 'm all, Peters. There's some pretty tough things in it—there ain't any getting around that—but you stick to them and think them out, and when once you get on the inside everything's plain as day."

"The miracles, too, captain?"

"Yes, sir! the miracles, too. Every one of them. Now, there's that business with the prophets of Baal; like enough that stumped you?"

"Well, I don't know but—"

"Own up now; it stumped you. Well, I don't wonder. You hadn't had any experience in raveling such things out, and naturally it was too many for you. Would you like to have me explain that thing to you, and show you how to get at the meat of these matters?"

"Indeed, I would, captain, if you don't mind."

Then the captain proceeded as follows: "I'll do it with pleasure. First, you see, I read and read, and thought and thought, till I got to understand what sort of people they were in the old Bible times, and then after that it was all clear and easy. Now this was the way I put it up, concerning Isaac —[This is the captain's own mistake][7]—and the prophets of Baal. There was some mighty sharp men among the public characters of that old ancient day, and Isaac was one of them. Isaac had his failings—plenty of them, too; it ain't for me to apologize for Isaac; he played it on the prophets of Baal, and like enough he was justifiable, considering the odds that was against him. No, all I say is, 'twa'n't any miracle, and that I'll show you so's't you can see it yourself.

"Well, times had been getting rougher and rougher for prophets— that is, prophets of Isaac's denomination. There was four hundred and fifty prophets of Baal in the community, and only one Presbyterian; that is, if Isaac was a Presbyterian, which I reckon he was, but it don't say. Naturally, the prophets of Baal took all the trade. Isaac was pretty low-spirited, I reckon, but he was a good deal of a man, and no doubt he went a-prophesying around, letting on to be doing a land-office business, but 'twa'n't any use; he couldn't run any opposition to amount to anything. By and by things got desperate with him; he sets his head to work and thinks it all out, and then what does he do? Why, he begins to throw out hints that the other parties are this and that and t'other—nothing very definite, maybe, but just kind of undermining their reputation in a quiet way. This made talk, of course, and finally got to the king. The king asked Isaac what he meant by his talk. Says Isaac, 'Oh, nothing particular; only, can they pray down fire from heaven on an altar? It ain't much, maybe, your majesty, only can they do it? That's the idea.' So the king was a good deal disturbed, and he went to the prophets of Baal, and they said, pretty airy, that if he had an altar ready, they were ready; and they intimated he better get it insured, too.

"So next morning all the children of Israel and their parents and the other people gathered themselves together. Well, here was that great crowd of prophets of Baal packed together on one side, and Isaac walking up and down all alone on the other, putting up his job. When time was called, Isaac let on to be comfortable and indifferent; told the other team to take the first innings. So they went at it, the whole four hundred and fifty, praying around the altar, very hopeful, and doing their level best.

They prayed an hour—two hours—three hours—and so on, plumb
till noon. It wa'n't any use; they hadn't took a trick. Of course they felt
kind of ashamed before all those people, and well they might. Now, what
would a magnanimous man do? Keep still, wouldn't he? Of course. What
did Isaac do? He graveled the prophets of Baal every way he could think
of. Says he, 'You don't speak up loud enough; your god's asleep, like
enough, or maybe he's taking a walk; you want to holler, you know'—or
words to that effect; I don't recollect the exact language. Mind, I don't
apologize for Isaac; he had his faults.

"Well, the prophets of Baal prayed along the best they knew how all
the afternoon, and never raised a spark. At last, about sundown, they
were all tuckered out, and they owned up and quit.

"What does Isaac do now? He steps up and says to some friends of his
there, 'Pour four barrels of water on the altar!' Everybody was astonished;
for the other side had prayed at it dry, you know, and got whitewashed.
They poured it on. Says he, 'Heave on four more barrels.' Then he says,
'Heave on four more.' Twelve barrels, you see, altogether. The water ran
all over the altar, and all down the sides, and filled up a trench around it
that would hold a couple of hogsheads—'measures,' it says; I reckon it
means about a hogshead. Some of the people were going to put on their
things and go, for they allowed he was crazy. They didn't know Isaac.
Isaac knelt down and began to pray; he strung along, and strung along,
about the heathen in distant lands, and about the sister churches, and
about the state and the country at large, and about those that's in authority in the government, and all the usual program, you know, till everybody
had got tired and gone to thinking about something else, and then, all of
a sudden, when nobody was noticing, he outs with a match and rakes
it on the under side of his leg, and pff! up the whole thing blazes like a
house afire! Twelve barrels of water? Petroleum, sir, PETROLEUM! that's
what it was!"

"Petroleum, captain?"

"Yes, sir, the country was full of it. Isaac knew all about that. You read
the Bible. Don't you worry about the tough places. They ain't tough
when you come to think them out and throw light on them. There ain't
a thing in the Bible but what is true; all you want is to go prayerfully to
work and cipher out how 'twas done."[8]

The voice of "Captain Saltmarsh," unmistakably Wakeman-esque, was first heard in chapter 77 of *Roughing It*. Called on to affirm the tall tale of a pathological liar, Saltmarsh instead shoots him down with salty succinctness.

*   *   *

From *Roughing It*, Chapter 77

"Beg your pardon, sir, beg your pardon, but it can only be considered remarkable when brought into strong outline by isolation. Sir, contrasted with a circumstance which occurred in my own experience, it instantly becomes commonplace. No, not that—for I will not speak so discourte-ously of any experience in the career of a stranger and a gentleman—but I am obliged to say that you could not, and you would not ever again refer to this tree as a large one, if you could behold, as I have, the great Yak-matack tree, on the island of Ounaska, sea of Kamtchatka—a tree, sir, not one inch less than four hundred and fifteen feet in solid diameter!—and I wish I may die in a minute if it isn't so! Oh, you needn't look so ques-tioning, gentlemen; here's old Cap'n Saltmarsh can say whether I know what I'm talking about or not. I showed him the tree."

Captain Saltmarsh—"Come, now, cat your anchor, lad—you're heav-ing too taut. You promised to show me that stunner, and I walked more than eleven mile with you through the cussedest jungle I ever see, a hunt-ing for it; but the tree you showed me finally warn't as big around as a beer cask, and you know that your own self, Markiss."[9]

Captain Saltmarsh shows up for a cameo appearance in chapter 16 of *The American Claimant* (1892), then goes away, leaving a small, intricate verbal profile of an old tar's parlance. The context of the scene is even more rococo in terms of plot, and need not be recounted here, because all that matters in this excerpt is the perfect idiom of Mark Twain's iconic Wakeman/Stormfield captain.

*   *   *

From *The American Claimant*, Chapter 16

Brady arrived with a box, and departed, after saying, "They're finishing one up, but they'll be along as soon as it's done."

Barrow took a frameless oil portrait a foot square from the box, set it up in a good light, without comment, and reached for another, taking a furtive glance at Tracy, meantime. The stony solemnity in Tracy's face remained as it was, and gave out no sign of interest. Barrow placed the second portrait beside the first, and stole another glance while reaching for a third. The stone image softened, a shade. No. 3 forced the ghost of a smile, No. 4 swept indifference wholly away, and No. 5 started a laugh which was still in good and hearty condition when No. 14 took its place in the row.

"Oh, you're all right, yet," said Barrow. "You see you're not past amusement."

The pictures were fearful, as to color, and atrocious as to drawing and expression; but the feature which squelched animosity and made them funny was a feature which could not achieve its full force in a single picture, but required the wonder-working assistance of repetition. One loudly dressed mechanic in stately attitude, with his hand on a cannon, ashore, and a ship riding at anchor in the offing, — this is merely odd; but when one sees the same cannon and the same ship in fourteen pictures in a row, and a different mechanic standing watch in each, the thing gets to be funny.

"Explain — explain these aberrations," said Tracy.

"Well, they are not the achievement of a single intellect, a single talent — it takes two to do these miracles. They are collaborations; the one artist does the figure, the other the accessories. The figure-artist is a German shoemaker with an untaught passion for art, the other is a simple-hearted old Yankee sailor-man whose possibilities are strictly limited to his ship, his cannon and his patch of petrified sea. They work these things up from twenty-five-cent tintypes; they get six dollars apiece for them, and they can grind out a couple a day when they strike what they call a boost — that is, an inspiration."

"People actually pay money for these calumnies?"

"They actually do—and quite willingly, too. And these abortionists could double their trade and work the women in, if Capt. Saltmarsh could whirl a horse in, or a piano, or a guitar, in place of his cannon. The fact is, he fatigues the market with that cannon. Even the male market, I mean. These fourteen in the procession are not all satisfied. One is an old 'independent' fireman, and he wants an engine in place of the cannon; another is a mate of a tug, and wants a tug in place of the ship—and so on, and so on. But the captain can't make a tug that is deceptive, and a fire engine is many flights beyond his power."

"This is a most extraordinary form of robbery, I never have heard of anything like it. It's interesting."

"Yes, and so are the artists. They are perfectly honest men, and sincere. And the old sailor-man is full of sound religion, and is as devoted a student of the Bible and misquoter of it as you can find anywhere. I don't know a better man or kinder hearted old soul than Saltmarsh, although he does swear a little, sometimes."

"He seems to be perfect. I want to know him, Barrow."

"You'll have the chance. I guess I hear them coming, now. We'll draw them out on their art, if you like."

The artists arrived and shook hands with great heartiness. The German was forty and a little fleshy, with a shiny bald head and a kindly face and deferential manner. Capt. Saltmarsh was sixty, tall, erect, powerfully built, with coal-black hair and whiskers, and he had a well tanned complexion, and a gait and countenance that were full of command, confidence and decision. His horny hands and wrists were covered with tattoo-marks, and when his lips parted, his teeth showed up white and blemishless. His voice was the effortless deep bass of a church organ, and would disturb the tranquility of a gas flame fifty yards away.

"They're wonderful pictures," said Barrow. "We've been examining them."

"It is very bleasant dot you like dem," said Handel, the German, greatly pleased. "Und you, Herr Tracy, you haf peen bleased mit dem too, alretty?"

"I can honestly say I have never seen anything just like them before."

"Schon!" cried the German, delighted. "You hear, Gaptain? Here is a chentleman, yes, vot abbreviate unser aart."

The captain was charmed, and said:

"Well, sir, we're thankful for a compliment yet, though they're not as scarce now as they used to be before we made a reputation."

"Getting the reputation is the up-hill time in most things, captain."

"It's so. It ain't enough to know how to reef a gasket, you got to make the mate know you know it. That's reputation. The good word, said at the right time, that's the word that makes us; and evil be to him that evil thinks, as Isaiah says."

"It's very relevant, and hits the point exactly," said Tracy. "Where did you study art, Captain?"

"I haven't studied; it's a natural gift."

"He is born mit dose cannon in him. He tondt haf to do noding, his chenius do all de vork. Of he is asleep, and take a pencil in his hand, out come a cannon. Py crashus, of he could do a clavier, of he could do a guitar, of he could do a vashtub, it is a fortune, heiliger Yohanniss it is yoost a fortune!"

"Well, it is an immense pity that the business is hindered and limited in this unfortunate way."

The captain grew a trifle excited, himself, now:

"You've said it, Mr. Tracy!—Hindered? well, I should say so. Why, look here. This fellow here, No. 11, he's a hackman,—a flourishing hackman, I may say. He wants his hack in this picture. Wants it where the cannon is. I got around that difficulty, by telling him the cannon's our trademark, so to speak—proves that the picture's our work, and I was afraid if we left it out people wouldn't know for certain if it was a Saltmarsh-Handel—now you wouldn't yourself—"

"What, Captain? You wrong yourself, indeed you do. Anyone who has once seen a genuine Saltmarsh-Handel is safe from imposture forever. Strip it, flay it, skin it out of every detail but the bare color and expression, and that man will still recognize it—still stop to worship—"

"Oh, how it makes me feel to hear dose oxpressions!—"

—"still say to himself again as he had said a hundred times before, the art of the Saltmarsh-Handel is an art apart, there is nothing in the heavens above or in the earth beneath that resembles it,—"

"Py chiminy, nur horen Sie einmal! In my life day haf I never heard so brecious worts."

"So I talked him out of the hack, Mr. Tracy, and he let up on that, and said put in a hearse, then—because he's chief mate of a hearse but don't own it—stands a watch for wages, you know. But I can't do a hearse any more than I can a hack; so here we are—becalmed, you see. And it's the same with women and such. They come and they want a little johnry picture—"

"It's the accessories that make it a 'genre'?"

"Yes—cannon, or cat, or any little thing like that, that you heave in to whoop up the effect. We could do a prodigious trade with the women if we could foreground the things they like, but they don't give a damn for artillery. Mine's the lack," continued the captain with a sigh, "Andy's end of the business is all right. I tell you he's an artist from way back!"

"Yoost hear dot old man! He always talk 'poud me like dot," purred the pleased German.

"Look at his work yourself! Fourteen portraits in a row. And no two of them alike."

"Now that you speak of it, it is true; I hadn't noticed it before. It is very remarkable. Unique, I suppose."

"I should say so. That's the very thing about Andy—he discriminates. Discrimination's the thief of time—forty-ninth Psalm; but that ain't any matter, it's the honest thing, and it pays in the end."

"Yes, he certainly is great in that feature, one is obliged to admit it; but—now mind, I'm not really criticising—don't you think he is just a trifle overstrong in technique?"

The captain's face was knocked expressionless by this remark. It remained quite vacant while he muttered to himself—"Technique—technique—polytechnique—pyrotechnique; that's it, likely—fireworks too much color." Then he spoke up with serenity and confidence, and said:

"Well, yes, he does pile it on pretty loud; but they all like it, you know—fact is, it's the life of the business. Take that No. 9, there, Evans the butcher. He drops into the stoodio as sober-colored as anything you ever see: now look at him. You can't tell him from scarlet fever. Well, it pleases that butcher to death. I'm making a study of a sausage-wreath to hang on the cannon, and I don't really reckon I can do it right, but if I can, we can break the butcher."

"Unquestionably your confederate—I mean your—your fellow-craftsman—is a great colorist—"

"Oh, danke schon!—"

—"in fact a quite extraordinary colorist; a colorist, I make bold to say, without imitator here or abroad—and with a most bold and effective touch, a touch like a battering ram; and a manner so peculiar and romantic, and extraneous, and ad libitum, and heart-searching, that—that—he —he is an impressionist, I presume?"

"No," said the captain simply, "he is a Presbyterian."

"It accounts for it all—all—there's something divine about his art, —soulful, unsatisfactory, yearning, dim hearkening on the void horizon, vague—murmuring to the spirit out of ultra-marine distances and far-sounding cataclysms of uncreated space—oh, if he—if he—has he ever tried distemper?"

The captain answered up with energy:

"Not if he knows himself! But his dog has, and—"

"Oh, no, it vas not my dog."

"Why, you said it was your dog."

"Oh, no, gaptain, I—"

"It was a white dog, wasn't it, with his tail docked, and one ear gone, and—"

"Dot's him, dot's him!—der fery dog. Wy, py Chorge, dot dog he would eat baint yoost de same like—"

"Well, never mind that, now—'vast heaving—I never saw such a man. You start him on that dog and he'll dispute a year. Blamed if I haven't seen him keep it up a level two hours and a half."

"Why captain!" said Barrow. "I guess that must be hearsay."

"No, sir, no hearsay about it—he disputed with me."

"I don't see how you stood it."

"Oh, you've got to—if you run with Andy. But it's the only fault he's got."

"Ain't you afraid of acquiring it?"

"Oh, no," said the captain, tranquilly, "no danger of that, I reckon."

The artists presently took their leave.[10]

Stormfield came back as the Admiral in "The Refuge of the Derelicts," which Mark Twain wrote in 1905 but did not publish. This description of him, delivered by the character named Shipman, echoes Herman Melville's observation, that "sailors only go *round* the world, without going *into* it."

∗   ∗   ∗

From "The Refuge of the Derelicts"

Now I will post you about the Admiral. He is a fine and bluff old sailor, honest, unworldly, simple, innocent as a child—but doesn't know it, of course—knows not a thing outside of his profession, but *thinks* he knows a lot—you must humor that superstition of course—and he *does* know his Bible, (just well enough to misquote it with confidence,) and frankly thinks he can beat the band at explaining it, whereas his explanations simply make the listener dizzy, they are so astronomically wide of the mark; he is profoundly religious, sincerely religious, but swears a good deal, and competently—you mustn't notice that; drinks like a fish, but is a fervent and honest advocate and supporter of the temperance cause, and does what he can to reclaim the fallen by taking the pledge every now and then as an example, with the idea that it is a great encouragement to them; he can't sing, but he doesn't know it—you must ask him to sing; is a composer—good land!—and believes he is a musician; he thinks he is deep, and furtive, and not to be seen through by any art, whereas he is just glass, for transparency—and lovable? he is the most lovable old thing in the universe. . . .

He was eighty years old. Tall; large; all brawn, muscle and health; powerful bass voice, deep and resonant. He was born at sea, in the family's home, which was a Fairhaven whaleship, owned and commanded by his father. He was never at school; such education as he had, he had picked up by odds and ends, and it was rather a junk-shop than a treasury; though that was not his idea of it. He had very decided opinions upon most matters, and he had architected them himself. Sometimes they were not sound, but what they lacked in soundness they generally made up in originality.

He spent seventy years at sea, and then retired. He had now been retired ten years. He had never served in a warship, and did not get his title from the government; it was a token of love and homage, and was conferred upon him by the captains of the whaling fleet.[11]

The Wakeman/Stormfield character made his final appearance in *Extract from Captain Stormfield's Visit to Heaven* (1909), in which the venerable captain has died and gone to the Pearly Gates riding on a spaceship with a ship's wheel and a propeller. Upon arriving, the captain discovers that his angel wings do not behave at all like sails.

*   *   *

From *Extract from Captain Stormfield's Visit to Heaven*

I saw I hadn't got the hang of the steering, and so couldn't rightly tell where I was going to bring up when I started. I went afoot the rest of the day, and let my wings hang. Early next morning I went to a private place to have some practice. I got up on a pretty high rock, and got a good start, and went swooping down, aiming for a bush a little over three hundred yards off; but I couldn't seem to calculate for the wind, which was about two points abaft my beam. I could see I was going considerable to looard of the bush, so I worked my starboard wing slow and went ahead strong on the port one, but it wouldn't answer; I could see I was going to broach to, so I slowed down on both, and lit. I went back to the rock and took another chance at it. I aimed two or three points to starboard of the bush—yes, more than that—enough so as to make it nearly a head-wind. I done well enough, but made pretty poor time. I could see, plain enough, that on a head-wind, wings was a mistake. I could see that a body could sail pretty close to the wind, but he couldn't go in the wind's eye. I could see that if I wanted to go a-visiting any distance from home, and the wind was ahead, I might have to wait days, maybe, for a change; and I could see, too, that these things could not be any use at all in a gale; if you tried to run before the wind, you would make a mess of it, for there isn't any way to shorten sail—like reefing, you know—you have to take it all in—shut your feathers down flat to your sides. That would land you, of course.

You could lay to, with your head to the wind—that is the best you could do, and right hard work you'd find it, too. If you tried any other game, you would founder, sure.

I judge it was about a couple of weeks or so after this that I dropped old Sandy McWilliams a note one day—it was a Tuesday—and asked him to come over and take his manna and quails with me next day; and the first thing he did when he stepped in was to twinkle his eye in a sly way, and say,—

"Well, Cap, what you done with your wings?"

I saw in a minute that there was some sarcasm done up in that rag somewheres, but I never let on. I only says,—

"Gone to the wash."[12]

Captain Wakeman's curtain call came a century after Samuel Clemens died, when the full *Autobiography of Mark Twain*, which he dictated in 1906, emerged at last, after the one hundred years he mandated. In it, the author reminisced fondly about the man.

* * *

From the *Autobiography of Mark Twain*

I first knew Captain Wakeman thirty-nine years ago. I made two voyages with him, and we became fast friends. He was a great burly, handsome, weatherbeaten, symmetrically built and powerful creature, with coal black hair and whiskers, and the kind of eye which men obey without talking back. He was full of human nature, and the best kind of human nature. He was as hearty and sympathetic and loyal and loving a soul as I have found anywhere, and when his temper was up he performed all the functions of an earthquake, without the noise. He was all sailor, from head to heel; and this was proper enough, for he was born at sea, and, in the course of his sixty-five years, he had visited the edges of all the continents and archipelagoes, but had never been on land except incidentally and spasmodically, as you may say. He had never had a day's schooling in his life, but had picked up worlds and worlds of knowledge at second-hand, and none of it correct. He was a liberal talker, and inexhaustibly interesting. In the matter of a wide and catholic profanity he had not his peer on the planet while he lived. It was a deep pleasure to me to hear him do his stunts in this line. He knew the Bible by heart, and was profoundly and sincerely religious. He was always studying the Bible when it was his watch below, and always finding new things, fresh things, and unexpected delights and surprises in it—and he loved to talk about his discoveries and expound them to the ignorant. He believed that he was the only man on the globe that really knew the secret of the Biblical miracles. He had what he believed was a sane and rational explanation of every one of them, and he loved to teach his learning to the less fortunate. . . .[13]

He was a most winning and delightful creature. When he was fifty-three years old he started from a New England port, master of a great clipper ship bound around the Horn for San Francisco, and he was not aware that he had a passenger, but he was mistaken as to that. He had never had a love passage, but he was to have one now. When he was out from port a few weeks he was prowling about some remote corner of his ship, by way of inspection, when he came across a beautiful girl, twenty-four or twenty-five years old, prettily clothed and lying asleep with one plump arm under her neck. He stopped in his tracks and stood and gazed, enchanted. Then he said,

"It's an angel—that's what it is. It's an angel. When it opens its eyes, if they are blue I'll marry it."

The eyes turned out to be blue, and the pair were married when they reached San Francisco. The girl was to have taught school there. She had her appointment in her pocket—but the Captain saw to it that that arrangement did not materialize. He built a little house in Oakland—ostensibly a house, but really it was a ship, and had all a ship's appointments, binnacle, scuppers, and everything else—and there he and his little wife lived an ideal life during the intervals that intervened between his voyages. They were a devoted pair, and worshiped each other. By and by there were two little girls, and then the nautical paradise was complete.[14]

Last Voyages of a Half-Century at Sea

Mark Twain continued to be impressed by advances in nautical architecture and engineering. He returned to the ocean, and to the United States, in October 1900, after a five-year absence, accompanied by Livy and his daughters Clara and Jean. He made this comment about the brand-new steamship *Minnehaha* during that crossing from England to New York: "Oct. 14, 1900, Sunday noon. About 500 miles to make. A spacious ship and most comfortable. Rides the seas level, hardly any motion, no seasickness aboard. No table racks."[1]

Over the next three years, the frail Livy Clemens continued to battle physical ailments, which had punctuated her life. Acting on her doctor's advice, she and Sam, along with the faithful Clara, left New York again on October 24, 1903, bound for Italy on the *Princess Irene*, hopeful of recouping Livy's health in a place she remembered fondly. But they had a very trying time aboard, and did not reach Genoa until November 7. Sam kept notes, while the family kept to their cabin.

* * *

From Mark Twain's Notebook

Sunday, Oct. 25. Heavy storm all night. Only two stewardesses. Ours served sixty meals in rooms, this morning. . . .

Oct. 28. Youth in smoking-chapel talking nursery German in loud voice, to be heard and envied of men. — The old familiar simple words of the textbook vocabulary, uttered with painful distinctness. Yet there are those who say there is not hell.

Thursday, Oct. 29. Two men—a giant and a Shetland pony—also a giraffe, six feet four, tramped the deck after midnight, talking loudly. On the port side four sat under Mrs. Miller's open port and told unclean an-

ecdotes, in the national yell, swore, laughed like demons, and sang. The
Captain is going to prevent these freedoms after 11:30 hereafter.

Oct. 30. There should be no first come, take choice, in location of
steamer chairs. The chair space outside of a stateroom should be the
property of the occupant. People under our port chatter till 11—if these
were our chairs we could have tranquility, for we retire at 9:30. . . .

Passed the Azores at 8.

Monday. Due at Gibraltar ten days from N.Y., three days to Naples,
one day to Genoa. . . .

Saw at Gibraltar Michael Benunes, our guide of 36 years ago—still the
most distinguished-looking person in that town. He took Jackson, Dan,
Jack, Miss Newell, and me into Spain—all dead now but me, I believe.

NEVER take a promenade-deck room again, at any price; a madhouse
is preferable. Get the Captain's apartment or go down cellar, and NEVER
travel in an emigrant ship.[2]

The respite promised in Italy did not materialize for Olivia Langdon Clemens, who
died in Florence on June 5, 1904. The grieving Samuel and Clara Clemens suffered
through the sudden and unwelcome return trip to the United States aboard the
Prince Oscar, sailing from Naples on June 28, with their beloved Livy, long-suffering
spouse and mother, in her coffin in the hold of the ship.

June 29. Sailed last night, at ten. The bugle called me to breakfast. I
recognized the notes, and was distressed. When I heard them last Livy
heard them with me; now they fall upon ears unheeded.

This ship is the *Oscar*, Hamburg American.

June 30. Clara keeps to her bed and cannot bear to see any strangers.

The weather is beautiful, the sea is smooth and curiously blue.

In my life there have been 68 Junes—but how vague and colorless 67
of them are contrasted with the deep blackness of this one.

July 1. I cannot reproduce Livy's face in my mind's eye—I was never
in my life able to reproduce a face. It is a curious infirmity—and now at
last I realize that it is a calamity.

July 2. In these 34 years we have made many voyages together, Livy
dear, and now we are making our last. You down below and lonely, I
above with the crowd and lonely.

July 3. Ship time 8 A.M. In 13¼ hours it will be four weeks since Livy died. 31 years ago we made our first voyage together and this is our last in company. Susy was a year old then. She died at 24 and has been in her grave 8 years.

July 4. We did not come out of our room during the day and evening. We were full of memories of other Fourths.

July 8. A wonderful day. Brilliant sun, brilliant blue water, strong and delightful breeze. In middle of Gulf Stream. Temperature of water 73½ degrees Fahrenheit. We had such days in the Indian Ocean, and Livy so enjoyed the exultation of spirits they produced.

July 10. Tonight it will be six weeks. But to me it remains yesterday as it has from the first. But this funeral march—how sad and long it is.

Two days more will be the second stage of it.

July 12. Due to finish this melancholy voyage at 7 or 8 this evening.

Smallpox discovered this morning; five cases in steerage; every soul on board vaccinated.

People who travel in an immigrant ship belong in an insane asylum.

July 13. Orders from President Roosevelt and the Secretary of the Treasury passed us swiftly ashore.[3]

In 1907, Clemens sailed to England aboard the steamship *Minneapolis* on June 8 to accept an honorary doctoral degree from Oxford University. The vessel was one of the four renowned "Minne class" sister ships of the Atlantic Transport Line, along with *Minnehaha*, which Clemens had admired during his trip from England to New York in October 1900. He dictated these recollections of the voyage for his autobiography on July 24, soon after he returned to Stormfield, his mansion in Redding, Connecticut, from his month in England:

* * *

From the *Autobiography of Mark Twain*

We had a lazy, comfortable, homelike, nine-day passage, over smooth seas, with not enough motion in a thousand miles to make a baby sick. The ships of that line are very large and very steady, and most satisfactorily slow and deliberate. They have spacious decks, and every passenger has a deal more room than he needs; they are freight ships, and have accommodations for only a handful of passengers. This one was full, with only a hundred and fifty-four. Fifty-one of them were college girls, with their protectors, going out on vacation to study Europe. This was pleasant to me, who am rather abnormally partial to young girls. . . .

At the end of nine days we reached the dock at Tilbury, and the hearty and happy and memorable English welcome began. Who began it? The very people of all people in the world whom I would have chosen: a hundred men of my own class—grimy sons of labor, the real builders of empires and civilizations, the stevedores! They stood in a body on the dock and charged their masculine lungs, and gave me a welcome which went to the marrow of me.[4]

Bermuda beckoned to Samuel Clemens until the end of his life. The island had enchanted him during his first "idle excursion" there in 1877. It was a convenient alternative to longer voyages, with comparable benefits. Lying five hundred miles east of North Carolina, Bermuda basks in the middle of the Gulf Stream, the greatest unleashed hot tub in the world, flowing north like an ocean river the size of a thousand Mississippis, but warmer and clearer, more widely diffused, and nearly invisible. After an absence of three decades, Clemens returned in early January 1907, then dictated the following observations while on board the RMS *Bermudian* on the way home.

That is a pleasant country—Bermuda—and close by and easy to get to. There is a fine modern steamer admirably officered; there is a table which even the hypercritical could hardly find fault with—not even the hypercritical could find fault with the service. On board there is constant communication with the several populations of the planet—if you want it—through the wireless telegraph, and the trip to Bermuda is made in two days.[5]

Clemens came back for a two-week stay in March 1907, and again in February 1908, when he recorded his regret at not rediscovering the island sooner.

I have been in Bermuda again; this is the fifth time; it was on account of bronchitis, my annual visitor for these seventeen or eighteen years. I have

FIGURE 6. The last time Mark Twain went to sea, it was on the elegant
Oceana (no relation to the P & O Line ship of the same name that took the
Clemens family from Australia to Ceylon). When he sensed his impending death
in April 1910, he left Bermuda and returned to Stormfield, his hilltop villa in
Redding, Connecticut. He died there on April 21, 1910, exactly one week
after the *Oceana* arrived in New York City.
"S. S. *Oceana*, New York–Bermuda Service," published by J. H. Bradley & Co.,
Hamilton, Bermuda, card no. 663 (undated). Courtesy of the Roorda/Doyle Collection.

not come out of any previous attack so quickly or pleasantly; the attack
has always kept me in bed five weeks, sometimes six, and once eight.
This time I got out of bed at the end of the first week, two days after a
ten-inch snow-storm, and took the chance and went to sea in bitter winter weather. We made the passage in forty-five hours and landed in lovely
summer weather. The passage itself came near to curing me, for a radical
change is a good doctor. A single day of constant and delightful exposure
to the Bermudian sun completed the cure; then I stayed eight days longer
to enjoy the spiritual serenities and the bodily rejuvenations furnished
by that happy little paradise. It grieves me, and I feel reproached, that I
allowed the physicians to send Mrs. Clemens on a horrible ten-day sea
journey to Italy when Bermuda was right here at hand and worth a hundred Italies, for her needs.[6]

From the time Mark Twain began his life's experience on the water, as a cub-pilot on a Mississippi River paddle-wheel steamboat, to the last voyage of his life, a week before he died, from Bermuda back home in 1910, a transformation in seafaring took place. This transformation took place on the river that Twain studied as a young man, and it took place on the oceanic highways that he traversed for more than four decades. Twain bore witness to that process, vividly capturing it at regular intervals throughout his prolific writing career, informed as it was by his wide-ranging wanderings on the watery parts of the world.

On Christmas Eve 1909, Clemens's youngest child, Jean, who had long battled worsening epilepsy, had a seizure in her bathtub in Stormfield and drowned at the age of twenty-nine. This sudden shock devastated her father, who was in the sprawling home when it happened. When the first, blackest waves of grief had crashed down on him and sizzled away grudgingly, he made his way to Bermuda, in hopes of reviving his spirits and his health. He left New York on January 3, 1910, just two weeks after Jean's death. But this time, Bermuda was no help. He declined further, and asked to go home to die. The last of Mark Twain's many sea voyages, from Hamilton, Bermuda, to New York City on the steamship *Oceana*, ended on April 14, 1910, exactly one week before his death (Fig. 6). While on board, he wrote these lines:

"It is a losing race. No ship can outsail death."[7]

The Dark Wilderness of the Sea— and of Life

After circumnavigating the globe, Mark Twain began, but did not finish, three "sea-disaster" stories. These disturbing rumina- tions concern two kinds of existential dread. The first, at the earthly level, is the visceral fear of being lost at sea. The second, at the level of the Hereafter, is the mind-bending prospect of facing death and the unknown afterlife—or afternot! The truncated tales were finally pub- lished in 1967.

Mark Twain's trilogy of despair is as much about the sublime ocean as it is about the writer's turbulent mind, which was especially tempes- tuous after his eldest—and favorite—daughter, twenty-four-year-old Susy, suddenly sickened of typhus while the rest of the family was at sea, and died two days after their return in August 1896. They learned of her death soon after completing their circumnavigation. Generated by Twain's emotional agony, the sea-disaster stories are unsettling feats of imagination. They rank with the earliest literature in the genre of sci- ence fiction. They are also exercises in fictional existentialism. In a later era, their abrupt endings might have been interpreted as intentional ef- forts on the part of the writer/philosopher to amplify their dreadfulness. Had these bleak visions found print earlier, Jean-Paul Sartre and Samuel Beckett might have been accused of being derivative of them.

While traversing the Indian Ocean, Mark Twain learned about areas of "the vast plain of the sea" where compasses fail and mariners become lost.[1] That inspired him to write "The Enchanted Sea-Wilderness," which begins portentously.

* * *

From "The Enchanted Sea-Wilderness"

Scattered about the world's oceans at enormous distances apart are spots and patches where no compass has any value. When the compass enters one of these bewitched domains it goes insane and whirls this way and that and settles nowhere, and is scared and distressed, and cannot be comforted. The sailor must steer by sun, moon and stars when they show, and by guess when they don't, till he gets past that enchanted region. The worst of these spots and the largest one is in the midst of the vast ocean solitudes that lie between the Cape of Good Hope and the south pole. It is five hundred miles in diameter, and is circular in shape; four-fifths of this diameter is lashed and tossed and torn by eternal storms, is smothered in clouds and fog, and swept by fierce concentric currents; but in the centre there is a circular area a hundred miles across, in whose outer part the storms and the currents die down; and in the centre of this centre there is still a final circular area about fifty–sixty miles across where there are but the faintest suggestions of currents, no winds, no whisper of wandering zephyr, even, but everywhere the silence and peace and solemnity of a calm which is eternal.

The storyteller is "a bronzed and gray sailor," with "experience of that strange place. . . . He said that the outer great circle where the currents are . . . is known as the Devils' Race-Track, and that they call the central calm Everlasting Sunday." His brig, sailing to Australia in December 1853, catches fire, forcing the crew to abandon ship. If the ship's dog had not alerted the captain, all on board would have died. Still, the "rough and hard-hearted" captain orders the heroic canine to be left behind to burn to death. Only four hours later, the stranded sailors spot a ship, which rescues them. It is their own sister ship, also en route to Australia. Their captain had died a month before. Taking control in this absence, the dog-murdering captain unleashes all hell:

The wind freshened, the sky grew dark, and inside of an hour there was a terrific gale blowing. We stripped the ship and she drove helpless before it, straight south-east. And so, night and day and day and night for eighteen days we drove, and never got a sight of the sun or the moon or the stars in all that time — hundreds and hundreds and hundreds of miles we wallowed through the wild seas, with never a notion of where we were but what we got from the dead reckoning. . . .

The compass was gone crazy, and we were in the whirl and suck of the Devil's Race-Track. . . . When the day was you could hardly tell, it so little differed from the night. . . .

We had nine days and nights like this—always the roaring gale and the wild sea and blustering squalls of snow and hail and sleet and the piping of the gulls and the flitting of the dim albatross; and then on the tenth morning the gale began to slacken and the seas to go down and the squalls to get wider apart and less furious, and the blackness to soften up and shred away, and the sea-birds to thin out; and about noon we drifted out of the lofty wall of gloom and clouds into a calm sea and the open day and deep, deep stillness. The sweep of that black wall described an enormous circle; and it was so high that the furthest side of it still stood boldly up above the sea, though it was fifty miles away. We were in a trap; and that trap was the Everlasting Sunday.

Mark Twain takes to new levels the literary motifs of the Sargasso Sea, which spins ships into the vortex of the North Atlantic gyre, and the ghost ship, the most famous of which is the *Flying Dutchman*.

One morning when we had been in there seven months and gradually getting further and further toward the middle, an inch at a time, there was a sudden stir and excitement. . . . A sailor came flying along the deck blubbering and shouting, "A ship! A ship!"

Not just one ship, but "a whole fleet." The sailors rowed to the nearest ship.

The nearer we got, the crazier she looked, and there was no sign of life or movement about her. We began to suspect the truth—and pretty soon we knew it, and our spirits fell. Why, she was just a naked old wreck, as you may say, a mouldy old skeleton, with her yards hanging every-whichway, and here and there a rotten rag of sailcloth drooping from the clews. As we passed under her stern, there was her name, in letters so dulled you could hardly spell them out. The *Horatio Nelson*! I gasped for breath.

I knew the ship. When I was a boy of ten my uncle Robert sailed in her as chief mate; and from that day to this she had never more been heard of—thirteen years.

They climbed on board, and found "men lying here and there and yonder, and two or three sitting, with elbow on knee and hand under chin—just as natural! No, not men—leathery shriveled-up effigies of them. Dead these dozen years." There was also a New England whaler, there for six years, an English convict ship bound for Australia, carrying 260 outcasts, there for thirty-three years, and "a Spanish ship [that] had been there sixty years; but the oldest one of all, and in almost the best repair, was a British man-of-war, the *Royal Brunswick*. She perished with all on board the first voyage she ever made, the old histories say—and the old ballads, too—but here she was; and here she had been, since November 10th, 1740—a hundred and thirteen years, you see."

At a little distance you might have thought some of the men in this ship were still alive, they looked so natural in their funny old uniforms. And the admiral was one—old Admiral Sir John Thurlow . . . had his big cocked hat on, and his big epaulettes, like as if he was gotten up for Madam Tussaud's; and his coat was all over gold lace; and it was real gold, too, for it was not tarnished. He was sitting on a gun carriage, with his head leant back against the gun in a sick and weary way; and there was a rusty old leather portfolio in his lap and a pen and an empty inkstand handy. He looked fine and noble—the very type of the old fighting British Admiral, the men that made England the monarch of the seas. By a common impulse, and without orders, we formed up in front of him and uncovered in salute. Then Captain Cable stepped up to take the portfolio, but in his awkwardness he gave a little touch to the Admiral's elbow and he fell over on the deck. Dear me, he struck as lightly and as noiseless as if he had been only a suit of clothes stuffed with wool; and a faint little cloud of leathery dust rose up from him, and we judged he had gone to pieces inside. We uncovered again and carried him very reverently to his own cabin and laid him to rest.

And here we had an instance of the difference between navy discipline and merchant marine. In this ship the log was kept up as long as an officer was left alive—and that was two months and sixteen days. That is the grip that authority and duty get upon a trained man, you see. When the men began to starve and die they were[2]

That's it. There's no telling how the Ishmaelian "bronzed and gray sailor" lived to tell the tale. Becalmed in the center of his own black mood, the grief-stricken father could not extricate his narrator from the Sargasso Sea he created in his story — or himself from the sea-wilderness of his life.

Mark Twain contended that he met an American named George Parker in New Zealand in 1895, an Ohio orphan who went to sea at eighteen, who related the following sea-disaster tale.

*   *   *

From "An Adventure in Remote Seas"

It was a sealing voyage to the far south. . . . We sailed in midsummer, toward the end of December, in blistering weather, and made a long course due south till we were well below Auckland island, then squared around and moved eastwardly two or three weeks through snow-storms and biting cold. And now we ran into a snow-storm which lasted six days and nights without a break. Of course we lost our reckoning. We knew we were somewhere in that empty vast stretch of ocean which lies southwest of Cape Horn, but that was all. We could not come within five hundred miles of guessing our position.

The snow stopped falling, one morning, just in time to save us from shipwreck. We found ourselves in a rock-bound bay and driving straight for the shore. A cast of the lead gave twenty-five fathoms, and we let go a couple of anchors, they took a good grip and we were all right.

The skies soon cleared, and outside the bay we saw an archipelago of rocks well peopled with seals. We recognized that we were in fine luck.

They sent a boat ashore and found they were on an island, "a dreary and forbidding place. As far as the eye could reach, on all sides, the vacant ocean stretched to the horizon." They found a cave entrance and "a rude and weather-beaten house, made of rough planks and ship timbers — a building of great age, apparently." Half the crew moved ashore, and turned their attention to their prey, the island's seals. "It was like murdering children, they were so gentle and trustful." After a week of killing seals, the crew calculated every sailor had made one hundred dollars. The captain's share was much more, "and he was feeling pretty rich."

That night, a storm blew in, and he said—

"We'll take a look at the vessel and see if she is all right," and we muffled ourselves up and took the lanterns and went outside. We took refuge from the bitter wind in the cave door, and from there we looked out upon the harbor, and saw the vessel's lights and dropped our apprehensions.

The group looked inside the cave, and the narrator "saw something glisten on the floor—a coin, I thought." They discovered a vast trove of treasure. "We counted and counted until we ached all over from fatigue, and were getting drowsy, and actually growing tired of it—a thing which looks impossible, but it is true." They quit for the night, then started the next morning, weighing coins by the shovel and putting them "into fifty-pound piles. . . . We weighed about a hundred piles an hour." Distracted by their labors, they were unconcerned by the fact that their ship was gone, the other half of the crew presumably having taken to sea during the storm to avoid being wrecked. "We weighed coin all day, and all the two following days, and then we were done. . . . We had more than a hundred and twenty tons of gold—more than sixty million dollars."

In the meantime, there was still no sign of the ship. With the weighing finished, the men's worries about the missing vessel mounted. "The hours began to drag on our hands." At last, one sailor uttered the unthinkable to the captain.

"With all deference, sir, I am a good deal troubled, myself."

"Why?"

"Because when we came here we hadn't had an observation for days and days, and hadn't any but a guesswork idea of where we were. Maybe twelve or fifteen hundred miles south-west-by-west from Cape Horn, but no telling—no sort of telling. A man might paddle around for two years on a guess like that and not find this little patch of rock. We got no observation here, the weather has been thick ever since. The mate hasn't any idea where this island is. He will get tired guessing around, presently, and give it up and strike for some of the old sealing-grounds and get what skins he can and go home."

That made me sick, it looked so true, but the others did not seem to realize the size of it, and the captain said it wasn't time yet to begin to worry about it. He seemed like a man infatuated; and pretty soon he was ciphering away again, just as usual."[3]

Again, the author did not—perhaps could not—finish the story, leaving readers to wonder how "George Parker" made it off that uncharted desert island, where there were tons of useless gold, but no precious food or water.

Mark Twain's untitled foray into science fiction is set aboard a minuscule passenger liner, sailing for years across the terrifying water-world of a microscope slide, where bacteria appear as enormous, hideous sea monsters. At one point, a "spider-squid" bigger than a whale eats the captain's son. The eminent Mark Twain scholar and editor Bernard DeVoto decided to call this story "The Great Dark" when he published it for the first time in 1968. A better title might be "Six Years under the Microscope."

The ship remains in the shadow outside the illuminated circle of the slide, in conditions resembling a stormy, moonless night. Among the few passengers is a family headed by the narrator, who believes it is all a dream that he got them into by making a deal with the "Superintendent of Dreams." But his wife and children are certain that they have always been on the ship, and that their life in a house was the dream. After a while, he himself accepts this version of reality.

Mark Twain considered two plans for ending the story: either everyone would perish in the nightmare world of the microscope slide, or everyone would perish and then wake up to find it was a dream. The unfinished version closes with the Wakeman-inspired Captain Davis sweet-talking his men out of a mutiny while humiliating its leader, the ship's carpenter.

*   *   *

From "The Great Dark"

"You have mutinied two or three times, boys. It is all right—up to now. I would have done it myself in my common-seaman days, I reckon, if my ship was bewitched and I didn't know where I was. Now then, can you be trusted with the facts? Are we rational men, manly men, men who can stand up and face hard luck and big difficulty that has been brought by nobody's fault, and say live or die, survive or perish, we are in for it, for good or bad, and we'll stand by the ship if she goes to hell!"

(The men let go a tolerably hearty cheer.) "Are we men—grown men—salt-sea men—men nursed upon dangers and cradled in storms—men made in the image of God and ready to do when He commands and die when He calls—or are we just sneaks and curs and carpenters!" (This brought cheers and laughter, and the captain was happy.) "There—that's the kind. And so I'll tell you how the thing stands. *I* don't know where this ship is, but she's in the hands of God, and that's enough for me, it's enough for you, and it's enough for anybody but a carpenter. If it is God's will that we pull through, we pull through—otherwise not. We haven't had an observation for four months, but we are going ahead, and do our best to fetch up somewhere."[4]

The benighted crew resolves to press forward, despite the uncertainties. But there is no resolution to their predicament; they continue sailing into trackless obscurity, because (as in life) they have no choice.

Mark Twain's Maritime Maxims
and Metaphors

A ship is precisely a little village, where gossips abound, & where every man's business is his neighbors.[1]

There isn't a Parallel of Latitude but thinks it would have been the Equator if it had had its rights.[2]

Disobedience is the flagship of the fleet of sin.[3]

Mrs. B. was arrayed in a superb speckled foulard, with stripes running fore and aft, and with collets and camails to match; also, a notable rotonde of Chantilly lace, embroidered with yellow and blue dogs, birds and things, done in cruel.[4] . . .
    Mrs. J. B. W. wore a rat-colored brocade silk, studded with large silver stars. . . .
    Miss A. H. wore a splendid Lucia de Lammermoon.[5] . . . Her *coiffure* was a simple wreath of sardines on a string.[6]

I warn you when they put beautiful clipper-built girls on the stage in this new fashion, with only just barely clothes enough on to be tantalizing, it is a shrewd invention of the devil.[7]

After years of waiting, it [the Sphinx] was before me at last. The great face was so sad, so earnest, so longing, so patient. There was a dignity not of earth in its mien, and in its countenance a benignity such as never any thing human wore. It was stone, but it seemed sentient. If ever image of stone thought, it was thinking. It was looking toward the verge of the landscape, yet looking at nothing — nothing but distance and vacancy. It was looking over and beyond every thing of the present, and far into the past. It was gazing out over the ocean of Time — over lines of century-waves which, further and further receding, closed nearer and nearer together, and blended at last into one unbroken tide, away toward the horizon of remote antiquity.[8]

We were spinning along through Kansas, and in the course of an hour and a half we were fairly abroad on the great Plains. Just here the land was rolling — a grand sweep of regular elevations and depressions as far as the eye could reach — like the stately heave and swell of the ocean's bosom after a storm. And everywhere were cornfields, accenting with squares of deeper green, this limitless expanse of grassy land. But presently this sea upon dry ground was to lose its "rolling" character and stretch away for seven hundred miles as level as a floor![9]

It was in the first days of June, and winter [in South Africa]; the daytime was pleasant, the nighttime nice and cold. Spinning along all day in the cars it was ecstasy to breathe the bracing air and gaze out over the vast brown solitudes of the velvet plains, soft and lovely near by, still softer and lovelier further away, softest and loveliest of all in the remote distances, where dim island-hills seemed afloat, as in a sea—a sea made of dream-stuff and flushed with colors faint and rich; and dear me, the depth of the sky, and the beauty of the strange new cloud-forms, and the glory of the sunshine, the lavishness, the wastefulness of it! The vigor and freshness and inspiration of the air and the sun—well, it was all just as Olive Schreiner had made it in her books.

To me the veldt, in its sober winter garb, was surpassingly beautiful. There were unlevel stretches where it was rolling and swelling, and rising and subsiding, and sweeping superbly on and on, and still on and on like an ocean, toward the faraway horizon, its pale brown deepening by delicately graduated shades to rich orange, and finally to purple and crimson where it washed against the wooded hills and naked red crags at the base of the sky.[10]

They are beautiful things, those diamonds, in their native state. They are of various shapes; they have flat surfaces, rounded borders, and never a sharp edge. They are of all colors and shades of color, from dewdrop white to actual black; and their smooth and rounded surfaces and contours, variety of color, and transparent limpidity make them look like piles of assorted candies. A very light straw color is their commonest tint. It seemed to me that these uncut gems must be more beautiful than any cut ones could be; but when a collection of cut ones was brought out, I saw my mistake. Nothing is so beautiful as a rose diamond with the light playing through it, except that uncostly thing which is just like it—wavy sea-water with the sunlight playing through it and striking a white-sand bottom.[11]

"Drifting to Starboard"

The little donkeys had saddles upon them which were made very high in order that the rider's feet might not drag on the ground. The preventative did not work well in the cases of our tallest pilgrims, however. There were no bridles—nothing but a single rope, tied to the bit. It was purely ornamental, for the donkey cared nothing for it. If he were drifting to starboard, you might put your helm down hard the other way, if it were any satisfaction to you to do it, but he would continue to drift to starboard all the same. There was only one process which could be depended on, and it was to get down and lift his rear around until his head pointed in the right direction, or take him under your arm and carry him to a part of the road which he could not get out of without climbing. The sun flamed down as hot as a furnace, and neck-scarfs, veils and umbrellas seemed hardly any protection; they served only to make the long procession look more than ever fantastic—for be it known the ladies were all riding astride because they could not stay on the shapeless saddles sidewise, the men were perspiring and out of temper, their feet were banging against the rocks, the donkeys were capering in every direction but the right one and being belabored with clubs for it, and every now and then a broad umbrella would suddenly go down out of the cavalcade, announcing to all that one more pilgrim had bitten the dust. It was a wilder picture than those solitudes had seen for many a day. No donkeys ever existed that were as hard to navigate as these, I think, or that had so many vile, exasperating instincts.[12]

With all solemnity I set it down here, that those horses [in Syria] were the hardest lot I ever did come across, and their accouterments were in exquisite keeping with their style. One brute had an eye out; another had his tail sawed off close, like a rabbit, and was proud of it; another had a bony ridge running from his neck to his tail, like one of those ruined aqueducts one sees about Rome, and had a neck on him like a bowsprit; they all limped, and had sore backs, and likewise raw places and old scales scattered about their persons like brass nails in a hair trunk; their gaits were marvelous to contemplate, and replete with variety under way the procession looked like a fleet in a storm.[13]

As the sun was going down [over Nebraska], we saw the first specimen of an animal known familiarly over two thousand miles of mountain and desert—from Kansas clear to the Pacific Ocean—as the "jackass rabbit." He is well named. He is just like any other rabbit, except that he is from one third to twice as large, has longer legs in proportion to his size, and has the most preposterous ears that ever were mounted on any creature but a jackass.

When he is sitting quiet, thinking about his sins, or is absent-minded or unapprehensive of danger, his majestic ears project above him conspicuously; but the breaking of a twig will scare him nearly to death, and then he tilts his ears back gently and starts for home. All you can see, then, for the next minute, is his long gray form stretched out straight and "streaking it" through the low sage-brush, head erect, eyes right, and ears just canted a little to the rear, but showing you where the animal is, all the time, the same as if he carried a jib.[14]

By and by to the elephant stables, and I took a ride; but it was by request—I did not ask for it, and didn't want it; but I took it, because otherwise they would have thought I was afraid, which I was. The elephant kneels down, by command—one end of him at a time — and you climb the ladder and get into the howdah, and then he gets up, one end at a time, just as a ship gets up over a wave; and after that, as he strides monstrously about, his motion is much like a ship's motion. [15]

The boon companion of the colossal elephant was a common cat! This cat had a fashion of climbing up the elephant's hind legs and roosting on his back. She would sit up there, with her paws curved under her breast, and sleep in the sun half the afternoon. It used to annoy the elephant at first, and he would reach up and take her down, but she would go aft and climb up again. She persisted until she finally conquered the elephant's prejudices, and now they are inseparable friends. The cat plays about her comrade's forefeet and trunk often, until dogs approach, and then she goes aloft out of danger. [16]

It was a long, low dog, with very short, strange legs — legs that curved inboard, something like parentheses turned the wrong way (. Indeed, it was made on the plan of a bench for length and lowness. It seemed to be satisfied, but I thought the plan poor, and structurally weak, on account of the distance between the forward supports and those abaft. With age the dog's back was likely to sag; and it seemed to me that it would have been a stronger and more practicable dog if it had had some more legs. It had not begun to sag yet, but the shape of the legs showed that the undue weight imposed upon them was beginning to tell. It had a long nose, and floppy ears that hung down, and a resigned expression of countenance. I did not like to ask what kind of a dog it was, or how it came to be deformed, for it was plain that the gentleman was very fond of it, and naturally he could be sensitive about it." [17]

Mr. Bolton was relieved, exactly as a water-logged ship is lightened by throwing overboard the most valuable portion of the cargo — but the leak was not stopped. [18]

So I said she must stop swearing and drinking, and smoking and eating for four days, and then she would be all right again. And it would have happened just so, I know it; but she said she could not stop swearing, and smoking, and drinking, because she had never done those things. So there it was. She had neglected her habits, and hadn't any. Now that they would have come good, there were none in stock. She had nothing to fall back on. She was a sinking vessel, with no freight in her to throw overboard and lighten ship withal. [19]

At last, a forest of graceful needles, shimmering in the amber sunlight, rose slowly above the pygmy housetops, as one sometimes sees, in the far horizon, a gilded and pinnacled mass of cloud lift itself above the waste of waves, at sea, — the [Milan] Cathedral! We knew it in a moment. . . .

Away above, on the lofty roof, rank on rank of carved and fretted spires spring high in the air, and through their rich tracery one sees the sky beyond. In their midst the central steeple towers proudly up like the mainmast of some great Indiaman among a fleet of coasters.

We wished to go aloft.[20]

Baker's boy is the famine-breeder of the ship. He is always hungry. They say he goes about the state-rooms when the passengers are out, and eats up all the soap. And they say he eats oakum.[21] They say he will eat any thing he can get between meals, but he prefers oakum. He does not like oakum for dinner, but he likes it for a lunch, at odd hours, or any thing that way. It makes him very disagreeable, because it makes his breath bad, and keeps his teeth all stuck up with tar.[22]

APPENDIX B

Mark Twain's Ships

Ajax: San Francisco, California, to Honolulu, Hawaii, March 1866

Boomerang: Oahu to the Island of Hawaii and back, June 1866

Smyrniote: Honolulu to San Francisco, July–August 1866

America: Accessory Transit Line, San Francisco to San Juan del Sur, Nicaragua, December 1866

San Francisco: Pacific Mail Steamship Company, Greytown, Nicaragua, to New York, January 1867

Quaker City: Privately chartered, New York to Europe and back, June–November 1867

Henry Chauncey: Pacific Mail Steamship Company, from New York to Aspinwall, Colombia (now Colón, Panama), March 1868

Sacramento: Pacific Mail Steamship Company, from Panama City, Colombia (now Panama), to San Francisco, March–April 1868

Montana: Pacific Mail Steamship Company, San Francisco to Panama City, July 1868

Henry Chauncey: Pacific Mail Steamship Company, Aspinwall to New York, July 1868

Scotia: Cunard Line, New York to Liverpool, England, August 1872

Batavia: Cunard Line, Liverpool to New York, November 1872

Batavia: Cunard Line, New York to Liverpool, May 1873

Batavia: Cunard Line, Liverpool to New York, October 1873

City of Chester: Inman Line, New York to Liverpool, November 1873

Parthia: Cunard Line, Liverpool to Boston, January 1874

Bermuda: New York to Hamilton, Bermuda, and back, May 1877

Holsatia: Hamburg-America Line, New York to Hamburg, April 1878

Gallia: Cunard Line, New York to Liverpool, May 1879

Gallia: Cunard Line, Liverpool to New York, August–September 1879

La Gascogne: French Line, New York to Le Havre, France, June 1891

Lahn: Hamburg-America Line, Hamburg to New York, March 1892

Lahn: Hamburg-America Line, New York to Hamburg, April 1892

Havel: Hamburg-America Line, Hamburg to New York, June 1892

Havel: Hamburg-America Line, New York to Hamburg, July 1892

Kaiser Wilhelm II: Hamburg-America Line, Genoa to New York, March–April 1893

Kaiser Wilhelm II: Hamburg-America Line, New York to Genoa, May 1893

Kaiser Wilhelm II: Hamburg-America Line, Genoa to New York, September 1893

La Gascogne: French Line, New York to Le Havre, March 1894

La Gascogne: French Line, Le Havre to New York, March 1894

La Gascogne: French Line, New York to Le Havre, May 1894

La Gascogne: French Line, Le Havre to New York, July 1894

La Gascogne: French Line, New York to Le Havre, July 1894

New York: Southampton, England, to New York, February 1895

Paris: New York to Southampton, March 1895

La Gascogne: French Line, Le Havre to New York, May 1895

Warramoo: Victoria, Canada, to Sydney, Australia, August–September 1895

Flora: Union Company, Lyttelton, New Zealand, to unnamed "way-port," November 1895

Mahinapua: Way-port to Auckland, New Zealand, November 1895

Mararoa: Wellington, New Zealand, to Sydney, December 1895

Oceana: Peninsular and Oriental Line, Sydney to Ceylon (now Sri Lanka), December 1895–January 1896

Rosetta: Ceylon to Bombay (now Mumbai), India, January 1896

Wardha: Calcutta, India, to Mauritius, March–April 1896

Arundel Castle: Union-Castle Line, Mauritius to Durban, South Africa, April–May 1896

Norham Castle: Union-Castle Line, East London, South Africa, to Cape Town, South Africa, June 1896

Norman: Cape Town to Southampton, July–August 1896

Minnehaha: Atlantic Transport Line, Southampton to New York, October 1900

Kanawha: Yacht owned by Mark Twain's friend and patron Henry Huttleston Rogers, Caribbean voyage, April 1902

Princess Irene: Hamburg-America Line, New York to Genoa, October–November 1903

Prince Oscar: Hamburg-America Line, Genoa to New York, June–July 1904

Bermudian: New York to Hamilton and back, January 1907

Bermudian: New York to Hamilton and back, March–April 1907

Minneapolis: Atlantic Transport Line, New York to Southampton, June 1907

Minnetonka: Atlantic Transport Line, Southampton to New York, July 1907

Bermudian: New York to Hamilton and back, February 1908

Oceana: New York to Hamilton, January 1910

Oceana: Hamilton to New York, April 1910

NOTES

1. Life on Brown Water

1. Mark Twain, *Life on the Mississippi* (Boston: James R. Osgood, 1883), 62–69.
2. Ibid., 70–78.
3. Mark Twain, *The Innocents Abroad* (Hartford, CT: American Publishing Company, 1869), 475.
4. Twain's footnote: "The term 'larboard' is never used at sea, now, to signify the left hand; but was always used on the river in my time."
5. Twain, *Life on the Mississippi*, 143–151.
6. Ibid., 236–245.

2. Hawaiian Passages

1. This is Twain's interpolation.
2. Mark Twain, *Roughing It* (Hartford, CT: American Publishing Company, 1872), 444–453.
3. The Confederate commerce raider *Shenandoah* burned whaleships in the waters of Russian Alaska in 1865.
4. Lon was a boy traveling with Captain Smith. "Captain Cuttle" was Twain's nickname for Captain Smith.
5. Dennis the pig liked to get among the densely populated poultry and walk on their backs.
6. Sixty-eight pounders are cannons that fire sixty-eight-pound balls. The *Great Republic* was a large ocean liner.
7. That is, a secessionist.
8. *Mark Twain's Notebooks & Journals*, vol. 1, *1855–1873*, ed. Frederick Anderson, Michael B. Frank, and Kenneth M. Sanderson (Berkeley: University of California Press, 1975), 111–113, 181–182, 186–188, 190–192.
9. Mark Twain, *Roughing It* (Hartford, CT: American Publishing Company, 1872), 459–464.
10. Ibid., 524–546.

3. Pacific Perils

1. Twain's footnote: "A young sister."
2. Twain's footnote: "Say a piece the size of an ordinary percussion-cap box."
3. Twain's footnote: "From this time forward Henry's log is used."

4. Mark Twain, "43 Days in an Open Boat," *Harper's New Monthly Magazine* December 1866–May 1867, 104–113.

4. From Hawaii to New York

1. Mark Twain, *Roughing It* (Hartford, CT: American Publishing Company, 1872), 558–559.

2. Damon was pastor of the Oahu Bethel Church.

3. That is, pumping the bilge during the two-hour "dog watch."

4. Meaning the three survivors he interviewed.

5. This entry is from a different notebook than the previous entry from the same day.

6. The full quotation from Herman Melville's *Redburn*, based on his first experience at sea at age nineteen, is this: "It was then I began to see that my prospects for seeing the world as a sailor were, after all, very doubtful; for sailors only go *round* the world, without going *into* it, and their reminiscences of travel are only a dim recollection of a chain of tap-rooms surrounding the globe, parallel with the Equator." *Redburn: Being the Sailor-boy Confessions and Reminiscences of the First Voyage of the Son of a Gentleman in the Merchant Service* (New York: Baudry, 1850), 60.

7. *Mark Twain's Notebooks & Journals*, vol. 1, *1855–1873*, ed. Frederick Anderson, Michael B. Frank, and Kenneth M. Sanderson (Berkeley: University of California Press, 1975), 132–141, 145–144, 148–149, 153, 158–159, 161–163.

8. This is Twain's interpolation.

9. *Mark Twain's Travels with Mr. Brown: Being heretofore uncollected sketches written by Mark Twain for the* San Francisco Daily Alta California *in 1866 & 1867, describing the adventures of the author and his irrepressible companion in Nicaragua, Hannibal, New York, and other spots on their way to Europe*, ed. Franklin Walter and Dane G. Ezra (New York: Alfred A. Knopf, 1940), 15–17.

10. Ibid., 22.

11. Miss Slimmens was the shipboard gossipmonger, and the "Thunderclap" was a fictional scandal sheet that Twain made up, saying she was its editor.

12. Meaning "ants."

13. This comment by Twain appears in brackets in the original.

14. To "cat" an anchor means to secure the anchor after it is weighed.

15. This comment by Twain appears in brackets in the original.

16. Ibid., 28–32.

17. Ibid., 36–38.

18. Ibid., 58–59, 61–68.

19. Ibid., 78–79, 80–81.

5. The Innocents Afloat

1. Mark Twain, *The Innocents Abroad* (Hartford, CT: American Publishing Company, 1869), 26–49.

2. Ibid., 62–65.

3. Ibid., 90, 92–95.

4. Ibid., 337–339.

5. "Ferguson" was the nickname that Mark Twain gave to all of his tour guides.

6. Twain, *Innocents Abroad*, 609–610.

7. Twain's footnote: "Afterwards presented to the Central Park."

8. Twain, *Innocents Abroad*, 635–637.

9. Ibid., 639–642.

10. Ibid., 648–650.

6. Back to California, and Back

1. "Letter from 'Mark Twain,'" *San Francisco Daily Alta California*, September 6, 1868. Available from the California Digital Newspaper Collection, accessed August 15, 2017, https://cdnc.ucr.edu/cgi-bin/cdnc?a=d&d=DAC18680906.2.8.

2. Twain's footnote: "The customary canal technicality for 'tie up.'"

3. Mark Twain, *Roughing It* (Hartford, CT: American Publishing Company, 1872), 369–375.

7. Voyages to Europe on Passenger Liners

1. *Mark Twain's Letters*, vol. 5, *1872–1873*, ed. Lin Salamo and Harriet Elinor Smith (Berkeley: University of California Press, 1997), 151.

2. Ibid., 588–591.

3. The ship was actually headed for Sunderland, England.

4. Twenty names follow, including the grandson of Ralph Waldo Emerson, Edward W. Emerson of Concord, Massachusetts. *Mark Twain's Letters*, 5:222–226.

5. Ibid., 277.

6. Ibid., 335–337.

7. Ibid., 371.

8. *Mark Twain's Letters*, vol. 1, ed. Albert Bigelow Paine (New York: Harper and Brothers, 1917), 209–210.

9. *Mark Twain's Letters*, ed. Salamo and Smith, 5:474.

10. Ibid., 475.

8. Escapes and Excursions

1. His "girl," Becky Thatcher.

2. Mark Twain, *The Adventures of Tom Sawyer* (Hartford, CT: American Publishing Company, 1876), 114–117.

3. Mark Twain, *The Adventures of Huckleberry Finn* (New York: Charles L. Webster, 1884), 173–175.

4. *Mark Twain's Notebooks & Journals*, vol. 2, *1877–1883*, ed. Frederick Anderson, Lin Salamo, and Bernard L. Stein (Berkeley: University of California Press, 1975), 9.

5. In his notebook, Twain went into greater detail about the European storm petrels he saw: "Mother Carey's chicks very beautiful; bronze, shiny, metallic, broad white stripe across tail; built & carry themselves much like swallows. After luncheon I commenced feeding crumbs to a few over the stern, & in 15 minutes had a thousand collected from nobody knows where. We are very far from land, of course. They never rested a moment. This stormy Petrel is supposed to sleep on the water at night." *Mark Twain's Notebooks & Journals*, 2:13, 16.

6. The next passage, which features Captain "Hurricane" Jones, is missing here, but appears in "Mark Twain's Iconic Captain," later in this book.

7. Mark Twain, "Some Rambling Notes of an Idle Excursion," *Atlantic Monthly*, October 1877–January 1878, 443–446, 586–591.

8. Mark Twain, *A Tramp Abroad* (Hartford, CT: American Publishing Company, 1880), 5.

9. Translations are the editor's. Strikethrough text appears crossed out in Twain's notebook.

10. See Gabriel Franchère, *Narrative of a Voyage to the Northwest Coast of America* (1854).

11. *Mark Twain's Notebooks & Journals*, 2:65–69.

12. Twain, *A Tramp Abroad*, 275–283.

13. Ibid., 580.

14. *Mark Twain's Notebooks & Journals*, 2:340–341. "Xtrees" are crosstrees, high up where the main mast joins the topmast.

9. About All Kinds of Ships

1. *Mark Twain's Notebooks & Journals*, vol. 3, *1883–1891*, ed. Robert Pack Browning, Michael B. Frank, and Lin Salamo (Berkeley: University of California Press, 1975), 640–643.

2. The *City of Paris* had survived a collision.

3. The "Johnstown disaster" was a flood in Pennsylvania on May 31, 1889.

4. Mark Twain, "About All Kinds of Ships," in *The Million-Pound Bank Note and Other New Stories* (New York: Charles L. Webster, 1893), 193–223.

5. *Mark Twain's Notebook*, ed. Albert Bigelow Paine (New York: Harper and Brothers, 1935), 229.

6. Ibid., 233.

7. Mark Twain, *The American Claimant and Other Stories and Sketches* (Hartford, CT: American Publishing Company, 1892), 157–158.

10. Equatorial Circumnavigation

1. The author jotted this observation in his notebook on the first day of the Pacific crossing: "Friday, Aug. 23. Sailed for Australia in the *Warramoo*. Strange how these great brown gulls (species of albatross) can scrape the tip of one wing along the surface of the water over all depressions and elevations and never touch it. Have watched them for hours." *Mark Twain's Notebook*, 249.

2. Mark Twain, *Following the Equator* (Hartford, CT: American Publishing Company, 1897), 25–28.

3. Ibid., 35.

4. Ibid., 60.

5. Ibid., 65–70, 73–76.

6. Ibid., 78–80.

7. Ibid., 91–93.

8. Ibid., 100.

9. Ibid., 109–113.

10. Ibid., 301–303.

11. Ibid., 309–312.

12. Ibid., 324. This notation from that same Friday the thirteenth would seem to belie this idyll: "Now let us have a storm, and a heavy one. This is the damnest menagerie of mannerless children I have ever gone to sea with." *Mark Twain's Notebook*, 262.

13. Twain, *Following the Equator*, 331–336.

14. Ibid., 345.

15. Ibid., 609–617.

16. Ibid., 630–636. In *Following the Equator*, Mark Twain did not mention a brief coastal passage he took in South Africa, but he did in his notebook: "Tuesday, June 16. Lying at anchor before East London, *Norham Castle*, a large and very fine ship. Smythe and I came aboard yesterday afternoon, although we are due to sail this afternoon; but the tug might not be able to cross the bar if a great sea should be running, and there is a considerable sea today; it dashes itself against the big stone breakwater

near the mouth of the river and bursts up in a very white volume with laced edges, apparently 100 feet high. Thursday, June 18. Cablegram saying the *Drummond Castle* has gone down off Plymouth, 400 lives lost. This at Port Elizabeth." *Mark Twain's Notebook*, 300.

17. Twain, *Following the Equator*, 712.

11. Mark Twain's Iconic Sea Captain

1. "Letter from 'Mark Twain,'" *San Francisco Daily Alta California*, September 6, 1868. Available from the California Digital Newspaper Collection, accessed August 15, 2017, https://cdnc.ucr.edu/cgi-bin/cdnc?a=d&d=DAC18680906.2.8.

2. Mark Twain, *Roughing It* (Hartford, CT: American Publishing Company, 1872), 353–355.

3. "Bight" means "loop."

4. *Autobiography of Mark Twain*, ed. Harriet Elinor Smith et al. (Berkeley: University of California Press, 2013), 2:192–193.

5. *Mark Twain's Notebooks & Journals*, 2:36.

6. Edgar Wakeman, *The Log of an Ancient Mariner* (San Francisco: A. L. Bancroft, 1878), 253–254.

7. Twain's interpolation.

8. Mark Twain, "Some Rambling Notes of an Idle Excursion," *Atlantic Monthly*, October 1877–January 1878, 588–589.

9. Twain, *Roughing It*, 552.

10. Mark Twain, *The American Claimant and Other Stories and Sketches* (Hartford, CT: American Publishing Company, 1892), 162–169.

11. Mark Twain, "The Refuge of the Derelicts," in *Fables of Man*, ed. John S. Tuckey, Kenneth M. Anderson, Bernard L. Stein, and Frederick Anderson (Berkeley: University Press of California, 1972), 166–167.

12. Mark Twain, *Extract from Captain Stormfield's Visit to Heaven* (New York: Harper and Brothers, 1909), 60–63.

13. Here Twain gives a synopsis of chapter 50 of *Roughing It*, the whole of which is included earlier in this book.

14. *Autobiography of Mark Twain*, 2:192–193.

12. Last Voyages of a Half-Century at Sea

1. *Mark Twain's Notebook*, ed. Albert Bigelow Paine (New York: Harper and Brothers, 1935), 374.

2. Ibid., 384.

3. Ibid., 388–389.

4. *Autobiography of Mark Twain*, ed. Harriet Elinor Smith et al. (Berkeley: University of California Press, 2013), 3:72–73.

5. Ibid., 2:361–362.

6. Ibid., 3:201.

7. Letter to Alfred Bigelow Paine, quoted in Geoffrey C. Ward, Dayton Duncan, and Ken Burns, *Mark Twain: An Illustrated History* (New York: Alfred A. Knopf, 2001), 252.

Afterword

1. Mark Twain, *Following the Equator* (Hartford, CT: American Publishing Company, 1897), 60.

2. *Mark Twain's "Which Was the Dream?" and Other Symbolic Writings of the Later Years*, ed. John S. Tuckey (Berkeley: University Press of California, 1967), 76–77, 81–86.

3. Ibid., 89–90, 92–94, 96–98.

4. Ibid., 150.

Appendix A

1. *Mark Twain's Notebooks & Journals*, vol. 1, *1855–1873*, ed. Frederick Anderson, Michael B. Frank, and Kenneth M. Sanderson (Berkeley: University of California Press, 1975), 270.

2. Mark Twain, "Pudd'nhead Wilson's New Calendar," in *Following the Equator* (Hartford, CT: American Publishing Company, 1897), 699.

3. Mark Twain, "A Cat-Tale," *Letters from the Earth*, ed. Bernard DeVoto (New York: Harper and Row, 1938), 119.

4. Twain is punning on "crewel," a kind of yarn used for embroidery.

5. Twain is punning on Gaetano Donizetti's 1835 opera, *Lucia di Lammermoor*.

6. Mark Twain, untitled, *San Francisco Golden Era*, September 27, 1863, quoted in Ron Powers, *Mark Twain: A Life* (New York: Free Press, 2005), 125.

7. Mark Twain, untitled, *San Francisco Daily Alta California*, March 28, 1867, quoted in Powers, *Mark Twain*, 180.

8. Mark Twain, *The Innocents Abroad* (Hartford, CT: American Publishing Company, 1869), 371.

9. Mark Twain, *Roughing It* (Hartford, CT: American Publishing Company, 1872), 54.

10. Twain, *Following the Equator*, 692.

11. Ibid., 708. Twain made these remarks about a small pile of diamonds shown to him at the DeBeers company offices in Kimberly in the Cape Colony.

12. Twain, *Innocents Abroad*, 310–11.

13. Ibid., 321.

14. Twain, *Roughing It*, 32.

15. Twain, *Following the Equator*, 411.

16. Twain, *Innocents Abroad*, 80.

17. Twain, *Following the Equator*, 413. The dog in question was a dachshund. A few pages later there is another nautical dog comparison, as Mark Twain estimates the length of a Saint Bernard to be "4 feet 2 inches, from stem to 'stern-post'" (416).

18. Ibid., 552.

19. Ibid., 32.

20. Twain, *Innocents Abroad*, 130, 139.

21. Oakum consisted of shreds of old rope and canvas combined with tar and hammered into the seams of ships to keep them watertight.

22. Ibid., 295.

BIBLIOGRAPHY

Maritime Writings Published in Clemens's Lifetime

"43 Days in an Open Boat," *Harper's New Monthly Magazine*, December 1866, 104–113.

Traveling with the Innocents Abroad: Mark Twain's Original Reports from Europe and the Holy Land. [Contains the *Alta California* letters that were first published in 1867.] Edited by Daniel Morley McKeithan. Norman, OK: University of Oklahoma Press, 1958.

Mark Twain's Travels with Mr. Brown: Being heretofore uncollected sketches written by Mark Twain for the San Francisco Alta California *in 1866 & 1867, describing the adventures of the author and his irrepressible companion in Nicaragua, Hannibal, New York, and other spots on their way to Europe.* Edited by Franklin Walter and Dane G. Ezra. New York: Alfred A. Knopf, 1940.

The Innocents Abroad. Hartford, CT: American Publishing Company, 1869.

Roughing It. Hartford, CT: American Publishing Company, 1872.

The Adventures of Tom Sawyer. Hartford, CT: American Publishing Company, 1876.

"Rambling Notes of an Idle Excursion." *Atlantic Monthly*, October 1877–January 1878.

A Tramp Abroad. Hartford, CT: American Publishing Company, 1880.

Life on the Mississippi. Boston: James R. Osgood, 1883.

The Adventures of Huckleberry Finn. New York: Charles L. Webster, 1884.

The American Claimant and Other Stories and Sketches. Hartford, CT: American Publishing Company, 1892.

"About All Kinds of Ships." In *The Million-Pound Bank Note and Other New Stories.* New York: Charles L. Webster, 1893.

Following the Equator. Hartford, CT: American Publishing Company, 1897.

Extract from Captain Stormfield's Visit to Heaven. New York: Harper and Brothers, 1909.

Maritime Writings of Mark Twain Published Posthumously

Mark Twain's Letters, vol. 1. Edited by Albert Bigelow Paine. New York: Harper and Brothers, 1917.

Mark Twain's Notebook. Edited by Albert Bigelow Paine. New York: Harper and Brothers, 1935.

Letters from the Earth. Edited by Bernard DeVoto. New York: Harper and
   Brothers, 1962.
*Mark Twain's "Which Was the Dream?" and Other Symbolic Writings of the Later
   Years.* Edited by John S. Tuckey. Berkeley: University of California Press, 1967.
Mark Twain's Fables of Man. Edited by John S. Tuckey. Berkeley: University of
   California Press, 1972.
Mark Twain's Notebooks & Journals. 3 vols. Vol. 1, *1855–1873*, edited by Frederick
   Anderson, Michael B. Frank, and Kenneth M. Sanderson. Vol. 2, *1877–1883*,
   edited by Frederick Anderson, Lin Salamo, and Bernard L. Stein. Vol. 3,
   1883–1891, edited by Robert Pack Browning, Michael B. Frank, and Lin Salamo.
   Berkeley: University of California Press, 1975–1979.
Mark Twain's Letters, vol. 5, *1872–1873*. Edited by Lin Salamo and Harriet Elinor
   Smith. Berkeley: University of California Press, 1997.
Autobiography of Mark Twain. 3 vols. Edited by Harriet Elinor Smith, Benjamin
   Griffin, Victor Fischer, Michael Barry Frank, Sharon K. Goetz, Leslie Diane
   Myrick, and Robert Hirst. Berkeley: University of California Press, 2010–2015.

Other Sources

Browne, Ray B. "Mark Twain and Captain Wakeman." *American Literature* 33,
   no. 3 (November 961): 320–329.
Ganzel, Dewey. *Mark Twain Abroad: The Cruise of the* Quaker City. Chicago:
   University of Chicago Press, 1968.
Hoffman, Donald. *Mark Twain in Paradise: His Voyages to Bermuda.* Columbia:
   University of Missouri Press, 2006.
Melton, Jeffrey Alan. *Mark Twain, Travel Books, and Tourism: The Tide of a Great
   Popular Movement.* Tuscaloosa: University of Alabama Press, 2002.
Meltzer, Milton. *Mark Twain Himself: A Pictorial Biography.* New York: Thomas
   Y. Crowell, 1960.
Newell, Gordon R. *Paddlewheel Pirate: The Life and Adventures of Captain Ned
   Wakeman.* Boston: Dutton, 1959.
Powers, Ron. *Mark Twain: A Life.* New York: Free Press, 2005.
Stiles, Owen. "Sounding Calls." EdgeEffects, June 21, 2016. http://edgeeffects.net
   /sounding-calls.
University of California at Berkeley. Mark Twain Project Online. www
   .marktwainproject.org.
Wakeman, Edgar. *The Log of an Ancient Mariner.* San Francisco: A. L. Bancroft,
   1878.
Ward, Geoffrey C., Dayton Duncan, and Ken Burns. *Mark Twain: An Illustrated
   History.* New York: Alfred A. Knopf, 2001.

Williams-Mystic: The Maritime Studies Program of Williams College and Mystic Seaport. Searchable Sea Literature. https://sites.williams.edu/searchablesealit.

Zacks, Richard. *Chasing the Last Laugh: Mark Twain's Raucous and Redemptive Round-the-World Comedy Tour*. New York: Doubleday, 2016.